Social Media Communication

Trends and Theories

Bu Zhong

The Pennsylvania State University
University Park, PA

Registered Office
John Wiley & Sons, Inc., 111 River Street, Hoboken, NJ 07030, USA

Editorial Office
The Atrium, Southern Gate, Chichester, West Sussex, PO19 8SQ, UK
For details of our global editorial offices, customer services, and more information about Wiley products visit us at www.wiley.com.

Wiley also publishes its books in a variety of electronic formats and by print-on-demand. Some content that appears in standard print versions of this book may not be available in other formats.

Library of Congress Cataloging-in-Publication Data
Names: Zhong, Bu, author.
Title: Social media communication : trends and theories / Bu Zhong, The Pennsylvania State University, University Park, PA.
Description: Hoboken, NJ : John Wiley & Sons, Inc., 2022. | Includes bibliographical references and index.
Identifiers: LCCN 2021009900 (print) | LCCN 2021009901 (ebook) | ISBN 9781119041610 (paperback) | ISBN 9781119041603 (adobe pdf) | ISBN 9781119041597 (epub)
Subjects: LCSH: Social media. | Communication.
Classification: LCC HM742 .Z47 2022 (print) | LCC HM742 (ebook) | DDC 302.23/1--dc23
LC record available at https://lccn.loc.gov/2021009900
LC ebook record available at https://lccn.loc.gov/2021009901

Cover image: © Karoon Cha/Shutterstock
Cover design by Wiley

Set in 9.5/12.5 STIXTwo Text by Integra Software Services, Pondicherry, India

10 9 8 7 6 5 4 3 2 1

Social Media Communication

Contents

Preface   *x*

Part I   Theoretical Foundation of Social Media Use   *1*

1   Why Study Social Media?   *3*
Overview   *3*
The Power of Social Media   *4*
Social Media in a Time of Distrust   *4*
The "Us vs. Them" Mentality   *5*
Digitization and Digitalization   *5*
Adoption Models of Media Technologies   *7*
Theory Highlight: Construal Level Theory   *9*
Summary   *10*
Looking Ahead   *10*
Discussion   *10*
References   *11*

2   Media Technology and Human Civilization   *12*
Overview   *12*
Definition of Social Media   *13*
Definition of Technology   *15*
Four Eras of Human Civilization   *16*
Theory Highlight: Technology Determinism   *21*
Summary   *23*
Looking Ahead   *23*
Discussion   *24*
References   *24*

3   Social Media and Computer-Mediated Communication   *26*
Overview   *26*
Social Change   *27*
Computer-Mediated Communication   *27*
Verbal and Nonverbal Cues   *29*

Interpersonal Communication *30*
Uncertainty Reduction Theory *31*
Social Information Processing Theory *32*
ICT and Communication *32*
Popularity of Social Media *33*
Group Communication *34*
Information Seeking *35*
Theory Highlight: Uses and Gratifications Theory *36*
Summary *37*
Looking Ahead *38*
Discussion *38*
References *38*

4   Social Media, Judgment, and Decision Making *42*
Overview *42*
Media Technology and Brain Activity *43*
Judgment and Decision-Making Research *44*
Selective Exposure *45*
JDM and Social Endorsement *47*
The Power of Social Context *49*
Social Media for Patient Support *50*
Theory Highlight: Cognitive Dissonance Theory *51*
Summary *52*
Looking Ahead *52*
Discussion *52*
References *52*

5   Social Media and Behavior *55*
Overview *55*
Social Media and News Consumption *56*
Social Media and Health Behavior *58*
The Culture of Sharing *60*
Knowledge Collaboration *61*
Theory Highlight: Social Cognitive Theory *62*
Summary *62*
Looking Ahead *63*
Discussion *63*
References *63*

6   Social Media and Privacy Concern *66*
Overview *66*
Internet Privacy Concern *67*
Scholarly Perspectives Toward IPC *67*
Four Epochs *68*
Social Media Surveillance *69*
Generation Gap in IPC *70*
Privacy Concern at the Workplace *71*

Privacy Risks and Coping Strategies   *72*
Theory Highlight: Need for Cognition   *73*
Summary   *74*
Looking Ahead   *75*
Discussion   *75*
References   *75*

7   Social Media and Culture   *78*
Overview   *78*
Cultural Diversity   *78*
Five Dimensions of Cultural Differences   *80*
Cultural Evolution   *82*
Cultural Influence on Social Media Usage   *83*
Cultural Differences in Social Media Activities   *84*
Theory Highlight: Cultivation Theory   *85*
Summary   *86*
Looking Ahead   *86*
Discussion   *87*
References   *87*

8   Problematic Use of Social Media   *90*
Overview   *90*
Warm Feelings in Social Media Use   *91*
Mechanism of PUSM   *92*
Reward System and Self-Control   *94*
FOMO and Phubbing   *95*
Cyber Troops and Social Media Manipulation   *96*
Relief of PUSM   *99*
Theory Highlight: Third-Person Effect   *101*
Summary   *102*
Looking Ahead   *102*
Discussion   *102*
References   *102*

Part II   Social Media for Social Change   *107*

9   Business Use of Social Media   *109*
Overview   *109*
Business Adoption of ICT   *110*
Business Use of Social Media and Benefits   *111*
Virtual Customer Environment   *114*
Work Performance   *115*
Social Capital   *116*
Information Benefits in Social Networks   *117*
Government Use of Social Media   *118*

Theory Highlight: Social Network Theory   *119*
Summary   *121*
Looking Ahead   *121*
Discussion   *121*
References   *122*

10   Social Media Reshape the News Industry   *124*
Overview   *124*
News Consumption Habit Change   *126*
The Power of News Media   *127*
News Decision Making   *129*
The Power of Facebook Algorithms   *129*
Fake News and Misinformation   *132*
Declining Trust in News Media   *133*
News Media and Social Media Giants   *135*
Theory Highlight: Agenda-Setting Theory   *136*
Summary   *137*
Looking Ahead   *137*
Discussion   *137*
References   *137*

11   Social Media and Healthcare   *139*
Overview   *139*
Health Information on Social Media   *140*
Patients' Use of Social Media   *141*
Health Professionals' Use of Social Media   *142*
Values of Social Media Support Groups   *143*
Health Information Support   *144*
Trust in Doctors   *146*
Theory Highlights: Health Belief Model and Crisis and Emergency
      Risk Communication Model   *147*
Summary   *148*
Looking Ahead   *148*
Discussion   *149*
References   *149*

12   The App Economy and Artificial Intelligence   *152*
Overview   *152*
1. The App Economy   *152*
   Apps Promote Business   *154*
   The App Intelligence   *155*
   App Store Optimization   *156*
   Trends of App Development   *157*
   Trends of Mobile Commerce Apps   *158*
Discussion   *158*
References   *159*
Overview   *160*

2. Artificial Intelligence   *160*
  AI Helps Social Media Penetration   *160*
  AI-Powered Business Solutions   *161*
  The Algorithm Experience   *162*
  Social Media and AI   *163*
  AI Empowers Marketers   *164*
Theory Highlight: Knowledge Gap Hypothesis   *164*
Summary   *165*
Looking Ahead   *166*
Discussion   *166*
References   *166*

13   Social Media and Social Movement   *168*
  Overview   *168*
  Social Media Speed Up Social Movements   *169*
  New Path to Social Power   *170*
  Mobilization and Coalition Building   *171*
  Networked Publics   *173*
  Social Media and Democracy   *173*
  Theory Highlight: Diffusion of Innovation Theory   *176*
  Summary   *178*
  Looking Ahead   *178*
  Discussion   *178*
  References   *178*

14   The Future of Social Media   *181*
  Overview   *181*
  Young and Old Fish   *181*
  Two Premises   *182*
  The Model of Two-Stage Development   *183*
  Digital Skills at the Workplace   *185*
  Ethical Social Media Sites   *186*
  Fake News on Social Media   *187*
  Social Connectivity   *188*
  Summary   *189*
  Discussion   *189*
  References   *190*

Index   *191*

Preface

It is never easy to live a year in a foreign city that is 8,000 miles away from home, especially for a 10-year-old.

Following his father's sabbatical leave to Asia, Skyler, 10, left his American school to attend, reluctantly, his 5th grade year in Guangzhou, China. This was the biggest challenge he has had so far. He was old enough to know that living there for a year could be quite different from visiting it for a couple of days. Unsurprisingly, Skyler's initial adjustment to his Guangzhou school was a disaster due to language barriers, cultural shocks, a different pedagogy, and "endless" homework, even on holidays.

The most unbearable, above all, was the detachment from his American friends, causing him a kind of "social pain." Social pain can be as bad as physical pain, if not worse. This is well supported by a growing body of evidence from studies by neuroscientists and psychologists (Almehmadi et al., 2013; Stafford & Bell, 2012; Viale, 2011). By analyzing magnetic resonance imaging (MRI) results, Matthew Lieberman (2013), a professor of psychology and biobehavioral sciences at the University of California, Los Angeles, found that both physical and social pains were linked to the same brain region. Looking at MRI scans from two studies side by side, one on physical pain and the other on social pain, Lieberman and colleagues could detect little difference between them. Next time he felt down, he said he might reach for Tylenol (Lieberman, 2013).

Skyler did not need Tylenol to relieve social pain. He felt better as soon as he made new friends. The pain was completely gone after he returned home one year later. Recalling the experience, he said the most scaring part was being there without "old" friends. His experience clearly exemplifies the importance of staying social. We all are essentially social beings that are driven by deep motivations to be connected with others (Lieberman, 2013). The mutual influence is critical to one's well-being.

This helps explain why social media have become such an integral part of modern life, transforming the world in almost every aspect, in particular, communication and business. The popularity of social media, to many, might be plausibly attributed to the influx of new media technologies. The vital driving force behind it, however, is nothing but the trait of people being socially wired. This is consistent with the ample evidence from psychologists, who have discovered that the desire to form and maintain interpersonal attachments – the need to belong – is a fundamental human motivation (Baumeister & Leary, 1995).

Fundamentally, our minds are hardwired to be social.

Nowadays, social media are an essential multifunctional platform for us to obtain information and knowledge, share thoughts and ideas, and, simply, communicate with one another. As we live much of our lives on social media, the knowledge of online tools is not just something "nice to have," but a capability we need to survive and excel in this social media era. At an individual level, social media know-how contributes to one's success in the twenty-first century, while at the societal level, the know-how adds up to "a more thoughtful society" (Rheingold, 2012, p. 2).

In other words, what you do not know may be too much to afford. However, a good knowledge concerning how social media work, especially the mechanism of social media use, does not happen to us automatically. Social media have brought about new ways of communication humans did not experience before. This is not to say that they have totally replaced the old ways. We may not be completely wired to social media, but there is no doubt that social media are playing a critical role in our daily lives.

This book is thus designed to explore the power of social media, how social media evolve and change the human mind and behavior, how they affect information processing, the media industry and business marketing, as well as interpersonal and group communication. In other words, it is about how people live and work through, with, and around social media in various communication and business contexts.

Each chapter will center on an important topic with the power to change the ways you see and use social media, – for example, how social media evolve and affect people's information processing, the media industry and business marketing, in particular interpersonal and group communication powered by social media. After reading the chapters in this book, the reader should have an in-depth understanding on how social media are transforming humanity, communication, and business.

This book, however, is not about the wonders of social media, even though it explores social media and their social implications. Nor does it use particular forms of social media as the focal point, whether it be Facebook, Twitter, or TikTok. Otherwise the book would be instantly outdated, as social media, like it or not, never stop evolving. Hence, this book focuses on two areas – an in-depth understanding of the social media mechanism and its impact on human communication and how people may make the best use of social media in the areas of communication and business.

The first half of the book provides a multidisciplinary examination of the social media mechanism by drawing on the latest research findings in communication studies, information sciences, neurosciences, psychology and sociology. The impact of social media on information processing, social networking, cognition, media industry, and business marketing will be thoroughly discussed in this part. A solid knowledge of the social media mechanism should serve readers well in making the best use of them no matter how social media might evolve, or what new platforms could emerge in the future.

The second half of the book is devoted to research-based strategies regarding how to use social media productively in communication and business settings. Designed as a principal textbook for undergraduate and graduate-level courses in schools of communications and business, this book constitutes original research findings in all its chapters, including those from the author and his colleagues. Specifically, this book has the following major features:

1. *The Underlying Mechanism.* This is not just another "how-to" book concerning social media use or their marketing potential. Rather, it provides an in-depth understanding of the mechanism underlying social media and their implications in various

communication settings. This approach should help readers to make the best use of social media tools while recognizing the individual, group, and cultural differences involved. The latter often plays a pivotal role in global communication and business practices.

2. *A Multidisciplinary Approach.* The book employs a multidisciplinary approach to study social media and their impacts by drawing on the latest research findings in communication studies, neuroscience, information science, and psychology. The approach should be able to empower those who have an interest in doing more research in this stream. Though this part is mainly designed for graduate students and researchers, it provides answers to anyone who likes to explore "why so" in using social media tools.

3. *Theory Highlights.* Over a dozen of theories in the areas of communication, psychology, and sociology will be introduced. The goal is to enable readers to be acquainted with the theoretical frameworks researchers frequently employ in their social media studies. After reading the theory highlights, readers should have a good grasp of what each of the theories is about. The highlights also serve as a springboard for anyone who would like to explore more theories of interest in studying the impact of social media.

Most of the content in this book is based on the author's research and teaching in social media at a US university in recent years. The author has designed and taught several social media courses for undergraduate and graduate students at The Pennsylvania State University and Hong Kong Baptist University. The four courses are: "Social Media for Social Change," "Social Media Research: Trends and Theories," "Social Media Communication," and "Social Media Marketing," all of which had never been taught at the two universities before, and were well received by the students who majored in communication, psychology, business, and information science and technology.

In addition to college students, this book should be a tremendous source for researchers, educators, journalists, small business owners, librarians, and practitioners in media management, advertising, public relations, and business marketing. This book, however, does not have all of the answers for social media. It is understandable that some readers wish for a book that provides all of the answers and dictates their learning about social media. Most readers still want to search out materials and answers of their own. In the latter case, the current book serves as a critical source for starting a journey to a better understanding of digital media technology and how it transforms social interaction. As media theorist Neil Postman said, "Technology doesn't just add something, it changes everything," though new technology can never substitute for human values (Hendrickson, 2000).

This book thus aims to provide its readers with an in-depth understanding of the social media mechanism, on which they may develop strategies in connecting with others and cope with the communication challenges in a networked society. The information benefits are manifold, including not only staying away from social pain, but also joining hands to change the world. If you care about the impact of social media – what social media usage reveals about us, what it is delivering and we fantasize it can supply, this book is for you.

References

Almehmadi, A., Bourque, M., & El-Khatib, K. (2013). A Tweet of the mind: Automated emotion detection for social media using brainwave pattern analysis. *The 2013 International Conference on Social Computing*, Alexandria, VA.

Baumeister, R. F., & Leary, M. R. (1995). The need to belong: Desire for interpersonal attachments as a fundamental human motivation. *Psychological Bulletin*, 117(3), 497–529. https://doi.org/.10.1037/0033-2909.117.3.497

Hendrickson, L. (2000). Communications technology and personal identity formation. *Educational Technology & Society*, 3(3), 27–38. https://www.jstor.org/stable/pdf/jeductechsoci.3.3.27.pdf?refreqid=excelsior%3A5ae5dcab75c12af810fa8ce76b5be48e.

Lieberman, M. D. (2013). *Social: Why our brains are wired to connect*. Crown Publishers.

Rheingold, H. (2012). *Net smart: How to thrive online*. The MIT Press.

Stafford, T., & Bell, V. (2012). Brain network: Social media and the cognitive scientist. *TRENDS in Cognitive Science*, 16(10), 489–490. https://doi.org/10.1016/j.tics.2012.08.001.

Viale, R. (2011). Brain reading social action. *International Review of Economics*, 58(3), 319–366. https://doi.org/10.1007/s12232-011-0130-0.

Part I

Theoretical Foundation of Social Media Use

1

Why Study Social Media?

LEARNING GOALS

This chapter will help you understand:

- What is the power of social media?
- Are social media the culprit of causing social distrust?
- Why do we need to study social media?
- How are traditional and digital media technology adopted differently?

KEY CONCEPTS

The "Us vs. Them" mentality   Silo effect

Echo chamber   Information cocoon

Digitization   Digitalization

THEORY HIGHLIGHT

Construal Level Theory

Overview

Even though Joe Biden won the United States presidency in 2020, Democrats in the House of Representatives suffered serious defeats in the election, falling far short of expectations and setting off infighting amongst themselves. Immediately after Election Day, some Democratic House members pointed fingers at colleagues for losing seats in the House of Representatives. One of their key concerns was lack of appreciation of the importance of social media strategies in political campaigns. No one argued about whether to incorporate social media into campaign strategies or not. Rather, they debated the consequences of failing to let social media play an important role in the political activities.

The Power of Social Media

Congresswoman Alexandria Ocasio-Cortez said that it was inadequate for her Democratic colleague, Conor Lamb, to spend merely $2,000 on Facebook the week before the election, although he did manage to win in Pennsylvania (Herndon, 2020). "If you're not spending $200,000 on Facebook with fund-raising, persuasion, volunteer recruitment, get-out-the-vote the week before the election, you are not firing on all cylinders," said Ocasio-Cortez (Herndon, 2020). To her, digital investment and advertising on Facebook was important because that's where voters gathered, and both positive and negative political rhetoric went viral all the time. In political campaigns, no one could afford to allow Facebook to radicalize things without fighting back, she said (Herndon, 2020).

Of course, there are many factors contributing to the success of a political campaign, but politicians agree that a major one is the way the campaign team uses social media to raise money, motivate voters, and win support. In a networked society, a revolutionary social media strategy must be an integral part of any political campaign. Despite the power of social media being widely recognized, many people lack a coherent and analytic account of why certain social media strategies work while others do not. Fewer understand the mechanism of social media usage, for instance, how political views, participation, and voter behavior may be swayed by information disseminated on social media.

Another big lesson we learned from the 2020 US election was that social media could be used as a venue to spread weaponized misinformation, making people lose confidence and faith in those with different political beliefs. There was a time of distrust after the election caused by a profound lack of trust in the US political system and the mainstream media. Some even exhibited distrust in the future, which shocked the world, as Americans have been known for their persistent optimistic belief in the future. As a hallmark of their nation, Americans have long held the rosy assumption that the arc of justice moves inexorably upwards, and that the future could be and should be brighter than the past (Short, 2020). After that optimism weakened, more people faced a fearful future filled with constant anxiety and indignation. Some people believe that social media caused the problem of social distrust.

Social Media in a Time of Distrust

Social scientists argue that social media should not be perceived as the culprit that caused a time of distrust. For many, the advantages of social media have been misdirected, which is in contrast to what we have known for decades about these information platforms. In those good old days, we marveled at how much social media had changed the way we lived. They changed how we communicated, how we consumed news and entertainment, and how we worked and conducted business. These changes have been taken for granted, especially for those who grew up with the rise of social media. However, many people fail to understand why hate speech, conspiracy theories, and other types of disinformation flourish on social media, thus compounding the surge of the exhausting period of distrust.

Hate speech is not merely a narrative that can hurt people's feelings. Such "hate stratagems" work, like tactics of war to inflame the emotions of followers, denigrate the outclass, and inflict permanent and irreparable harm on an opponent (Kirk & Martin, 2020).

The abusive, insulting, intimidating, and harassing disinformation could easily lead to violence, hatred, discrimination, or distrust. By using labels, epithets, threats, and lies, producers of misinformation could destroy political opponents, manipulate public opinion, and disrupt a democratic system like an election. Unfortunately, such misinformation and disinformation can go viral easily on social media.

The "Us vs. Them" Mentality

The proliferation of falsehood and conspiracy theories on social media is partially due to the mechanism of these platforms, which can easily promote self responses, self beliefs, and selfish recognition. Because millions of users can stay connected on social media, scholars used to applaud the fact that social media could promote the return of a "public sphere" proposed by Habermas (1991), where "private people come together as a public" for the purpose of using reason to further critical knowledge that may lead to political change (p. 27).

The public sphere requires unlimited access to information, equal and protected participation, and the absence of institutional influence (Kruse et al., 2018). The idea is integral to the healthy existence of a participatory democracy, leading to action in the way of social movements (Habermas, 1991). Some scholars argued that social media are organized in ways that meet the requisites of a public sphere (Fuchs, 2008).

As shown in the 2020 US presidential election, social media have failed to promote unlimited access to information, equal access and participation, and these spaces have not been free of institutional influence. Instead, the platforms were ideal for developing an "*us vs. them*" mentality among users, especially in an election year. Heavy social media users are more likely to shut down media channels offering information from "their side," reinforce selective exposure and the silo effect, and drive us into echo chambers or information cocoons.

Some go even further and believe that an unworthy other side can be a threat against "us." They must be defeated politically, destroyed, or locked up, which requires "us" to cast aside traditional norms and commitments like trusting others and diversity. "Us vs. them" opposes these commitments as it does not fit an "us vs. them" mentality.

Digitization and Digitalization

Since the first digital message was sent out from a computer at the University of California in Los Angeles to another at the Stanford Research Institute in Menlo Park, California on October 29, 1969, marking the start of the internet, the world has been significantly transformed by the internet and computer-based technologies, including social media (Zhong, 2020). It is hard to predict the future of social media and how they will advance. Problematic use of social media may be a growing social concern, for example, hate speech or cyberbullying. Social media were not originally designed to protect users from abuse, misinformation, or disinformation. As a result, people will be vulnerable to more harm on social media in the coming decades. These digital nuisances, unfortunately, will keep harassing users for a long time.

Facing the potential perils on social media, users are encouraged to search for solutions for new challenges and overcome them. One of the solutions is to study them.

However, the future of social media usage can be exciting, too. There are ample positive effects associated with using them. Many researchers believe that social media usage can change the world for good. It will be interesting to witness how social media-dependent human societies will evolve in coming decades.

What is the future of social media? Niels Bohr, Danish physicist and Nobel Laurate, once said, "It is difficult to predict, especially the future." However, if we have to predict the future of a social media-dependent human society, people in such a society will universally embrace the trend of digitization and digitalization. The use of social media represents the digital transformation development of social life, a societal process requiring people to prepare, adopt, and integrate digital changes. Meanwhile, people are subject to develop and are confronted with old and new digital models in life and business.

To understand the future of social media, it is useful to define and differentiate digitization and digitalization. *Digitization* describes the analog-to-digital conversion of existing data and documents, in which the data are not changed in any substantial way, but simply are encoded in a digital format. For example, when an old black-and-white movie is converted to a digital version, the resolution may be improved and even colors can be added, but the movie remains the same movie, just in a digital format. Digitization can reap efficiency benefits when the digitized data are easily circulated and shared over the internet.

In the business world, *digitalization* is defined as "the use of digital technologies to change a business model and provide new revenue and value-producing opportunities; it is the process of moving to a digital business" (Garner, 2021). In this vein, we define digitalization at the societal level as the use of digital technologies to change human communication and social life, providing new benefits and value-added opportunities for human societies. Thus, digitalization moves beyond digitization (see Table 1.1), leveraging digital information technology to transform social life and business models – evaluating, reengineering, and reimagining the way we live and do business.

Table 1.1 The differences between digitization and digitalization.

	Digitization	Digitalization
Definition	*Digitization* describes the analog-to-digital conversion of existing data and documents, in which the data are not changed in any substantial way but simply are encoded in a digital format.	*Digitalization* refers to the use of digital technologies to change human communication and social life and provide new benefits and value-added opportunities for human societies.
Examples	<ul><li>Converting a black–white movie into a colored one with better resolution</li><li>Scanning a paper book to a digital book</li><li>Recording a live lecture to keep as a digital file</li></ul>	<ul><li>Analyzing Google search results to understand flu season trends</li><li>Using digital tools to monitor the quality of telemedicine visits</li><li>Using analytics tools to study customers' feedbacks on services</li></ul>

The synchronization of human communication in real-time through advanced digitalization has transformed our social life since the birth of the internet in 1969, causing a series of epoch-making changes in the current social media-dependent society that is dramatically different from previous eras, like the agricultural and industrial ages. In the coming decades, we should see a growing integration of multiple technologies into various aspects of our societies that will be increasingly digital. Some examples of digitalization include: smart homes, e-learning, e-healthcare, smart mobility, and smart cities, which are largely powered by computer-based technology, including information science and mobile technology.

Many domains will benefit from digitalization; cultural artifacts like artwork and historical relics can be digitized and therefore preserved and shown to the public, even if they are stolen, damaged, or are just not conveniently accessible. As more and more information and data are easily shared and accessed due to digitalization, more knowledge can be shared and produced like never before, adding new values to human societies. The widespread impact of digitalization affects everything from interpersonal communication and relationships augmented by social media and their services, to other relationships, such as how citizens interact with support services in e-government. Both digitization and digitalization are critical to the digital transformation of our social life. It is important to note that the process of digital transformation is not about data or information, but it is about people. The use of social media represents a key component of digital transformation, which in turn will define the future of social media, a topic we will revisit in the last chapter.

Adoption Models of Media Technologies

Digital media technology, also known as information and communication technology (ICT), has a different adoption model from traditional media technologies used for manufacturing televisions, land-line phones, or boomboxes. Late users of devices powered by traditional media technology can easily catch up with early users. This means that late users can use tech products as well as early users. When a user gets a TV set a couple of years after neighbors, it is possible to learn how to use the TV remote control within a day or two and begin to use it as well as the neighbors. The same results can apply to using a land-line phone or a boombox.

However, it can be dramatically different in terms of using ICT applications like the internet, social media, or a smartphone. The early and late users of ICT applications may always have a gap between them. Think about it. Do you think your grandparents could use the internet or their smartphone as well as you can? When they increase their level of using digital media technologies, you will not always stop at the same level and, quite likely, you will have reached a higher stage. This makes it difficult for any late adopters, like your grandparents, to catch up with most early users.

As shown in Figure 1.1, A and B are early and late users of ICT. When early user A starts to use ICT applications, A's technology level will keep going up, making B, a late user, hard to catch up. Thus, the technology levels between A and B may have a gap all the time. As for C and D, who are the users of traditional media technologies, their technology levels may easily merge at some point. This indicates that one can press the

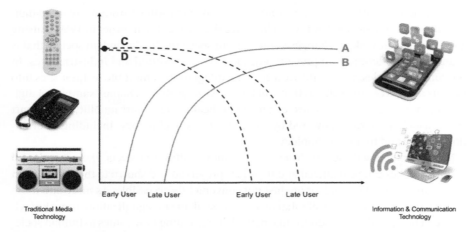

Figure 1.1 Adoption models of traditional media technology and information and communication technology (illustration by Moxin Qian).

buttons of a TV remote control or a telephone as well as the other. The lesson is simple. No one can afford waiting for a long time to learn new digital technologies. Any delay could make someone a late user who would eventually have a difficult, if not impossible, time catching up with early users.

Unlike traditional media technologies used in radio and television, social media became a global phenomenon as soon as they were developed. Both radio and television were first adopted in developed countries and then spread to developing countries. For example, color television was introduced to the United States in the 1950s, but it did not go to China until late 1970, where color television became a vmass medium in the 1980s. As social media sites were developed, they immediately won internet users around the world, making it a global phenomenon in a very short time (see Figure 1.2).

Today, social media are already everywhere around us and no one can afford the consequences of delaying the learning process. At this moment, if anyone asks, "Why study social media?"

It's the social media, stupid!

Social Media – A Global Phenomenon

Figure 1.2 Social media are a global phenomenon (Illustration by Moxin Qian).

Theory Highlight: Construal Level Theory

Construal level theory (CLT) is proposed to study how people can think about events that extend beyond the immediate context. It proposes that in order to look beyond here and now and understand distal objects, humans form varyingly abstract mental construals of them. These distal entities do not occur in present time, space, social realm, or actuality. While people cannot experience what is not present, they can rely on mental constructions such as prediction, memories, and speculation to transcend beyond the immediate situation and understand psychologically distant objects (Trope & Liberman, 2010). So there is a psychological distance between what people can feel here and now and the dimensions and measurements of "distance" of future events, remote places, distant others, and alternative realities. Here "psychological distance" can be a uniquely human ability, which is about the removal of an object or event from direct experience.

In other words, the theory holds that humans have the unique capacity to think about future events, remote places, distant others, and alternative realities. The CLT research shows that regardless of the psychological distance dimensions of an object, such as time, space, social distance, or hypotheticality, the mental construal processes are quite consistent, so as to be understood as cognitively related to each other (Maglio et al., 2013).

The basic premise of CLT is based on the link between distance and the level of mental construal. Objects viewed as more distant will be understood at a higher, more abstract level, which will then bring to mind more distant objects (Trope & Liberman, 2010). This notion of abstract versus concrete construal as it relates to distance is perhaps best understood through the proverbial distinction between the trees and the forest. When standing at a physical distance from a group of trees, one sees a forest in its entirety. When this distance is reduced, the large abstraction of a forest becomes individual trees. While this example focuses solely on spatial distance, the same logic can be applied to the other dimensions of psychological distance as well. For any dimension, Trope and Liberman (2010) explain that "as psychological distance increases, construals would become more abstract, and as level of abstraction increases, so too would the psychological distances people envisage" (p. 440).

Events can differ in terms of dimensions such as time, space, social distance, and hypotheticality as they happen. Human minds tend to treat these varying dimensions of distance in a mentally similar manner. For example, although time and space may be very different types of information, CLT suggests that people treat them interchangeably. Thus, from a psychological vantage point, just as an event one month from now is more distant than an event tomorrow, an event occurring to you is more distant than one occurring directly to me. As events become psychologically closer, information about detailed specifics becomes more available and reliable. CLT suggests that people incorporate this information by engaging in a low-level construal, representing events in terms of their more concrete and idiosyncratic features.

CLT is a widely applicable theory that allows researchers to examine the relationship between psychological distance from an object or entity and the corresponding level of thought, as either abstract or concrete. Scholars have applied CLT to varying domains in recent years through examining the distinction between abstractness and concreteness on individuals evaluations, predictions, and behaviors, including political attitudes (Alper, 2020). Studies examining CLT and political attitudes are broad in scope and have measured how CLT's psychological distance influences: political polarization, ideological differences, moral values, and political sophistication. Beyond political analysis, CLT has been applied to research studying new mobile and social technological use (Tseng & Hsieh, 2019; Young, 2015).

Summary

This chapter introduces the power of social media through the perspectives of some politicians. It then highlights how social media are used in a time of distrust, which may strengthen the "us vs. them" mentality. Social media are a global phenomenon, which were widely adopted by users around the world almost as soon as they were developed. For a better understanding of the social media age, digitization and digitalization are discussed in detail. Finally, the adoption models of traditional media technologies and digital media technologies are compared. The results should serve a reminder that there are serious consequences if some people choose not to study social media in a timely fashion as later users of digital media technologies may not reach the tech level of early users.

Looking Ahead

In Chapter 2, we will study "Media Technology and Human Civilization." The chapter will define the terms "social media" and "technology." It will then analyze the four eras of human civilization, which should lay a solid ground for studying the mechanism of social media impacts. It will also introduce the theory of technological determinism.

Discussion

1. Where does the power of social media come from?
2. How do social media affect your daily life? Please provide one or two examples.
3. Is the use of social media becoming more important to you this year than last year? Why so?
4. Some people did an experiment of staying away from social media for one full year. Can you imagine you can spend one day or one week without using any social media platforms?

5. Do you notice how traditional and digital media technology are adopted differently in our society?
6. Can you propose a research idea involving social media usage by employing the construal level theory as its theoretical framework?

References

Alper, S. (2020). Explaining the complex effect of construal level on moral and political attitudes. *Current Directions in Psychological Science, 29*(2), 115–120. https://doi.org/10.1177/0963721419896362.

Fuchs, C. (2008). *Internet and society: Social theory in the information age*. Routledge. http://www.loc.gov/catdir/toc/ecip0719/2007021600.html

Gartner. (2021). *Digitalization. Gartner Glossary: Information Technology*. Retrieved January 1, 2021, from https://www.gartner.com/en/information-technology/glossary/digitalization.

Habermas, J. (1991). *The structural transformation of the public sphere: An inquiry into a category of bourgeois society*. MIT Press.

Herndon, A. W. (2020, November 9). Some House Democrats were "sitting ducks." *New York Times*. https://www.nytimes.com/2020/11/07/us/politics/aoc-biden-progressives.html.

Kirk, R., & Martin, S. A. (2020). Stratagems of hate: Decoding Donald Trump's denigrating rhetoric in the 2020 presidential campaign. In D. Jackson, D. S. Coombs, F. Trevisan, D. Lilleker, & E. Thorsen (Eds.), *U.S. election analysis 2020: Media, voters and the campaign* (p. 58). Centre for Comparative Politics and Media Research, Bournemouth University. https://www.electionanalysis.ws/us

Kruse, L. M., Norris, D. R., & Flinchum, J. R. (2018). Social media as a public sphere? Politics on social media. *Sociological Quarterly, 59*(1), 62–84. https://doi.org/10.1080/00380253.2017.1383143.

Maglio, S. J., Trope, Y., & Liberman, N. (2013). Distance from a distance: Psychological distance reduces sensitivity to any further psychological distance. *Journal of Experimental Psychology: General, 142*(3), 644–657. https://doi.org/10.1037/a0030258

Short, J. R. (2020). An election in a time of distrust. In D. Jackson, D. S. Coombs, F. Trevisan, D. Lilleker, & E. Thorsen (Eds.), *U.S. election analysis 2020: Media, voters and the campaign* (p. 41). Centre for Comparative Politics and Media Research, Bournemouth University. https://www.electionanalysis.ws/us.

Trope, Y., & Liberman, N. (2010). Construal-level theory of psychologial distane. *Psychological Review, 117*(2), 440–463. https://doi.org/10.1037/a0018963.

Tseng, T. H., & Hsieh, S. H. (2019). Determinants of emoticon usage in mobile instant messaging: A construal level theory perspective. *Behaviour & Information Technology, 38*(3), 289–301. https://doi.org/10.1080/0144929X.2018.1531927.

Young, R. (2015). Source similarity and social media health messages: Extending construal level theory to message sources. *Cyberpsychology, Behavior, and Social Networking, 18*(9), 547–551. https://doi.org/10.1089/cyber.2015.0050.

Zhong, B. (2020). Social consequences of internet civilization. *Computers in Human Behavior. 107*, Article 106308. https://doi.org/10.1016/j.chb.2020.106308.

2

Media Technology and Human Civilization

LEARNING GOALS

This chapter will help you understand:

- What are social media and their major social features?
- What is technology determinism?
- What are the four eras of human civilization?

KEY CONCEPTS

Social media	Technology determinism
Agricultural civilization	Industrial civilization
Information civilization	Internet civilization

THEORY HIGHLIGHT

Technological Determinism

Overview

Social media matter more today than before as they are encroaching on all sorts of human activities, for better or worse. Look around and it is evident that social media have been imposing a revolutionary effect on numerous aspects of human society, bringing us a new life largely inconceivable to those who came before. Today our lives are so saturated with social media that few could afford not to use them. How much are our lives are being changed by social media? We may not come up with a good answer to the question until we pause for a moment and see how much we rely on them every day.

Each semester when I taught a social media course, the first assignment was "Without Social Media," requiring my students not to use social media for 24 hours and to write a reflection on it. No Facebook, Twitter, Snapchat, or Instagram, but they could still make phone calls, send emails or text messages, and of course, use traditional media like books, TV, and radio. Before the experiment, they were instructed to inform their parents and friends of this assignment so that no one got panicky in the hours when they were out of reach on social media.

Social Media Communication: Trends and Theories, First Edition. Bu Zhong.
© 2022 John Wiley & Sons, Inc. Published 2022 by John Wiley & Sons, Inc.

For this project, most students in past years chose to stop using social media on a Friday night before going to bed. This made it easier for them to survive the time without social media. When they woke up the next day, about one-third of the required time was gone. Each year the one-day social media ban still stunned most students. In their reports, the students wrote that they knew it was hard not to use social media, but never expected everything would be so different and difficult without them. Most of the complaints had to do with the inconvenience, stress, anxiety, and detachment caused by the social media ban. This assignment seemed even more trying for my recent students as more of them told me, honestly, that they failed the assignment – getting back on social media sooner than required, for no particular reason. Yes, during those hours, students could make phone calls, send emails, or text messages. "But without social media, much of my life is lost," one student concluded.

Social media, apparently, provide users with convenience in communicating with others, sharing, and accessing information. The convenience may be better viewed as a kind of freedom as many get so used to it in the twenty-first century. Without it, they no longer feel free in this networked society. On the other hand, an extensive use of social media results in dependence on technology. Once people are accustomed to the online life powered by social media, any slight disruption of the status quo becomes a major impediment. Similar dependence on prior technologies from mobile phones to cars has been well documented by researchers.

Thus, social media are not so much about media per se but more about being *social*.

Inherently, all forms of media are *social* because they store and transmit information and knowledge that originate in social relations in society (Fuchs, 2014). Social media are no exception, as they connect people and their social activities in technological artifacts by facilitating information flows between users. Sociality, in essence, is a key feature of media consumption and production. For instance, when you read the news, watch TV, send a text message, or update your Facebook status, these activities are social, as they are related to other people and their social activities. In this sense, everyone's thinking is social as it relies on other people's ideas.

Like other media platforms, social media are profoundly transforming our society, from accessing news to doing business. While Facebook, Twitter, Snapchat, and Instagram get a lot of attention in the United States, Weibo, WeChat, and Line attract millions of daily users in Asian countries like China, Japan, and Taiwan. We should also not forget the popularity of Flickr, Slack, LinkedIn, Path, Pinterest, Tumblr, Vine, and many more. An important reason behind the popularity of social media is that they facilitate a social need for people, not only to connect with others in real-time at a marginal cost but also to create and share information in a similar fashion, which has never happened before in human history.

Definition of Social Media

This book treats social media as a plural term, not a singular one, because the word *media* originating from Latin is the plural of *medium*. The word *media* is also taken as a plural noun not only in major English dictionaries, such as *The Merriam-Webster Dictionary* and *Oxford English Dictionary*, but in popular stylebooks used by news media, such as the Associated Press, Cable Network News (CNN), *New York Times*, and *Wall Street Journal*. Another reason is that social media in this book refer to not just one but various social network sites (SNS) and the related information and communication technologies (ICTs). Hence, this book uses a plural verb with *social media* despite some writers treating it otherwise, which is not necessarily wrong.

A more significant question is: How do we define social media?

Scholars have faced a recognized challenge in trying to define what constitutes social media. Researchers often adopt one or more characteristics to describe social media and other forms of new media. The characteristics they investigate include digitalization, interactivity, virtuality, dispersion, automation, variability, networking, and real-time access. Among the characteristics, digitalization is the key technology that reduces information to something that can be easily fragmented, handled, distributed, and shared, which enable networking, multimedia, collaborative, and interactive communication.

The fact that social media continue to proliferate and evolve at a surprising speed is another reason why a widely accepted definition of the term is hard to find. Some of the features that initially distinguished various forms of social media have faded in significance, while others have been reproduced by new genres of social media (Fuchs, 2014). Yet, in much of what researchers and practitioners discuss, the answer is more often assumed, rather than specifically defined. To many, it is like a kind of good art. People may not know what makes good art, but they know it when they see it.

Social media should not be called new media. Rather, they are part of new media that are powered by the advances of computer-based technologies, including ICT, mobile, and network technologies. Scholars tend to agree that new media refer to any media platforms that are not analog, like television, radio, magazines, newspapers, and books (Baym et al., 2012). New media thus consist of various digital media forms, such as online news (e.g., news content on CNN.com or NYTimes.com), user-generated content (e.g., blogs, personal podcasts), and social media (Zhong et al., 2014).

The term "social media" often overlaps with "social network sites" as there is some connection and integration between them. Both terms refer to the same media platforms and technology involved. As a result, social media users and researchers often use the two terms interchangeably (boyd, 2009). To Rodriguez (2013), for instance, "Social media encompass a diversity of tools and platforms (Facebook, Twitter, YouTube, blogs, Wikipedia, Tumblr, etc.) ..." (p. 1053). Following Rodriguez and other scholars, this book uses "social media" as a catch-all term, referring to various social network sites.

Since the late 1990s, a growing number of popular SNS have been created, first in the United States and later around the globe. Launched in 1997, Six Degrees was the first modern SNS allowing users to create a profile and make friends with other users. The site had attracted almost one million members at its peak, though it was shut down in 2001, although 2003 marked an important benchmark in social media development. During that year, scholars saw SNS start to rise to a cultural significance, such as when Friendster became a popular social network site that caught media attention (Ellison & boyd, 2013). Launched in 2002, Friendster was the first SNS with over 100 million registered users, though it was redesigned in 2011 as a social gaming platform. More SNS mushroomed after that: LinkedIn was launched in 2003, Facebook in 2004, Twitter in 2006, Instagram in 2010, and the rest, as we know, is history.

Generally speaking, social media are "the collection of software that enables individuals and communities to gather, communicate, share, and in some cases collaborate or play" (boyd, 2009). As hybrid media platforms for both interpersonal and group communication, social media have key characteristics of digitalization, interactivity, and real-time access to information that can be easily created, distributed and shared by users. Specifically,

> (Social media are) a networked communication platform, in which participants 1) have uniquely identifiable profiles that consist of user-supplied content, content provided by other users, and/or system-level data; 2) can publicly articulate connections that can be viewed and traversed by others; and 3) can consume, produce, and/or interact with streams of users-generated content provided by their connections on the site.
>
> (Ellison & boyd, 2013, p. 158)

In other words, social media are the means of interactions among users, organizations, and businesses, in which users create and share information in virtual communities. In this sense, social media have relevance not only for users, organizations, and businesses, but also human society as a whole.

Applications that have developed within and around social media are endless in number and functionality, but all make sharing and searching information online easier. The result is an enormous amount of information that can be easily created, shared, distributed, promoted, and searched. Social media became an important source of information in the era of internet civilization. As a result, social media help create an endless number of niche social communities where members can gather around common topics, resulting in social movements from raising awareness of climate change in a local community to the Arab Spring, a revolutionary wave of demonstrations, and protests spreading to 19 Arab countries.

For individuals or businesses that do not invest time in understanding what social media are and their implications in society, they will have to make it up in the near future. Researchers contend that like other forms of new media, social media can be best understood and analyzed when they are positioned as ICT applications in various social contexts (Cheong et al., 2012; Lievrouw & Livingstone, 2006). For a better understanding of social media functions, we must ask: What is technology?

Definition of Technology

The notion of technology is not foreign to human beings. Today, people tend to think about technology in terms of such novel innovations as VR (virtual reality), 3D printers, or drones, but technology is also as old as a stone axe and as simple as paper making in the history of human civilization (see Thurlow et al., 2004). In this view, social media are just one of the new applications in a long line of technologies invented by human beings.

We all know what technology is, or we think we do. The same term, nonetheless, may mean different things to different people. Before we review the role of technology, it is helpful to define what technology is. A widely cited definition of technology is from the International Technology Education Association (ITEA) in the United States:

> Broadly speaking, technology is how people modify the natural world to suit their own purposes. From the Greek word *techne*, meaning art or artifice or craft, technology literally means the act of marking or crafting, but more

generally it refers to the diverse collection of processes and knowledge that people use to extend human abilities and to satisfy human needs and wants.

(ITEA, 2007, p. 2)

Technology thus can be best understood as an intrinsic human faculty, which is one of
human beings' basic, even defining characteristics (Heidegger, 1977). Heidegger noted
that technology and sciences are distinct, but they strongly influence each other, and
technology is often the cause of scientific breakthroughs. To Heidegger, there are several essential facts about what technology is; i.e., technology, as a human activity, is a
means of transforming nature; technology is the art of solving practical problems, not
an application of abstract theory. In essence, the technological act of creation is the act
of revealing the truth out of the many possibilities offered by nature.

In human history, technological innovations have had wide-ranging effects across
numerous domains of society. One of the most significant outcomes of the progress of
technology is its impact on social activities and the environment these activities have.
For example, the progress of information and communication technology has brought
long-lasting consequences to people's interpersonal relations, and access to and afford-
ability of information.

Human civilization has gone through numerous changes in history, and in recent
years ours has been profoundly affected by the diffusion of ICT. Today, people still
need to communicate by phone or meet others face-to-face, but social media are providing yet one more means of engaging with people in society. If used effectively,
social media can give all of us a greater choice in how we communicate and do business in the world. To better understand the underlying mechanism of social media, it
is important to review the role of technology in the four eras of human civilization.

Four Eras of Human Civilization

One powerful approach to analyzing the role of technology is to treat the progress of
technology as a succession of rolling waves of change. This requires us to focus less on
the continuities of technology progress and more on the discontinuities or breakthroughs in it. The approach is particularly helpful in identifying key patterns of technology changes as they emerge and unfold so that we can take full advantage of them.

In this book, technology refers to information and communication technologies
(ICT), which may also be used interchangeably with media technologies. Each passing
day provides new and imperative reasons to review the role of information and communication technology in the twenty-first century. Social media powered by the
advances in information and communication technology have brought a radical and
pervasive change to human society. The basis of the change is the observation of the
broad use of social media, mobile technology, or ICT as a whole. The technology
behind social media has impacts comparable to Gutenberg's improvement of printing
technology, resulting in a broad social use of the technology by dramatically reducing
the cost of using it. The changes caused by social media, however, are not well understood by either average users or practitioners, including journalists, marketing manag-
ers, or public relations personnel.

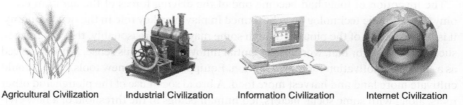

Agricultural Civilization Industrial Civilization Information Civilization Internet Civilization

Figure 2.1 Four eras of human civilization. (Illustration by Moxin Qian).

Technology, an intrinsic human faculty, is assumed to play a pivotal role in the process of humanity development (Calder, 1962). The progress of human civilization driven by technology may be loosely divided into four eras, i.e., the eras of agricultural, industrial, information, and internet civilization (see Figure 2.1). It must be noted that the four broad divisions are proposed in the hope of dividing the complex history of civilization into more easily understood phrases, in which the role of technology in each era of civilization can be better apprehended. Technology is, in essence, a truth revealing, creative activity. It is also, for the most part, a problem-solving activity (Heidegger, 1977). Polish scientist Andrzej P. Wierzbicki (2007) perceptively comments on the role of technology in human society, noting that "No matter how we define humanity, we would stop being human if we stopped creating technology" (p. 400).

1. Agricultural Civilization
The first era of human civilization emerged due to the rise of agriculture, which is "the first turning point in human social development" (Toffler, 1980, p. 29). The agricultural civilization should not be taken as a social structure consisting of discrete objects and distinctive events, but rather as a series of cumulative social changes moving at uneven speeds, during which hunting and gathering were transformed into agriculture – the cultivation of animals and plants for food and clothing.

The era of agricultural civilization dates back to the Neolithic period (around 10,000 B.C.), starting a long period of social transition from the pre-agricultural period, characterized by a Paleolithic diet, to an agricultural period characterized by a diet of cultivated food and domesticated animals (Barker, 2006). Leaving behind the hardships of nomadic life, human beings began the journey of civilization by settling down in fixed locations as soon as they knew how to gather seeds from plants and grew them periodically. In an agricultural community, farming was more economical and less labor-intensive than hunting, fishing, or searching for fruit in the wild. The development of farming provided people with fixed meals each day for the first time in history. The new lifestyle enabled people to live longer and healthier lives, and be less vulnerable to nature, especially when it turned harsh.

Once families started to produce more food than all the members could consume, people could then have time and opportunities to develop specialized knowledge, instead of producing food. When information can be communicated to others in written form, it can also be transmitted to future generations. The amount of knowledge then increased greatly in society, which supported philosophers, mathematicians, artists, and tool inventors, etc., resulting in widespread social changes.

The invention of tools had become one of the driving forces of the agrarian economy. If one single technology can be named in playing a key role in the new economy, it is the invention of the plough, though some may argue, reasonably, that other tools, such as the sickle or flail, were also essential innovations. In this sense, farming served as a source of motivation for tool invention. Equipped with the new tools, people could cultivate more land and harvest more food. A broad social use of the plough and other tools, along with some social factors, led human beings to the threshold of a new civilization era – the era of industrial civilization, which was sparked by the Industrial Revolution, starting in the late eighteenth century.

2. Industrial Civilization

The Industrial Revolution, marking another turning point in the history of human civilization, altered almost every aspect of human society, largely because of the advances in the technologies of industry. Multiple technological innovations at that time had liberated human beings by diminishing physical labor with mechanical work, supporting the injection of capitalist practices and principles into what had been an agrarian society. Human beings thus entered into the era of industrial civilization, the product of the Industrial Revolution.

Historians (e.g., Braudel, 1981) tend to agree that the preindustrial era, marking the beginning of capitalism, started in 1440, thanks to two new technologies – navigation technology, resulting in geographic discoveries, and Gutenberg's invention of printing technology. The latter, in a sense, was even more far-reaching. The broad social access to the printing press made it possible for more people to read and write in Europe, where printed books and manuscripts became less expensive and commonly accessible. Cumulatively, Europe witnessed a record high literacy rate, eventually contributing to the full blossom of the Renaissance.

Broad social access to steam machines, another new technology at that time, terminated the preindustrial era in 1760, and marked the beginning of the industrial civilization era. Some argue that neither Gutenberg nor Watt brought the world any new inventions, but instead adaptations of older inventions that existed somewhere else. The Chinese, for instance, had invented and developed movable type printing technology much earlier than Gutenberg. Four hundred years later, Gutenberg repeated, perhaps independently, the Chinese invention and added new values to the technology, making printing more mechanically efficient (Calder, 1962). However, what Gutenberg had contributed was broad social access to books, first in Europe and later in the rest of the world.

Watt's invention was not new either, but he added automatic control of rotary speed, a big improvement, to older steam machines that were unstable, unreliable, and unsafe. Again, Watt's contribution resulted in broad social access to the safe and reliable use of steam power, which would not easily explode like before. Mass media, both print and broadcast, in this era grew more powerful. The set of systematic changes to human society eventually amounted to a new era of civilization – information civilization, which is highly significant as a global civilization, integrating all parts of the globe into a single unit for the first time.

3. Information Civilization

Since the 1960s, numerous scholars have contributed insights on the subjects of the information society and the informational revolution, including Bell (1973), Castells

(2000), Drucker (1993), McLuhan (1964), Mattelart (2003), Naisbitt (1982), and Toffler (1980). Though holding diverse views, analyses, and research backgrounds, they share the same belief that we are living in times of an information revolution that is leading us into a new civilization era, which is dramatically different from the preceding era of industrial civilization. If the Industrial Revolution had significantly replaced physical labor with mechanical work, the information revolution brings about the dematerialization of work: automation, computerization, and robotization relieving humans from heavy or tedious work (Wierzbicki, 2007).

This new epoch is the era of information civilization, in which information plays a more essential role than industrial products. The main feature of the era is its high information intensity of all activities. Dijk (2012) argues that in such a society, "the information intensity of all activities becomes so high that it leads to:

- an organization of society based on science, rationality and reflexivity;
- an economy with all values and sectors, even the agrarian and industrial sectors, increasingly characterized by information production;
- a labor market with a majority of functions largely or completely based on tasks of information processing requiring knowledge and higher education;
- a culture dominated by media and information products with their signs, symbols and meanings" (p. 19).

It is generally accepted that 1980 marked the beginning of the information civilization era due to the improvement of personal computers (PC), network technology, and new protocols of computer networks (2007). The broad civil use of information technology, especially internet technologies, started with the definition of seven ISO/OSI and TCP/IP protocols in the 1980s, which by chance paralleled the development of the first personal computers (Wierzbicki & Nakamori, 2005). Broad access to PCs, network technology, and other information technology laid the ground for the development of social media.

The technology of the industrial civilization era was developed to such a degree that, for the first time in history, it promised the possibility of freeing people from hard work, while, on the other hand, it created the very real possibility of the total destruction of life on the Earth. Entire societies have become blinded by the seemingly unlimited power over nature given to them by industrial technology, leading to a great overexploitation of natural resources and degradation of the natural environment (Wierzbicki, 2007, p. 391).

In this era, information has become the fundamental productive resource, sometimes more important than raw materials or energy in the industrial economy. In the preindustrial and the industrial eras, the dominant medium for recording human heritage was printed books. Informational technology will soon make possible the fully multimedia recording of the human heritage; in other words, instead of a book, we will have electronic records including films, music, interactive exercises, and virtual environments. This change will have impacts exceeding that of Gutenberg's printing technology.

Like the rise of information civilization, a new era with distinct features follows, irresistibly, by the end of the second millennium. This is called the era of internet civilization, which is becoming the mainframe of the newly established networked society that is shaped socially, culturally, economically, and psychologically by media technologies, particularly in the areas of network technology and information and communication technologies.

4. Internet Civilization

At the dawn of the third millennium, networked society, characterized by a broad use of network technology and information and communication technology, has fully risen on a global scale (Castells, 2010), marking the beginning of the internet civilization era. "Networks are becoming the nervous system of the society," having more influence on the entire society and personal lives than the road system for transportation of people and goods (Dijk, 2012, p.2). The social use of ICT has made wide-ranging connectivity possible, including broadband, the cloud, and mobile technology. When people are brought closer like never before, their joint effort not only redefines boundaries of geopolitical entities, but also makes significant economic, social, and environmental progress.

The hallmark of internet civilization is the broad social use of ICT that provides innovative ways for people to collaborate, share, and get informed. By incorporating ICT into their lives, individuals have changed the ways they collaborate, innovate, and interact with each other. Knowledge in this era plays an even more important role than information (Wierzbicki, 2007). Unlike the technologies dominating prior eras of civilization, ICT differs in complexity by proposing an unlimited number of diversified technological possibilities, oriented toward both products and services (p. 413).

Another hallmark of the new era is unprecedented wide-ranging connectivity. In the internet civilization era, everyone and everything will be connected everywhere in real time. Media networks, social networks, and economic networks reach into the farthest corners of the world on a global scale (Dijk, 2012). In many respects, connectivity serves as the starting point for social developments, which creates freedom, empowerment, and opportunity to transform the world into a network society. While individuals and communities empowered by connectivity are driving fundamental social change, connectivity opens up new hope and opportunities for finding solutions to the toughest challenges in the world.

The era of internet civilization started in 2010, the year Apple Inc. launched its first iPad, representing another revolutionary media device following smartphones that bring people closer to information and to each other. The technology of the era makes it easy for people to create various networks in which they can easily exchange knowledge, capital, and cultural communication, in addition to creating and sharing information. The networks, or simply nets, enable new modes of informational flow. Those who control the information flow are in charge of the nets, and thus have enormous power to control anyone who relies on the flow of information.

As individuals are increasingly networked, rather than embedded into hierarchical groups, a networked individualism emerges, guiding how people connect, communicate, and exchange information, and, more importantly, providing opportunities, constraints, rules, and procedures. For the first time in history, technology offers seemingly unlimited possibilities of previously unavailable products and services than ever before (Wierzbicki, 2007).

The internet civilization era also requires people to develop new skills and strategies for collaborating, innovating, and problem-resolving. Meanwhile, a rising number of high-tech companies and businesses are fundamentally dependent on knowledge, with the capability of analyzing and making the best use of data. Other knowledge creators, in academia and in small firms, are also fundamentally dependent on knowledge. In the internet civilization era, we need social science that really understands how knowledge is created in the hard sciences and technology, and we, the representatives of the latter cultural spheres, cannot find such understanding in the arguments of social scientists today.

Foucault maintains that each era of civilization, or great "turn" in philosophy, was based on a distinctive cultural platform of new information, ideas, and concepts, which were formed before the beginning of the era, but affected the era after its formation for a period of time (Foucault, 1971). Internet civilization is no exception. Generally, internet civilization is based on the progress made in computing, network technology, and ICT, eventually bringing about a larger economic transformation since the 1970s.

Central to this transformation was the salience of digitally encoded information as the primary driver for economic, cultural, and social change. This occurred because within an increasingly competitive global system, knowledge began to replace labor as the most valuable component and, consequently, the production of services, as opposed to manufacturing, became centrally important. For Castells (1996), the nature of this change constituted a paradigm shift of information and communication technology, during which the cheap economic input of information is the most significant feature of change.

Castells (1996) identifies five primary features of the ICT paradigm: (1) information is the raw material of new forms of production and consumption; (2) digital information is all pervasive; (3) the logic of digital information affects society; (4) flexibility is a fundamental part of what information enables; and (5) networked information tends to converge into highly integrated systems. The network society is a product of these processes; networks provide the basis for organizing and expansion in the information age. The expansion of computing was due to the enabling effects of the networking process itself – the ability to link and spread and diffuse information flows on an unprecedented scale.

Hence, information is no longer taken as the vehicle of knowledge; it is now possible to think that knowledge might be something beyond information. A paradigmatic change of understanding is needed both in technology development and in assessing its social impacts. We will not be sufficiently prepared for the future if we adhere to old concepts and disciplinary paradigms, but must be ready to question them, preserving an open and critical mind in the era of internet civilization.

Theory Highlight: Technology Determinism

Any discussion on the role of technology in human civilization would not be complete without mentioning a key concept – *technological determinism* – since it offers a useful framework for understanding the interplay of technology and communication. Scholars who study technology, such as communication researchers, historians of technology, sociologists, economists, political scientists, anthropologists, and computer scientists, share a central concern about how far technology does or does not condition social change. The topic can be controversial as each commentator emphasizes different factors in the interaction between technology and social development.

Technological determinism can be a hard sell since few can produce a widely accepted explanation of it with rigorous and verifiable evidence.

The term *technological determinism* was coined by the American sociologist and economist Thorstein Veblen (1857–1929) in the early twentieth century (Veblen, 1933) and was later expanded on and developed by his student Clarence Ayres (Kte'pi, 2011). British scholars Castree et al. (2013) define technological determinism as:

> A reductionist, theoretical position in which technology is understood to determine, in fairly linear simple cause-and-effect ways, the social, cultural, political, and economic aspects of people's lives. Here, technology is seen as independent, active, and determining, and society is dependent, passive, and reactive. From this perspective, technical advancements are the key drivers of social and economic change. For example, technological determinists argue that new technical developments such as rail, telegraph, cars, telecommunications, elevators, and computers are key factors determining the shape and functioning of modern societies. Moreover, they would suggest that social, economic, and environmental issues can be solved purely through technological solutions.
>
> (p. 505)

Today, few scholars would accept such an extreme position. Rather, most researchers hold that social and economic institutions strongly determine the shape taken by technology, instead of the other way around (Kte'pi, 2011). Like other social activities, technology and its uses are socially constructed, their effects vary across space and time, and social problems cannot simply be solved by technology alone, but also need social and political solutions (Castree et al., 2013).

In addition to technology determinism, British scholar Chandler (1995) observes that there are various kinds of "determinism" featured in social and natural sciences. For example, there is *linguistic determinism*, suggesting that people's thinking is determined by language. Then there is *biological* (or *genetic*) *determinism*, proposing that human behavior is controlled solely by an individual's genes. Such a belief goes against most scientists who agree that all physical traits and behaviors are the result of complex interactions between both biology and the environment (Dubos, 1998; Ridley, 2003). Both theories can be linked to certain forms of technological determinism (Chandler, 1995). All these deterministic theories, including technological determinism, seek to explain social and historical phenomena in terms of one principal or determining factor.

Apparently, these approaches are oversimplistic and have been challenged since their introduction. A good reminder concerning technological determinism comes from Thurlow and colleagues (2004): It is always useful to remind you of the trap of being too deterministic about technology whenever you come across someone making a claim about the overwhelming effect of technology on certain aspects of social activities, no matter if the technology is a steam engine or social media.

It is worth noting that this book aims to explore the impact of social media and the latest application of media technology on people and their social activities. However, this approach may not be labeled as technological determinism because the book does not intend to ignore or overlook the dynamics of social, cultural, and psychological influences on human society. Rather, it sidesteps the complexities of the process of social influences by addressing the impact of technology on social media users and related social implications. During the process, social, political, and cultural activities have imposed an essential effect on social development, but, obviously, it is out of the scope of the current book.

Summary

This chapter lays the groundwork for a detailed discussion on how social media are transforming human communication and businesses in the coming chapters. It first defines two key terms: social media and technology. Both terms will be thoroughly examined later in the context of analyzing the sociality features of social media. For a better understanding of the social media impact on people and their societies, this chapter proposes the four eras of human civilization and investigates the broad social use of new technologies in each of the eras:

1. Agricultural civilization – farming, printing, geographic discoveries
2. Industrial civilization – steam machines, electricity, mobile transportation
3. Information civilization – PC, mobile communication, network technology
4. Internet civilization – ICT, social media, Wi-Fi, mobile technology

This chapter suggests that a profound knowledge of the social media mechanism is critical to one's life, career, and social activities in the era of Internet Civilization. Like it or not, social media are starting to exert a growing impact on human society, something that no one can ignore. The chapter also reminds us of the trap of technological determinism. In this chapter, technological determinism is discussed as a useful theoretical framework for studying the technological perspectives in social media activities.

Looking Ahead

In Chapter 3, a theoretical background is presented to study how people process information in the context of computer-mediated communication (CMC). It analyzes the significant differences between CMC and face-to-face communication. CMC users are often active information processors who can accrue accurate impressions of others and build high-quality relations with them in an online environment. This chapter also introduces the Uncertainty Reduction Theory and Social Information Processing Theory. Both theories should help to understand how people interact with others and process information on social media. Finally, the chapter reviews why social media use sometimes can be quite addictive.

Discussion

Suppose you would like to spend one day (24 hours) without using any social media, including, but not limited to, Instagram, Snapchat, Facebook, Slack, Signal, and LinkedIn. You can use phone, email, text message, and traditional media – radio, magazines, newspapers, and television. For minimizing any interruption, please inform your parents and friends in advance after you choose a date for the experiment so that no one panics when they cannot find you on social media. Then write an essay about how you survive the 24 hours without social media. Your essays should address the following questions. If you cannot write such an essay, please imagine such a day without social media and then answer the following questions:

1. How difficult is it not to use social media for 24 hours?
2. Which social media platform do you miss the most, and why?
3. What happens to you during the experiment? What feelings do you have after you make it?
4. Do you experience any mood or behavior changes, positive or negative?

References

Barker, G. (2006). *The agricultural revolution in prehistory: Why did foragers become farmers?* Oxford University Press. http://www.loc.gov/catdir/toc/ecip0615/2006018538.html.

Baym, N., Campbell, S. W., Horst, H., Kalyanaraman, S., Oliver, M. B., Rothenbuhler, E., Weber, R., & Miller, K. (2012). Communication theory and research in the age of new media: A conversation from the CM Cafe. *Communication Monographs, 79*(2), 256–267. https://doi.org/10.1080/03637751.2012.673753.

Bell, D. (1973). *The coming of post-industrial society: A venture in social forecasting.* Basic Books.

boyd, d. m. (2009). *Social media is here to stay ... now what?* Microsoft Research Tech Fest. http://www.danah.org/papers/talks/MSRTechFest2009.html.

Braudel, F. (1981). *Civilization and capitalism, 15th–18th centuries.* Harper & Row.

Calder, R. (1962). *Living with the atom.* University of Chicago Press.

Castells, M. (1996). *The rise of the network society: The information age: Economy, society and culture* (Vol. 1). Blackwell.

Castells, M. (2000). *End of millennium* (2nd ed.). Blackwell.

Castells, M. (2010). *The rise of the network society* (2nd ed.). Wiley-Blackwell.

Castree, N., Kitchin, R., & Rogers, A. (2013). *A dictionary of human geography.* Oxford University Press. https://10.1093/acref/9780199599868.001.0001.

Chandler, D. (1995). *Technological or media determinism.* Retrieved November 28, 2014, from http://visual-memory.co.uk/daniel/Documents/tecdet.

Cheong, P. H., Martin, J. N., & Macfadyen, L. P. (Eds.). (2012). *New media and intercultural communication: Identity, community, and politics.* Peter Lang.

Dijk, J. (2012). *The network society* (3rd ed.). SAGE.

Drucker, P. F. (1993). *Post-capitalist society.* Harper Business.

Dubos, R. J. (1998). *So human an animal: How we are shaped by surroundings and events.* Transaction Publishers.

Ellison, N. B., & boyd, D. M. (2013). Sociality through social network sites. In W. H. Dutton (Ed.), *The Oxford handbook of internet studies* (pp. 151–172). Oxford University Press. https://doi.org/10.1093/oxfordhb/9780199589074.013.0008.

Foucault, M. (1971). *The order of things: An archeology of human sciences*. Pantheon.

Fuchs, C. (2014). *Social media: A critical introduction*. Sage. https://doi.org/10.4135/9781446270066.

Heidegger, M. (1977). *The question concerning technology, and other essays*. Harper & Row.

ITEA. (2007). *Standards for technological literacy: Content for the study of technology* (3rd ed.). International Technology Education Association. http://www.iteaconnect.org/TAA/PDFs/xstnd.pdf.

Kte'pi, B. (2011). Technological determinism. In D. Mulvaney (Ed.), *Green technology: An A-to-Z guide* (pp. 403–405). Sage.

Lievrouw, L. A., & Livingstone, S. M. (2006). *Handbook of new media: Social shaping and social consequences of ICTs* (Updated student ed.). Sage.

Mattelart, A. (2003). *The information society: An introduction*. Sage.

McLuhan, M. (1964). *Understanding media: The extensions of man*. McGraw-Hill.

Naisbitt, J. (1982). *Megatrends: Ten new directions transforming our lives*. Warner Books.

Ridley, M. (2003). *Nature via nurture: Genes, experience, and what makes us human*. HarperCollins.

Rodriguez, S. (2013). Making sense of social change: Observing collective action in networked cultures. *Sociology Compass, 7*(12), 1053–1064. https://doi.org/10.1111/soc4.12088.

Thurlow, C., Tomic, A., & Lengel, L. B. (2004). *Computer mediated communication: Social interaction and the Internet*. Sage.

Toffler, A. (1980). *The third wave* (1st ed.). Morrow.

Veblen, T. (1933). *The engineers and the price system*. Viking.

Wierzbicki, A. (2007). Technology and change: The role of technology in the knowledge civilization era. In A. Wierzbicki & Y. Nakamori (Eds.), *Creative environments: Issues of creativity support for the knowledge civilization age* (pp. 385–416). Springer. https://doi.org/10.1007/978-3-540-71562-7.

Wierzbicki, A. P., & Nakamori, Y. (2005). A vision of the new civilization era. In A. Wierzbicki & Y. Nakamori (Eds.), *Creative space: Models of creative processes for the knowledge civilization age* (Vol. 10, pp. 127–157). Springer. https://doi.org/10.1007/11508083_5.

Zhong, B., Huang, Y., & Zhou, Y. (2014). The current trends of online journalism research in the new media era. *Communication & Society, 29*, 235–265.

3

Social Media and Computer-Mediated Communication

LEARNING GOALS

This chapter will help you understand:

- What is computer-mediated communication?
- What is social information processing theory?
- How do social media affect personal interaction?
- How do social media affect interaction with information?

KEY CONCEPTS

Social change	Social movement
Social media	Computer-mediated communication

THEORY HIGHLIGHT

Uses and Gratifications Theory

Overview

Nowadays few could imagine that social media were once considered a fad in the early 2000s when they first appeared. Rather, it is evident that social media are here to stay, penetrating various aspects of people's daily lives and social activities. Researchers agree that social media are all about us. We can fence ourselves in, but can hardly fence them out. Like it or not, social media, functioning as a form of computer-mediated communication (CMC), have profoundly changed the dynamics of human communication and business models. At a societal level, social media help bring about social movements around the globe, ranging from hotel bookings to Hong Kong's Umbrella Movement in 2014.

Social movements, aiming to "establish a new order of life" (Blumer, 1955, p. 19), refer to any organized collective activity to bring about or resist fundamental change in an existing group or society. Schaefer (2012) notes that social movements are more structured than other forms of collective behavior and persist over a longer period. A series of social changes usually come as a result of social movements, for instance, the Industrial Revolution in Europe or the Civil Rights Movement in the United States.

Social Media Communication: Trends and Theories, First Edition. Bu Zhong.
© 2022 John Wiley & Sons, Inc. Published 2022 by John Wiley & Sons, Inc.

Social Change

Sociologists define social change as any "significant alteration over time in behavior patterns and culture, including norms and values," and social change is more often "the unintended effect of technology progress" (Schaefer, 2012, p. 412). In many cases, social change yields profound social consequences, having long-term effects on human developments at a societal level. To better understand the nature of social change, such as the patterns and possible causal relations, sociologists propose three basic theories of change: evolutionary, functionalist, and conflict theories.

The theories of change admit that social change and resistance to the change are inevitably connected, which is a normal phenomenon during social developments. The resistance to change tends to be strong among those who feel that their vested interests are threatened by potential changes. The resistance to using social media will exist for a period of time among some individuals, though it is not nearly as strong as in the 2000s.

In the era of internet civilization, social media evolve to be a new genre of computer-mediated communication (Ellison & boyd, 2013), connecting our world in a fashion we have never seen before. If we merely say social media are playing a role in shaping today's world, that would be, obviously, an understatement. Studying social media is to explore the social process of the ICT-powered platforms, wherein significant flows of information are produced, apprehended, shared, and used for a better understanding of human communication. The communication on social media is mediated by how we perceive and use computer-based technologies in general, such as smartphones, mobile technology, artificial intelligence, and robotics (Zhong, 2020).

Computer-Mediated Communication

The classic definition of computer-mediated communication (CMC) comes from Susan Herring: "CMC is communication that takes place between human beings via the instrumentality of computers" (Herring, 1996, p. 1). Simpson (2002) notes that CMC can be divided into two major modes: synchronous and asynchronous CMC. The former refers to real-time interaction and the latter is about latent interaction, during which users are not online simultaneously. Synchronous CMC includes various types of text-based online chatting, messaging, audio, and video conferencing, while asynchronous CMC is about using emails, discussion forums, and listservs. CMC can take place through local area networks (LANs) or the internet. Social media as a form of CMC afford both synchronous and asynchronous interaction, which will be discussed in detail later.

CMC, however, is not something new in the twenty-first century; it can be dated back to World War II when the first electronic digital computer was invented (Thurlow et al., 2004). From then on, CMC never stopped gathering momentum around the world as more people communicate with one another by means of computer-based technology. In the United States, scientists began to exchange text-based prototype emails in the 1960s. In those early days, scientists were not supposed to send any personal emails as the email system was government property. By the 1990s, when personal computers had become mass-marketed consumer electronic devices, appearing in schools, businesses, offices, and homes around the world, a new information economy and network society began to emerge, in which information and communication technology played a critical role (Warschauer, 2003). The diffusion of ICT, in turn, promotes the social use of CMC.

In the early 1990s, CMC, consisting mainly of email and asynchronous discussion groups, such as newsgroups, mailing lists, and bulletin board systems, had not yet attracted much attention, except among early adopters and researchers. It is important to remember that the internet had yet to be introduced to the general public until the mid-1990s. As a result, there were no blogs, wikis, text messages, or audio or video chats, let alone social media. Email, one of the earliest CMC forms, just started to be popular beyond college campuses and research institutes. Of course, the interface of email systems then, such as Pine, looked very different from what we have become used to today (see Figure 3.1).

In the mid-1990s, when the impact of the internet started to become more pervasive and tangible around the globe, it was clear that CMC could offer much potential for rich discovery, such as virtual communities, virtual teams, e-commerce, and online relationship formation, along with less desirable online developments, including spam, phishing, deception, trolling, cyberstalking, and cyberbullying (Herring, 2014). At a societal level, CMC provides a new venue to promote *social inclusion*, engaging those who are cut off in some way from the benefits of mainstream society through lack of adequate access to ICT.

On the other hand, CMC is also accused of being both asocial and antisocial. When people communicate amongst themselves, it is not simply delivering arguments, facts, ideas, or opinions to one another, but it also involves nonverbal socioemotional cues, such as charisma, humor, voice intonation, facial expressions, body posture, gestures, eye movement, and the use of space, etc. Rice and Gattiker (2001) argue that CMC differs from face-to-face communication because CMC limits the level of synchronicity of interaction, causing a reduction of interactivity, while also overcoming time and space dependencies. Together with these arguments, the overall use of CMC results in multiple differences from face-to-face communication.

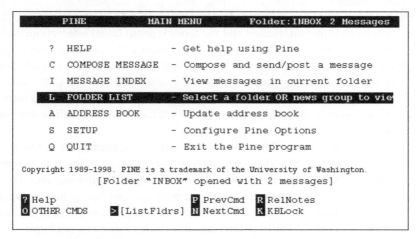

Figure 3.1 Pine, a prototype email system developed at the University of Washington in 1989.

Empirical evidence shows that most people could identify and interpret these nonverbal cues in face-to-face communication, but not as much in a CMC context that contains few nonverbal cues.

Verbal and Nonverbal Cues

Compared with face-to-face communication, CMC users could lose lots of nonverbal cues, which could cause them to "become self-focused and resistant to influence, disinhibited, belligerent, and affectively negative" (Walther, 2011, p. 446). CMC is thus labeled as "impoverished, impersonal and emotionally cold," and it is generally seen to be more uninhabited, more anti-normative, and aggressive (Thurlow et al., 2004). The allegation of asociality suggests that "CMC is bad because the quality of communication is reduced as a result of the technological restraints of the internet" and CMC has "a negative impact on offline communication and offline relationships" (Thurlow et al., 2004, p. 46).

The lack of social context cues was, indeed, the key concern of CMC's impact on interpersonal and group communication. Some early researchers specified that CMC occluded the cues to individuality and normative behavior that face-to-face interaction transacts nonverbally (Siegel et al., 1986; Sproull & Kiesler, 1986). For example, Rice and Case (1983) predicted that CMC contained less social–emotional cues than face-to-face communication, resulting in a lack of social presence. They argued that human communication also relied on processing nonverbal information; CMC devoid of nonverbal cues must lack dynamic facial expression and could even lead users to antagonism and hostility with one another (Walther et al., 2015). Hence, the assumption is that since CMC filters out many nonverbal cues that are available in traditional communication, it reduces the socioemotional quality of communication.

The "cues-filtered-out" proposition of CMC seems to assume that CMC users are passive, rather than active, information receivers. New findings, however, suggest that CMC users are able to accrue impressions of others in an online community and build new relations with them. Imagine this: when you compare meeting someone face-to-face with meeting online for only two or three times, it is possible that you know more of him or her in person than in an online context. However, if you compare meeting the same person online or offline for half a year, the difference between the two scenarios may be marginal. Many even report they know the person better in an online environment, where people often disclose their political views and other controversial thoughts that are seldom shared in a face-to-face meeting.

Some students also said that they developed online friendships with people they never met in real life, and, quite possibly, would never meet in the future. However, the friendship became very rewarding to them, which was never experienced in offline life. Meanwhile, some "strangers" online could hurt them even more severely than anyone they knew in real life. These anecdotes indicate that the current obscure set of assumptions of CMC may not be sufficient to explain the relationship between verbal and nonverbal cues in CMC, which is still evolving rapidly.

Other researchers challenged the social presence explanation of CMC dynamics by arguing that several assumptions of the social presence model were problematic (Lee & Spears, 1995; Walther, 1992, 2011). These researchers articulated alternative assumptions and employed different research designs, leading to the development of second-generation theories of CMC. These latter positions predict different social and interpersonal effects of CMC media depending on other contextual factors.

Later research also challenges the methods used in earlier studies, particularly the use of transcribed speech as the stimulus for measuring the effectiveness of CMC. Recent studies also challenge the previous findings concerning the absence of nonverbal cues in CMC that prevent communicators from detecting nonverbal cues. New studies indicate that CMC users often adapt to the medium by altering their language in a way that compensates for the absence of nonverbal cues. Several more studies on compliance gaining and social influence in CMC also discovered that CMC users often process messages based on argument strength, and they experience less overall attitude change than do offline communicators (Walther, 2011). Guadagno and Cialdini (2002) found, for instance, that the model of face-to-face interaction producing more communicator-relevant thoughts than CMC interaction may only extend to short-term interactions with strangers. Their finding suggests that a prior relationship with the communicator supersedes the communication mode, no matter whether the mode is CMC or face-to-face communication.

Overall, contemporary relationships are not conducted through one medium or another but often through a great variety of channels. Multimodality has become the primary channel characteristic of interpersonal and social relationships. The questions researchers raised about CMC in the 1990s may not fit how most of us use social media today, although those questions are of help in exploring how people form impressions and attitudes toward others in a social media environment.

Interpersonal Communication

Human communication becomes possible when its process involves three rudimentary components in a communicative relationship, i.e., a *communicator* sending a *message* to a *receiver*. Other elements, including noise (i.e., any distortion to the message), feedback, channel, and context, also play a role in shaping the process – in particular, the meaning of the message. The message itself, however, has no meaning unless it is interpreted by humans. Thus, the meaning of the message relies on how people interpret it, which is in turn mediated by their social and cultural learnings (Mooij, 2014).

Scholars refer to a communicative exchange of information among people as *interpersonal communication*. Knapp and Daly (2011) define interpersonal communication as the ability to relate to people in written as well as verbal communication. The most common functions of interpersonal communication are listening, talking, and conflict resolution, while eye contact, body movement, and hand gestures are also part of interpersonal communication (Knapp & Daly, 2011). Put simply, interpersonal communication emphasizes sharing or exchanging both verbal and nonverbal information, as well as various behavioral, cognitive, and cultural cues. Hence, interpersonal communication is a mutual, relational, co-constructed process, as opposed to something that one person does "to" someone else (Stewart et al., 2004, p. 131).

In the process of interpersonal communication, people obtain and process information about their environment and interpersonal relationships, including forming impressions and attitudes toward others. It is both challenging and rewarding to achieve predictable outcomes of a communicative exchange with target individuals, especially when no prior relationship exists. Such a relationship is full of uncertainty, but it is possible to obtain attributional certainty by processing information so that people may anticipate subsequent communication and increase interpersonal attraction toward their communication partner (Berger, 1979; Carr & Walther, 2014). Thus, interpersonal communication may be described as the ways people build up beneficial interpersonal relationships by gradually reducing uncertainty to achieve certainty.

Uncertainty Reduction Theory

To study how people obtain and process information to reducing uncertainty, Berger and Calabrese (1975) propose Uncertainty Reduction Theory (URT), an influential theoretical mechanism that guides research in various areas of interpersonal communication as well as other areas of the field (e.g., intercultural, organizational, and health communication), and stimulated alternative theories focused on uncertainty reduction. According to URT, the primary concern of strangers when they first meet is to reduce uncertainty about each other as most of them have a need to reduce uncertainty about others by gaining and processing the information available. The results, based on information processing, can then be used to predict the behavior of others, which is crucial to relationship development. Hence, those who intend to develop a relationship often choose to use more effort to reduce uncertainty about a target individual than those who have no intention to build up a relationship, or vice versa.

To reduce uncertainty about others and the interaction, people employ three basic strategies to seek information about target individuals: interactive, active, and passive information seeking (Berger, 1987). Interactive information-seeking strategy refers to direct communication with target individuals, having a conversation with them, or seeking their feedback. Active strategy involves asking others about the target individual or trying to set up a situation where the target's reactions to the environment can be observed and assessed. Finally, passive information seeking entails observation of target individuals by watching them interact with others at a social gathering (Berger & Calabrese, 1975).

Empirical research has confirmed that the three information-seeking strategies work well as communicative means of uncertainty reduction and thereby increase confidence in one's attributions of a target (Carr & Walther, 2014). Given the influx of social media and other online information sources, researchers add another uncertainty reduction strategy – extractive information seeking – to account for technological advances and affordances enabled by CMC (Ramirez et al., 2002), in particular, how people obtain and process online information, including information shared through social media.

Nowadays people can simply Google or pay a small fee to search personal information, including court and public records, if they seek to learn more about target individuals. Among the online sources, social network sites like Twitter and Facebook are particularly rife with uncertainty-reducing information as users often populate sites with personal information, including demographic information, personal beliefs, calendars and events, acquaintances, and photographs, detailing several years of the user's life across multiple social contexts (Carr & Walther, 2014). Given the richness of online information about individuals, most employers do a routine search on social media platforms about their job applicants before scheduling a face-to-face interview.

Social Information Processing Theory

Another theory addressing people's interactions and information sharing on social media is Social Information Processing Theory (SIP) (Walther, 1992). The theory suggests that people can overcome limitations of communication channels to accomplish their communication goals. SIP assumes that communicators make attempts to achieve communication goals in online settings as much as in offline settings. When the lack of cues available in an online setting presents obstacles to accomplishing their goals, users adapt their behaviors to the cues that are available. Given enough time, people can utilize these circumventions to accomplish goals online as well as face-to-face (FtF).

CMC lacks many of the nonverbal cues that are prevalent in FtF. Because nonverbal cues are heavily utilized in the impression formation process (Berger & Calabrese, 1975), their shortage in CMC poses a problem for impression formation online. However, consistent with SIPT, Tidwell and Walther predicted that individuals adapt to the barriers that CMC presents for uncertainty reduction by finding other ways of getting to know someone that compensates for the limitations that CMC technology imposes. Consistent with their predictions, they found that individuals communicating with a stranger through CMC asked more direct questions and disclosed more than those interacting FtF.

Past research by Westerman and Tamborini (2008) has also examined the relationship between the nonverbal information available in a communication mode and the use of questions and disclosures for uncertainty reduction. Westerman and Tamborini (2008) measured questions and disclosures as indicators of interactive uncertainty reduction strategies (IURS). Their research proposed that mode-based differences in the availability of nonverbal cues would influence the use of IURS to reduce uncertainty, and tested a model of uncertainty reduction across different communication modes. Their results showed that upon initial contact with strangers in both FtF and CMC interactions, uncertainty was not only high, but was equivalent across the two modes.

After five minutes of interaction, uncertainty had decreased in both modes; however, the rate at which uncertainty decreased differed across conditions. Uncertainty was lower in FtF than CMC at this point in time. These results were consistent with SIPT claims (Walther, 1992) that uncertainty reduction goals can be accomplished through similar processes both in FtF and CMC, but these processes take longer in CMC due to the lack of available nonverbal cues. However, the use of IURS was not related to uncertainty, as predicted in this study.

ICT and Communication

Before social media emerged, there was a long list of ICT applications, including audio or video chat, email, instant messaging, and listserv. Each of the ICT applications brings "communication hope" to users so that they may "overcome the distinct finitude of local civil society and bring about a far-flung, nationwide community" (Simonson, 1996). ICT developments have been expected to strengthen personal networks, community activities, and democracy. In this perspective, social media are bringing users "ICT hope." The latest ICT applications, such as social media, might generate new types of communication that eventually help overcome "systematically distorted communication" (Habermas, 1970), a critical challenge the world faces today. New types of communication mean new hope for social change. Therefore, it is useful to investigate what social media add to previous ICT applications that bring about social change.

Research has discovered that social media, like other CMC forms, are not neutral. In fact they have caused many changes in the way people communicate with one another, altering their communication patterns and social networks (Fulk & Collins-Jarvis, 2001). In other words, social media may lead to social effects on interpersonal communication, group communication, and information seeking.

The advent of social networking sites is rapidly changing human interaction, enabling millions of people worldwide to live much of their lives on SNS, like Facebook, Twitter, and LinkedIn (Zhong et al., 2011). Perhaps because social media are designed for interpersonal communication, users often report that they use the new media platforms primarily for maintaining or strengthening existing relationships, while initiating new relationships is the second function (Bryant et al., 2011). Other research reports that SNSs may be used to seek information about potential relationships or partners, construct individual or multiple identities, manage interpersonal impressions and relationships, and add in relational reconnection. The trend exemplifies that the Internet, "by its very nature, is powered by human interaction" (Amichai-Hamburger & Vinitzky, 2010, p. 1290).

Meanwhile, social networking is rewiring "our social DNA, making us more accustomed to openness" (Fletcher, 2010, p. 33). Korean researchers found that SNS have created a new space for users, and they view the space as an aspect of reality that is inseparable from their "real" lives because it is within those spaces that users search for and construct their true identities (Kim & Yun, 2007). Users also tend to develop increased levels of intimacy and liking with those they often interact with on SNS. Other research also show that the SNS use has an impact on the tendency of engaging in elaborative thinking (Zhong et al., 2011). The fact that more and more people connect with each other via social media poses a tremendous pressure on nonusers. Those who choose not to use social media due to lack of knowledge, access, or disinterest often find themselves withdrawn or isolated in a networked society.

Popularity of Social Media

Social media have been noted to reduce the costs, such as time, effort, or expense, that are associated with relational maintenance, and therefore enable users to maintain relationships with an extremely large number of people (Bryant et al., 2011). Research also discovered ample evidence on the impact of social media on intrapersonal communication, which refers to the communication involving all of the internal thought processes, including thinking, perceiving, sensing, evaluating, and interpreting events within oneself. These skills are vital to problem solving, reasoning, and analyzing. The relationship between the use of social media and cognition will be further examined in Chapter 4.

Another reason for the popularity of social media might be its asynchronous nature, meaning users do not have to be on SNS at the same time in order to communicate. Though few studies have been conducted to prove this, prior studies on other forms of CMC, such as emails and text messages, have demonstrated that this feature can facilitate relational maintenance between users with different schedules and provide them with increased control over their impressions by allowing extra time to communicate with one another (Walther & Boyd, 2002). Therefore, it is safe to assume that users enjoy using social media because they are able to gratify their communication needs, which can be explained by the theoretical framework of uses and gratification (see Theory Highlight in this chapter).

The concept of "friends" was significantly altered after Facebook was created in 2004. In those good old days, people used to interact with a few dozen friends regularly. Back in 2007, when a student of mine told me she had over 600 "friends" on her Facebook, I was appalled, as I had only 50. Today, with the development of social media, numerous students have told me that they had several thousand Facebook friends, which is no longer a surprise to me at all. Meanwhile, the information that used to be shared only amongst friends in an inner circle may go viral at lightning speed on social network sites.

Earlier, these were a matter of embarrassment and people used to hide such instances. Now, people announce them on Facebook with fanfare. The concept of interpersonal communication is now fading as people have created numerous groups on Facebook. Anything and everything is communicated among all group members.

Group Communication

Information and communication technologies have long been conceptualized as a means of enabling not only two-way communication, or interpersonal communication, but also multichannel communication, or group communication. Like other forms of mass media, such as newspapers, radio, and television, social media have been increasingly used as an effective tool to mobilize community members and organize collective actions in a series of social movements. Social media can be used to create a more collaborative culture among users, offering new means of collaboration among those who may be otherwise sporadic outside formal activist organizations (Rodriguez, 2013).

Collaboration was once brutally difficult in the era of Industrial Civilization. Today it remains difficult to manage collective actions and organizations, but things are starting to get easier. With the help of social media, various new platforms of collaboration are being built, empowering a more efficient group communication around the world to go against the hierarchy that is deeply ingrained in our society.

With enhanced group communication, people and institutions do not just collaborate more, but also share more with others. In this new context, some US companies share their own intellectual property with competitors, which made little sense in the era of Industrial Civilization. For example, few would understand why IBM gave away $400 million worth of software to Linux. It saved them $900 million a year by developing their own proprietary systems and created a platform for creating a hardware and service business and other opportunities (Olson, 2012). In essence, group communication encourages different thinking. In a more collaborative society, empowerment also means giving up power. It is about achieving power *through* people rather than *over* people. It is about letting go to build more successful organizations and a more open society, in which group communication plays a critical role.

Group communication powered by social media often brings about contentious social consequences. There are plenty of cases in which social media were used to help engage voters, like in Obama's Facebook campaign in 2008, and motivate and organize young people, like in the Twitter Revolution in Moldova in 2009, the "Arab Spring" protests in 2011, and Occupy Central in Hong Kong in 2014.

On the other hand, there are a series of online practices developed by terrorist groups, as well as cyber-dissident movements, such as Wikileaks or Anonymous. There is an ongoing debate about whether social media can themselves foment or produce social movements and revolutions. For most scholars, there is no doubt that social media are creating a new kind of social order and strengthening human communication.

Many people are used to the role that social media, like Twitter, Facebook, and Instagram, play in their everyday lives. However, watching them during social movements, like the protests or uprisings in Ukraine, Venezuela, or Hong Kong in 2014, reminds us that social media are quickly becoming a real-time, crowd information source. Twitter, for example, had been a powerful crowd-sourced media platform broadcasting breaking news about the riots in Ferguson, MO after the shooting of an unarmed black man. Anyone could see video clips posted by participants, live tweets on the arrest of journalists, and so on. Similarly, for many who searched for information about the ongoing protests in Ukraine, Venezuela, or Hong Kong, social media often mattered more than traditional media outlets.

The world saw the same kind of phenomenon in Turkey, Egypt, and other Arab countries, where anti-government demonstrations erupted and quickly turned into mass protests lasting for months. In those cases, Twitter, Facebook, and other forms of social media became a crucial source of information for protestors and activists, in part because the pro-government media in those countries avoided covering the news. In other words, social media often serves users like a citizen-powered version of CNN during a social crisis, where they can seek real-time information that the news media are unwilling or unable to cover. The above cases unveil another function of social media, which is *information seeking*.

Information Seeking

Information seeking can be defined as "the pursuit of desired information about a target" (Ramirez et al., 2002, p. 217). Social media essentially function as archives of social information at the disposal of users in pursuit of information about a target (Bryant et al., 2011). Sanders (2008) explains that active, passive, and interactive strategies function to reduce uncertainty on Facebook, and found that interactive strategies most effectively reduced uncertainty, passive strategies were only mildly effective at reducing uncertainty, and active strategies were unimportant in reducing uncertainty on Facebook.

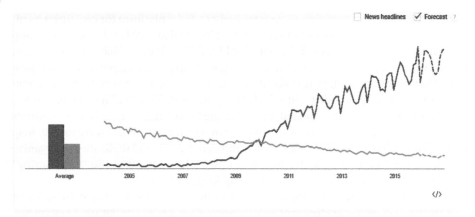

Figure 3.2 The search results of the term "social media" in blue and "new media" in red on Google Trends (Data generated by the author on November 20, 2015).

Additionally, intense Facebook users reported more confidence in their ability to reduce uncertainty with information collected on Facebook, signaling that intense users might view Facebook as a valuable source of social information. Social media might also enable a mixture of passive and active strategies to the extent that users gather information that third parties have posted on a person of interest's profile, yet do not directly ask that third party for information (Bryant et al., 2011). Social media users who are skeptical of other members' identity claims might strategically seek information to confirm or discredit claims made by other users or new relational partners (Walther et al., 2009).

Google Trends reveals that few people searched the term "social media" in 2004. It was only toward the end of 2009 that the term enjoyed an explosion of interest from 2010 onwards, while the term "new media" shows a steady drop of interest since 2000 (see Figure 3.2). As social media increase in popularity, they will likely continue to serve as a primary source of information, not only about users that create a file, but also as a news source in daily life.

Theory Highlight: Uses and Gratifications Theory

Uses and Gratifications Theory measures how people use the media and what kind of functions the media serves for audience members as active receivers (Katz, 1959), instead of what the media does to audiences. The theory suggests that the message is only one possible influencer as even the most powerful messages cannot have an effect on an individual who does not consume it. On the other hand, audience members deliberately choose to use specific types of media to gratify their needs. Uses and gratifications focuses on: "(1) the social and psychological origins of needs (2), which generate expectations (3) of the mass media or other sources (4), which lead to differential patterns of media exposure (5), resulting in need gratifications (6) and other consequences (7), perhaps mostly unintended ones" (Katz et al., 1974, p. 20). Rubin (2002) includes seven elements in uses and gratifications: psychological and social environment, needs and motives to communicate, the media, attitudes and expectations about the media, functional alternatives to using the media, communication behavior, and the outcomes or consequences of behavior.

Mass communication studies used to emphasize what the media does to the audience. Audience members were treated as passive receivers, who were directly influenced by media messages. Such a traditional mechanistic approach emphasized short-term, immediate changes in audience members' thoughts, attitudes, or behaviors. However, later studies showed that the media actually do less to the audience than what was expected; thus the pioneers in this field started to lose interest in communication research. Communication scholar Bernard Berelson claimed that communication research might be dead.

In 1959, American and Israeli sociologist Elihu Katz introduced a functional approach to the media, known as "uses and gratifications." Uses and gratifications shifted the focus of research from media's direct effects on receivers as a mechanistic approach instead to measuring how people use the media.

The emphasis of this theory is on individual differences and active audience members (Haridakis, 2002), indicating gratifications obtained from media are mostly based on the preexisting needs of individual users. Katz (1959) concludes that individual differences constrain direct media effects, which means the same media message does not have an identical effect on everyone. Different intentions, selectivity, and involvement of the audience lead to different media effects.

Uses and gratification is considered to be a starting point when new media technologies are introduced. It examines why people adopt some specific types of media (newspaper, radio, TV, internet) or certain genres of media (entertainment, news, talk shows) to meet their different needs. By comparing motives across media, and with newer media, new emerging media could provide better viewer satisfaction.

Summary

For a better understanding of social media's impact, this chapter presents a theoretical background for information processing in the context of CMC. Social media, in essence, are part of CMC. A detailed introduction was thus devoted to CMC, especially the significant differences between CMC and face-to-face communication. CMC provides new opportunities to those who have not fully enjoyed the benefits in a network society due to lack of access to media technologies. However, CMC is also blamed for being asocial and antisocial as it contains fewer nonverbal cues than face-to-face communication. It is problematic if CMC users are assumed to be passive information receivers. They are often active information processors who can accrue accurate impressions of others and build high-quality relations with them in an online environment.

This chapter also introduces the Uncertainty Reduction Theory that addresses how people obtain and process information for reducing uncertainty. The URT claims that individuals who intend to develop a relationship with others would make more effort to reduce uncertainty about them than those who have no such intention. Social Information Processing Theory is also discussed and argues that individuals often work hard to achieve communication goals in both online and offline settings. Both theories should help to understand how people interact with others and process information on social media. Finally, the chapter reviews how ICT applications transform communication, including interpersonal and group communication. Social media, as one of the latest ICT applications, are becoming a real-time, crowd-sourced information source for users. This may explain why many users are beginning to find that using social media can be quite addictive.

Looking Ahead

Chapter 4 will cover how people process information on social media, which could be quite different from processing news information from traditional media outlets. The social media use may affect judgment and decision making (JDM). It will introduce how scholars study JDM, in particular, people's selective exposure. The main features of JDM are empirically investigated in those areas, and these results should help explain some important information-processing strategies and phenomena, such as selective exposure. The chapter also addresses the important role a social context plays in affecting JDM, which can change people's purchase decisions and the ways they express opinions.

Discussion

1. Have you seen some social changes unfolding on social media recently? What is the role of social media play in those social changes, if any?
2. How do you think that computer-mediated communication is affecting our lives and work now and in the coming years?
3. Can you design a research project measuring the effects of social media by employing the Social Information Processing Theory?

References

Amichai-Hamburger, Y., & Vinitzky, G. (2010). Social network use and personality. *Computers in Human Behavior*, *26*(6), 1289–1295. https://doi.org/10.1016/j.chb.2010.03.018.

Berger, C. R. (1979). Beyond initial interaction: Uncertainty, understanding, and the development of interpersonal relationships. In H. Giles & R. N. St. Clair (Eds.), *Language and social psychology* (pp. 122–144). Blackwell.

Berger, C. R. (1987). Communicating under uncertainty. In M. E. Roloff & G. R. Miller (Eds.), *Interpersonal processes: New directions in communication research* (pp. 39–62). Sage.

Berger, C. R., & Calabrese, R. J. (1975). Some explorations in initial interaction and beyond: Toward a developmental theory of interpersonal communication. *Human Communication Research, 1*(2), 99–112. https://doi.org/10.1111/j.1468-2958.1975.tb00258.x.

Blumer, H. (1955). Collective behavior. In A. M. Lee (Ed.), *Principles of sociology* (2nd ed., pp. 165–198). Barnes and Noble.

Bryant, E. M., Marmo, J., & Ramirez, A. (2011). A functional approach to social networking sites. In K. B. Wright & L. M. Webb (Eds.), *Computer-mediated communication in personal relationships* (pp. 3–20). Peter Lang.

Carr, C. T., & Walther, J. B. (2014). Increasing attributional certainty via social media: Learning about others one bit at a time. *Journal of Computer-Mediated Communication, 19*(4), 922–937. https://doi.org/10.1111/jcc4.12072.

Ellison, N. B., & boyd, d. m. (2013). Sociality through social network sites. In W. H. Dutton (Ed.), *The Oxford handbook of internet studies* (pp. 151–172). Oxford University Press. https://doi.org/10.1093/oxfordhb/9780199589074.013.0008.

Fletcher, D. (2010, May 31). Friends without borders. *Time, 175* (21), 32–38.

Fulk, J., & Collins-Jarvis, L. (2001). Wired meetings: Technological mediation of organizational gatherings. In F. M. Jablin & L. L. Putnam (Eds.), *The new handbook of organizational communication* (2nd ed., pp. 624–703). Sage. https://doi.org/10.4135/9781412986243.

Guadagno, R. E., & Cialdini, R. B. (2002). Online persuasion: An examination of gender differences in computer-mediated interpersonal influence. *Group Dynamics: Theory, Research, and Practice, 6*(1), 38–51. https://doi.org/10.1037//1089-2699.6.1.38.

Habermas, J. (1970). On systematically distorted communication. *Inquiry: An Interdisciplinary Journal of Philosophy, 13*(1–4), 205–218. https://doi.org/10.1080/00201747008601590.

Haridakis, P. M. (2002). Viewer characteristics, exposure to television violence, and aggression. *Media Psychology, 4* (4), 323–352. https://doi.org/10.1207/S1532785XMEP0404_02.

Herring, S. C. (1996). *Computer-mediated communication: Linguistic, social and cross-cultural perspectives*. Benjamins.

Herring, S. C. (2014). Research: Computer-mediated communication. *Bulletin of the Association for Information Science and Technology, 41–44*(3), 41. https://doi.org/10.1002/bult.2014.1720400313.

Katz, E. (1959). Mass communications research and the study of popular culture: An editorial note on a possible future for this journal. *Studies in Public Communication, 2*, 1–6. https://repository.upenn.edu/cgi/viewcontent.cgi?article=1168&context=asc_papers.

Katz, E., Blumber, G. H., & Gurevitch, M. (1974). Utilization of mass communication by the individual. In G. H. Blumber & E. Katz (Eds.), *The uses of mass communication: Current perspectives on gratifications research*. Sage.

Kim, K.-H., & Yun, H. (2007). Crying for me, crying for us: Relational dialectics in a Korean social network site. *Journal of Computer-Mediated Communication, 13*(1), 298–315. https://doi.org/10.1111/j.1083-6101.2007.00397.x.

Knapp, M. L., & Daly, J. A. (2011). *The Sage handbook of interpersonal communication* (4th ed.). Sage.

Lee, M., & Spears, R. (1995). Love at first byte? Building personal relationships over computer networks. In J. T. Wood & S. Duck (Eds.), *Under-studied relationships: Off the beaten track* (pp. xvi, 280 pp.). Sage Publications.

Mooij, M. K. d. (Ed.). (2014). *Human and mediated communication around the world – A comprehensive review and analysis.* Springer. https://doi.org/10.1007/978-3-319-01249-0.

Olson, P. (2012). *How the internet will reboot civilization.* Forbes. http://www.forbes.com/sites/parmyolson/2012/2006/2026/heres-how-the-internet-will-reboot-civilization.

Ramirez, A., Jr., Walther, J. B., Burgoon, J. K., & Sunnafrank, M. (2002). Information-seeking strategies, uncertainty, and computer-mediated communication: Toward a conceptual model. *Human Communication Research, 28*(2), 213–228. https://doi.org/10.1111/j.1468-2958.2002.tb00804.x.

Rice, R. E., & Case, D. (1983). Electronic message systems in the University: A description of use and utility. *Journal of Communication, 32*(1), 131–152. https://doi.org/10.1111/j.1460-2466.1983.tb02380.x.

Rice, R. E., & Gattiker, U. E. (2001). New media and organizational structuring. In F. M. Jablin & L. Putnam (Eds.), *The new handbook of organizational communication: Advances in theory, research, and methods* (pp. 544–583). Sage. https://doi.org/10.4135/9781412986243.n14.

Rodriguez, S. (2013). Making sense of social change: Observing collective action in networked cultures. *Sociology Compass, 7*(12), 1053–1064. https://doi.org/10.1111/soc4.12088.

Rubin, A. M. (2002). Media uses and effects: A uses-and-gratifications perspective. In J. Bryant & D. Zillman (Eds.), *Media effects: Advances in theory and research* (pp. 525–548). Lawrence Erlbaum Associates.

Sanders, W. S. (2008, November 21–24). Uncertainty reduction and information-seeking strategies on Facebook [Paper presented]. The 94th National Communication Association Annual Convention, San Diego, CA.

Schaefer, R. T. (2012). *Sociology: A brief introduction* (10th ed.). McGraw-Hill.

Siegel, J., Dubrovsky, V., Kiesler, S., & McGuire, T. W. (1986). Group processes in computer-mediated communication. *Organizational Behavior and Human Decision Processes, 37*(2), 157–187. https://doi.org/10.1016/0749-5978(86)90050-6.

Simonson, P. (1996). Dreams of democratic togetherness: Communication hope from Cooley to Katz. *Critical Studies in Mass Communication, 13*(4), 324–342. https://doi.org/10.1080/15295039609366985.

Simpson, J. (2002). Computer-mediated communication. *ELT Journal, 56*(4), 414–415. https://doi.org/10.1093/elt/56.4.414.

Sproull, L., & Kiesler, S. (1986). Reducing social context cues: Electronic mail in organizational communication. *Management Science, 32*(11), 1492–1512. https://doi.org/10.1287/mnsc.32.11.1492.

Stewart, J. R., Zediker, K. E., & Witteborn, S. (2004). *Together communicating interpersonally: A social construction approach* (6th ed.). Oxford University Press.

Thurlow, C., Tomic, A., & Lengel, L. B. (2004). *Computer mediated communication: Social interaction and the internet.* Sage.

Walther, J. B. (1992). Interpersonal effects in computer-mediated interaction: A relational perspective. *Communication Research, 19*(1), 52–90. https://doi.org/10.1177/009365092019001003.

Walther, J. B. (2011). Theories of computer-mediated communication and interpersonal relations. In M. L. Knapp & J. A. Daly (Eds.), *The Sage handbook of interpersonal communication* (4th ed., pp. 443–479). Sage.

Walther, J. B., & Boyd, S. (2002). Communication technology and society: Audience adoption and uses. In C. A. Lin & D. J. Atkin (Eds.), *The Hampton Press communication series* (pp. 153–188). Hampton Press.

Walther, J. B., Van Der Heide, B., Hamel, L. M., & Hillary C. Shulman. (2009). Self-generated versus other-generated statements and impressions in computer-mediated: A test of warranting theory using Facebook. *Communication Research, 36*(2), 229–253. https://doi.org/10.1177/0093650208330251.

Walther, J. B., Van der Heide, B., Ramirez, A., Burgoon, J. K., & Peña, J. (2015). Interpersonal and hypersonal dimensions of computer-mediated communication. In S. S. Sundar (Ed.), *The handbook of the psychology of communication technology* (pp. 3–22). Wiley-Blackwell.

Warschauer, M. (2003). *Technology and social inclusion: Rethinking the digital divide*. MIT Press.

Westerman, D., & Tamborini, R. (2008, May 22–26). Uncertainty reduction over time in initial stranger interactions: A Social Information Processing Theory approach [Paper presented]. The 58th Annual Conference of the International Communication Association, Montreal, Quebec, Canada.

Zhong, B. (2020). Social consequences of internet civilization. *Computers in Human Behavior*. https://doi.org/10.1016/j.chb.2020.106308.

Zhong, B., Hardin, M., & Sun, T. (2011). Less effortful thinking leads to more social networking? The associations between the use of social network sites and personality traits. *Computers in Human Behavior, 27*(3), 1265–1271. https://doi.org/10.1016/j.chb.2011.01.008.

4

Social Media, Judgment, and Decision Making

LEARNING GOALS

This chapter will help you understand:

- How do scholars study judgment and decision making?
- What is selective exposure?
- How do people process social media information?
- Does social media information affect judgment and decision making?

KEY CONCEPTS

Selective exposure	Crescendo effect
Information processing	Online healthcare support

THEORY HIGHLIGHT

Cognitive Dissonance Theory

Overview

A global trend is emerging which shows that people are consuming more and more information through social media. People get on social media to communicate with others, send messages, update statuses, post "likes," tweet or retweet, make comments, review products, obtain or share news, photos, and video, etc. All of the online behaviors show that social media have increasingly become platforms for users to exhibit their daily lives. On social media, what is shared, in essence, is information, which can be in textual, audio, or video form.

British sociologist Anthony Giddens (1999) said, "Globalization isn't only about what is 'out there,' remote and far away from the individual. It is an 'in here' phenomenon too, influencing intimate and personal aspects of our lives." Similarly, it is problematic to view the information on social media as only affecting something "out there," like interpersonal or group communication. The information also has an "in here" impact on social media users, including evaluation of interpersonal relationships, information processing, and perception of social environment, etc. In other words, socially based information may influence people's judgment and decision making (JDM).

Information has long been found to play a vital role when people reconstruct the world, interpret it, and respond to it adaptively. As social media become an important social milieu that enables interpersonal and group communication by allowing users to create and share information, the use of social media, or, more exactly, the information shared through various social media platforms, could shape people's judgment and decision making. Despite a growing body of social media scholarship, research regarding cognitive and behavioral factors that influence users' JDM is still in its early stage. Some direct links have been discovered between the use of social media and JDM, mainly due to the increased connectedness that is facilitated by digital media technologies.

In the business world, social media are also found to play an important role in consumers' purchase decisions. A study from the Advertising Research Foundation, for example, showed that much of consumer spending was influenced by the information on social media, such as "likes," reviews, and tweets. Social media not only introduced consumers to a brand they were previously unfamiliar with, but helped change their existing opinions of that brand during their buying decision process (ARF, 2012). That is why anyone who comes to "the world of work these days needs to have an intelligent opinion about media technology" (Thurlow et al., 2004, p. 3).

Media Technology and Brain Activity

The internet-based digital media technologies, including social media, are the most widespread and rapidly adopted technology in human history. Almost instantly, these digital media technologies have revolutionized how people search for information, consume news content, and manage their social lives in the era of the internet civilization. For centuries, scientists have developed an intense interest in understanding how media technology use may affect brain development and activities, such as decision-making and emotional processing functions (see Figure 4.1). It is not yet clear about the impact of the emerging digital media technologies for connection, information, communication, and screen time is having on human brains and cognitive functioning (Firth et al., 2019). Prior to the birth of the internet, a large body of research had convincingly demonstrated that the brain is somewhat malleable to environmental

Media Technology and Brain

1900	1950	1980	2000	2010	2020
Book	Movie	Computer	Email	Podcast	App
Journal	Radio	Video game	Internet	Smartphone	Chatbot
Play	Television	Walkman	Texting	Social media	Digital assistant

Figure 4.1   Scientist have an intense interest in studying how the media technology use affects brain activities.

demands and stimuli, particularly with regards to learning new processes, due to its capacity for neuroplasticity (Firth et al., 2019).

Scientists know that human brains have been very adaptive and sensitive to environmental and stimuli, for example, the constant interaction with social media content through the smartphone's touchscreen interface. The external stimuli due to the use of digital media technology may cause profound neural changes in the brain's cortical regions associated with sensory and motor processing of the hand and thumb (Small et al., 2009). Some of the changes may affect the brain's structure and function, inducing both positive and adverse neurocognitive changes. Scientific evidence indicates the possibility that various types of media technology usage could affect the brain and cognitive processes in both adverse and beneficial ways (Firth et al., 2019).

Research has identified that digital media technologies are influencing users' brains and cognitive processes in several specific areas: (a) attention span and tendency of distraction. The multifaceted stream of incoming information encouraging users to engage in attentional-switching and media multitasking behaviors, rather than sustained focus; (b) the ubiquitous and rapid access to online factual information outcompeting previous transactive systems, and potentially even internal memory processes; and (c) the online social world paralleling "real world" cognitive processes, and becoming meshed with our offline sociality, introducing the possibility for the special properties of social media to impact on "real life" in unforeseen ways (Firth et al., 2019, p. 126). This chapter will particularly examine the impact of social media use on people's judgment and decision making, especially in the areas of consuming news and healthcare information.

Judgment and Decision-Making Research

Judgment and decision making pervade human experience, which happen everywhere all the time in people's daily lives. Every day people need to assess the information and make decisions on what actions should be taken. For example, one needs to make daily decisions on what to wear for the day, what needs to be done at work, where can be a good lunch place, etc. Some decisions, like buying stocks or choosing a career, are more important than others, such as which shirt to put on, due to the possible consequences caused.

Early scholars of JDM designed a rational actor model to study how people make decisions, which assumes that decision makers are "impartial and unflawed thinkers who have an unlimited capacity for analysis and calculation" (Dunning, 2012, p. 252). According to this model, decision makers often have fixed preferences about what they want and complete information they need for decision making. Their top concern is their material self-interest; the interest of other actors do not matter and are given little thought, if any. They are so rational that they are unmoved by incidental passions, emotions, or moods during the process of decision making. Thus, rational decision makers always choose the most optimal behavior possible (Dunning, 2012).

To today's readers, such a rational decision maker may sound more like a robot than a human being. By employing this model, economists had achieved certain surprising success in the analysis of human behavior for over a century (Becker, 1976). To make it more realistic, later scholars started to revise the model, and some tried to change it dramatically by explaining people's judgments and decisions in their everyday world.

Psychologists began to provide an alternative model of human decision making in the 1950s (Edwards, 1954; Simon, 1957). The new model suggests that people often do not have the cognitive capacity or sufficient time to do all the thinking that the rational actor model often demands or assumes. Simon (1957) discovered that, in reality, people frequently fail to conduct an exhaustive analysis of any decision, but stop well before they have thoroughly analyzed all the information they have. Edwards (1968) found that decision makers seldom revise their beliefs when new information is available. Even when they revise, many only do so by following a few basic and simple principles, which do not require a lot of effortful thinking.

Dunning (2012) noted that it was with the "heuristics and biases" work of Kahneman and Tversky that the JDM research started to take off in the 1970s. The core idea of the heuristics and biases program is that judgment under uncertainty is often based on a limited number of simplifying heuristics rather than more formal and extensive information processing, and these heuristics typically yield accurate judgment, but can give rise to systematic error (Gilovich et al., 2002). According to Dunning (2012), there are five central insights of JDM research:

1. People follow crude and quick heuristics rather than exhaustive analysis to make decisions. In other words, most decisions do not involve intense, exhaustive, and analytical thinking.
2. Reference points in the environment sway judgments in decisive ways. Unlike the rational actor model, JDM research shows that people's preferences during the process of decision making are often not well formed before making a decision. Their decisions often change based on features of the choice presented to them.
3. People use the information available to them to make a decision, but often fail to recognize that there is other relevant information they may use as well.
4. People lean heavily on confirmatory evidence and neglect disconfirming information. They thus tend to favor information that confirms that conclusion over information that would disconfirm or contradict it.
5. When thinking about JDM outcomes, people give disproportionate weight to outcomes that happen now or in the near future, rather than in the more distant future. When risky options are evaluated, the possible losses are weighted more than potential gains.

For a better understanding of the social media impact on JDM, this chapter will investigate more about Item 4 listed above by analyzing the concept of "selective exposure."

Selective Exposure

In the era of internet civilization, so-called "information overload" has become one of the biggest irritations in modern life. Anyone could be easily confused by never-ending threads of information such as emails, tweets, Facebook updates, YouTube videos, etc. Facing such an enormity of information, people sometimes feel overwhelmed and confused.

On the other hand, people are not just passive absorbers of the information shared on social media, but selectively search, process, and analyze the information they obtain. This is typically done to avoid irrelevant or useless information. There are occasions when information is selected based on its agreeable nature (Cotton, 1985). For instance, people tend to systematically add friends, join Facebook groups, or follow tweets that disseminate consistent information supporting their standpoints. In other words, they choose to receive information that supports rather than conflicts with their existing beliefs, ideas, or values because this type of information is more preferred. The preference for supportive information over opposing information has been termed selective exposure (Fischer et al., 2012). The tendency has also been labeled confirmation bias (Jonas et al., 2001). It occurs in both individual (Fischer et al., 2008) and group (Van Ginkel & van Knippenberg, 2008) decision making. The effect gets stronger for emotionally charged issues and deep-rooted beliefs.

The explanation of selective exposure can be classified as either motivational or cognitive accounts (Fischer et al., 2012). Motivational approaches stress that people prefer consistent information and neglect inconsistent information because they wish to defend their perspectives (Olson & Stone, 2005). It has also been argued that selective exposure reduces cognitive dissonance (Festinger, 1957), threats to self-esteem (Pyszczynski & Greenberg, 1987), and the complexity of information processing (Ditto & Lopez, 1992). Motivational approaches reveal that negative mood increased one's preference for consonant over dissonant information during the process of decision making, and selective exposure alleviated negative mood (Jonas et al., 2006).

Cognitive explanations for selective exposure focus on biases in information processing, such as an asymmetric attention to consistent information or obtaining such information (Fischer et al., 2012). One tends to experience mental stress or discomfort when being confronted by contradictory information that challenges one's beliefs, ideas, or values. Psychologists call the stress or discomfort "cognitive dissonance" (Festinger, 1957). People are motivated to seek out information that is consistent with their attitudes and to avoid or ignore information that is attitudinally inconsistent (or dissonant).

Festinger (1957) developed the theory of cognitive dissonance, proposing that one way the dissonance can be reduced is through selective exposure. When inconsistency (dissonance) is experienced, individuals tend to become psychologically uncomfortable and are motivated to attempt to reduce this dissonance, as well as actively avoid situations and information that are likely to increase it. Over time, this behavior is likely to become habituated so that users turn to their preferred sources automatically, no matter what the subject matter is.

A long stream of research has been devoted to the understanding of dissonance-motivated selective exposure to information, but several key questions concerning the tendency of information search remain unanswered. First, according to Cotton (1985), previous studies in this area did not clearly differentiate seeking consistent information from avoiding inconsistent information. Thus, it is not clear whether selective exposure is primarily about seeking consistent information or actively avoiding inconsistent information, or if both occur simultaneously. Another question that is not fully investigated is how individual differences may modify selective exposure. Are some people more likely than others to seek out or avoid information? A third unanswered question is whether selective exposure to information changes over time. The final question, with no convincing answer, is how widespread selective exposure exists in people's JDM.

JDM and Social Endorsement

Empirical evidence suggests that the impact of social media use on individual, group, and organizational decision making can be extensive (Power & Phillips-Wren, 2011). What concerns researchers is not whether social media information alters users' JDM but how, especially in a positive or negative way. Recent research reveals that consuming information on social media can positively or negatively impact the rationality and effectiveness of decision making. For example, some who rely heavily on information from social networks rather than expert opinion and facts may make more biased decisions. This chapter will particularly examine how the information disseminated through social media may influence users' decisions in news choice and healthcare behavior.

Perhaps because of a more polarized political environment, Americans and their news use are showing a general trend of moving toward divergent political orientations (Messing & Westwood, 2014). Evidence suggests that Americans are increasingly polarized along partisan lines. For example, research shows "a substantial increase in partisan polarization" during US House elections, in which there has been a substantial increase in partisan voting" (Abramowitz et al., 2008, p. 87).

As for people's news use, Iyengar and Hahn (2009) found that Americans showed selective exposure effects to news information: conservatives and Republicans tended to get the news from Fox News and to avoid news reports from CNN and NPR, while liberals and Democrats displayed exactly the opposite tendency, dividing their attention equally between CNN and NPR, but avoiding Fox News. They also found that the pattern of selective exposure based on partisan affinity held true for both news stories involving controversial issues and those of relatively "soft" subjects, such as crime and travel (Iyengar & Hahn, 2009). Some voters' increased exposure to one-sided news coverage indicates an "echo chamber" effect – the news serves to reinforce existing beliefs and attitudes (Iyengar & Hahn, 2009). This suggests a strong connection between the polarization of news audiences and their choice of news information.

Nowadays, social media are playing a growingly important role in how people find news. A 2020 national survey shows that over half of US adults (53%) relies on social media for news, among which Facebook is the news powerhouse – being a regular source of news for a third of Americans (Shearer & Mitchell, 2021). The trend is especially pronounced among young people who prefer to get news through social media rather than traditional media like newspapers or television.

The pervasive use of social media, to some researchers, is presumed to reinforce people's selective exposure to news information, where users could easily customize their information flow so that they may obtain more consistent information supporting their existing beliefs, and filter out as much inconsistent information as they like. Like other ICT applications, social media not only help disseminate more information at a faster speed, but also enable users to access information more selectively. Although facing an infinite variety of information, social media users may limit their exposure to certain information they find disagreeable. Thus, social media use could exacerbate the fragmentation of the media and the citizenry, narrowing rather than widening people's political horizons.

Iyengar and Hahn (2009) argue that information overload in the new media environment may further bolster selective exposure. Compared to traditional news information, the audience may not so easily avoid coverage of political candidates they dislike because news reports typically assign equal coverage to each (Iyengar & Hahn, 2009). They stressed that when candidates, interest groups, and voters all converge on the internet, the possibility of selective exposure to political information increases.

Other researchers, however, hold that this concept has ignored fundamental changes in the way that the public uses ICT, specifically with respect to social media and news consumption (Messing & Westwood, 2014). They argue that socially based information like online news fundamentally alters the context in which news reading occurs. Social media provide a venue that promotes exposure to news from politically heterogeneous individuals, and which serves to emphasize social value rather than partisan affiliation (Messing & Westwood, 2014).

Messing and Westwood (2014) found that the social endorsement generated among social media users increases the probability that people select information, and that the mere presence of social endorsement serves to reduce political selectivity to levels indistinguishable from chance. Their findings suggest that social endorsement could change the ways in which people select news information in the context of social media.

As a result, they argue that social media should be expected to increase users' exposure to a variety of news and politically diverse information and that social media may constitute a force that drives citizens to read news from various sources (Messing & Westwood, 2014). The two researchers also caution that social endorsement is not a panacea – de facto selective exposure and partisan polarization will continue to occur offline if users choose to limit their news consumption to partisan sources and maintain a politically homogeneous network of contacts (Messing & Westwood, 2014).

Power and Phillips-Wren (2011) also reported the impact of social media use on people's decision making. They found that people's participation in online communities facilitated through social media could accelerate decision process and information development. Bulmer and Dimauro (2009) found that social network participation increasingly affects executive decision making at companies. They found that most respondents (80%) were able to accelerate the decision process and information/strategy development by participating in online communities. At the same time, endorsement (e.g., like, read, share, retweet) is found to be at the center of collaboration in social media communities.

Auditore (2011) uses the term "crescendo effect" to describe the phenomenon of how much feedback can be generated in a social media community in the form of tweets, Facebook "Likes," LinkedIn mentions, and other digital means of notification. This is paramount because the new flow of influence acts like a crescendo through the ecosystem of social media. The crescendo effect in social media environments has a great impact on consumers' buying decisions. Specifically, it is not the number of clicks that an online article gets, but the ecosystem of the viewers, how they collaborate, and how the influence flows from it (Auditore, 2011). This also holds true in the area of healthcare, where social media are transforming the patient–physician relationship (Nelson et al., 2013).

The Power of Social Context

By now it is clear that social interactions with others, online or offline, have a substantial impact on people's judgment and decision making. This indicates that environmental cues often strongly influence people's JDM. For example, consumers reported that their purchase decisions and satisfaction with their shopping experience were affected by the presence of other consumers, no matter if the others were their friends or strangers (Moe & Schweidel, 2014). People are found to process information differently when others are present, an effect that is not limited to offline environmental factors (Moe & Schweidel, 2014). Even when others are present in a virtual environment, like in a social media network, people's JDM can also be affected.

The power of social context can alter the ways people express opinions. People tend to voice more agreeable opinions in certain social contexts so as to conform to social norms. Generally, people living in Asian countries are more sensitive to the cues of a social context than Westerners, in that Asians try not to express opinions that may be different from those in the same setting. Still, both Asians and Westerners show a general tendency to avoid direct conflict with others when they interact.

Yet, similar social dynamics have been found to exist in large and anonymous online opinion environments (Moe & Schweidel, 2014). The dynamics are termed *adjustment effects* in online opinion expression, where the opinions that have been previously expressed by others can shape how we express opinions on social media. The social media comments of others can affect our own opinions on two different levels. At the deepest level, we may actively take in the opinions of others and process this new information, and combined with our prior opinion, we may reevaluate our beliefs. In such circumstances, the social context influences our opinion formation process and the opinion we hold fundamentally changes as a result of our social encounters. Alternatively, we may find ourselves altering only the opinion that we express. In these cases, our opinion has not actually changed and the social context affects only our opinion expression, indicating the limits of the social context power (Moe & Schweidel, 2014).

In an online environment, social media allow people to easily connect with others, regardless of whether they belong to the influential elite or the mass market. When these connections form a networked community, information, ideas, and opinions can spread easily. This process can be initiated either by a few influential individuals or it can emerge from a broader population. The structure of our social networks and the paths that word-of-mouth take over these social ties are more transparent with social media than ever before. As a result, the socially based information distributed through social media may have a profound influence on people's JDM and behavior, and the latter will be further discussed in Chapter 5.

Social Media for Patient Support

Social media, like Facebook, are becoming an important support community online, where patients and caregivers can connect, especially in various disease-specific groups. For patients with chronic or rare diseases, using social media to seek health information and connect with others who share similar experiences are an invaluable part of patientcare (Walker, 2013). Social integration are important not only to the able-bodied, but even more so to those with disabilities and chronic or mental illness because they face a growing risk of isolation. It is well established that social isolation causes feelings of loneliness, low self-esteem, and hopelessness, while social support helps patients maintain positive mood and optimism, increases optimism and self-esteem, and decreases depression (Symister & Friend, 2003).

Online patient support communities often provide social support in ways their physical world may not (Preece & Maloney-Krichmar, 2003). Such communities provide patients with access to individuals who are willing to share experiences and insights with a level of empathy that "may encourage strong relationships to develop making these communities some of the most important on the Internet" (p. 35). Online health communities are particularly valuable to anyone who is isolated or lacks mobility, where patients could "ask difficult questions," and "gain support and wisdom" from others (Bonniface & Green, 2007, p. 67).

Another benefit of online support is that it helps patients who may not be able to or do not have the desire to attend face-to-face sessions (White & Dorman, 2001, p. 693). Comparing online and offline support groups to cancer support communities, a study reveals little difference between cancer patients' perceptions of the listserv and their perceptions of their face-to-face partner regarding support for their specific illness (Turner et al., 2001). It is also found that the face-to-face interaction makes some people reluctant to fully disclose their medical conditions. Contrarily, Turner, Grube, and Meyers concluded that the "online support members may be less concerned with preserving face and may communicate support in a more 'bald on record' way" (p. 246), a quality in the communication that patients wanted.

Although the benefits are numerous, some participants could get lost in the virtual world, which is one of their major potential challenges. Other challenges or barriers for those seeking social support online are technical functions. As more organizations begin to identify potential strengths and weaknesses of providing support or information in virtual worlds, perhaps the technical challenges will be resolved rapidly.

In conclusion, as cost and access to healthcare and social support is already challenging for millions of individuals around the globe, access to online support through social network sites is becoming more popular. A growing number of groups and organizations are set to provide online support, which is viewed as a tremendous help to patients and their families. The trend also calls for a better understanding of long-term implications of social media use for healthcare purposes.

Theory Highlight: Cognitive Dissonance Theory

People tend to seek and maintain consistency in their beliefs and behaviors. However, when they conflict with each other, or with what's been previously embraced, they experience cognitive dissonance – a discomfort caused by conflicting attitudes, beliefs, or behaviors. The discrepancy between beliefs and behaviors often causes mental stress or tension, which drives people to change conflicting beliefs or behaviors in order to relieve or eliminate the dissonance.

Psychologist Leon Festinger (1957) proposed cognitive dissonance theory to study how people cope with conflicting attitudes, beliefs, or behaviors (cognitive dissonance). The theory suggests that people seek to reduce or eliminate inconsistency between attitudes or behaviors (dissonance) whenever they can. Dissonance occurs when people have to choose between two conflicting beliefs or actions. The strength of the dissonance depends on two factors: the perceived importance of the subject and the number of dissonant beliefs. To cope with dissonance, people tend to: (1) reduce the importance of dissonant beliefs or behaviors; (2) add more consonant beliefs that outweigh the existing dissonance; or (3) change the dissonant beliefs or behaviors. Here is an example:

"Consider someone who buys an expensive car but discovers that it is not comfortable on long drives. Dissonance exists between their beliefs that they have bought a good car and that a good car should be comfortable. Dissonance could be eliminated by deciding that it does not matter since the car is mainly used for short trips (reducing the importance of the dissonant belief) or focusing on the cars strengths such as safety, appearance, handling (thereby adding more consonant beliefs). The dissonance could also be eliminated by getting rid of the car, but this behavior is a lot harder to achieve than changing beliefs."

(Aïmeur, 2002, p. 230)

As shown in this example, people are more likely to change their belief to accommodate behavior in the case of a discrepancy between them. Since the late 1950s, cognitive dissonance theory has been extensively used by researchers in psychology and communication areas in studying decision making, attitude formation, and factors contributing to their changes. Findings in this stream of research also suggest that some people may change their attitudes, say, to a political candidate or a controversial event, if they are manipulated into certain activities or behaviors. Thus, the theory is of particular interest to researchers of judgment and decision making.

Summary

This chapter focuses on how people process information on social media, especially the practical implications when they obtain, produce, and distribute information on the digital platforms. It is important to understand how social media users process information because these information and processing strategies influence people's judgment and decision making.

The strategies of information processing on social media platforms could be quite different from processing news information from traditional media outlets. The research on JDM is introduced to examine how the information on social media may affect JDM, including news use, purchase decisions, and healthcare support. Some key features of JDM are empirically investigated in those areas, whose results should help explain some important information processing strategies and phenomena, such as selective exposure. The chapter also addresses the important role a social context plays in affecting social media users' JDM, which not only changes people's purchase decisions but also the ways they express opinions.

Looking Ahead

Chapter 5 will center on how the social media usage affects a wide range of behaviors and habits, which can be either positive or negative. For analyzing the inaction between the social media use and behavior change, this chapter introduces the Social Ecological Model, suggesting that people's behavior can be strongly influenced by multiple environmental and situational factors. As the global-scale knowledge collaboration takes shape with the help of social media, the freedom of accessing social media should be viewed as a basic human right as it belongs to the freedom of speech.

Discussion

1. How does the use of social media affect judgment and decision making?
2. What are selective exposure and confirmation bias? How do they affect the social media use?
3. What is social endorcement and how does it affect the news use?
4. Do you think using social media provides support to the users who are not patients?

References

Abramowitz, A. I., Alexander, B., & Gunning, M. (2008). Incumbency, redistricting, and the decline of competition in U.S. House elections. *Journal of Politics, 68*(1), 75–88.

Aïmeur, E. (2002). Strategic use of conflicts in tutoring systems. In C. Tessier, L. Chaudron, & H. J. Müller (Eds.), *Conflicting agents conflict management in multi-agent systems* (pp. xiii, 335 pages). Kluwer. http://alias.libraries.psu.edu/eresources/proxy/login?url=http://www.netLibrary.com/urlapi.asp?action=summary&v=1&bookid=67554.

ARF. (2012). *Digital & social media in the purchase decision process.* Advertising Research Foundation. http://thearf-org-aux-assets.s3.amazonaws.com/research/ARF_Digital_Social_Media_Purchase_Process.pdf.

Auditore, P. (2011). *The social media crescendo effect*. http://marketinginfluence.typepad. com/marketinginfluence1/2011/2004/the-social-media-crescendo-effect.html.

Becker, G. S. (1976). *The economic approach to human behavior*. University of Chicago Press.

Bonniface, L., & Green, L. (2007). Finding a new kind of knowledge on the HeartNET website. *Health Information and Libraries Journal, 24*(Supplement 1), 67–76 https://doi. org/10.1111/j.1471-1842.2007.00742.x.

Bulmer, D., & Dimauro, V. (2009). *The new symbiosis of professional networks: Social media's impact on business and decision-making*. http://sncr.org/wp-content/ uploads/2010/2002/NewSymbiosisReportExecSumm.pdf.

Cotton, J. L. (1985). Cognitive dissonance in selective exposure. In D. Zillmann, & J. Bryant (Eds.), *Selective exposure to communication* (pp. 11–34). Lwrence Erlbaum Associates.

Ditto, P. H., & Lopez, D. F. (1992). Motivated skepticism: Use of differential decision criteria for preferred and nonpreferred conclusions. *Journal of Personality and Social Psychology, 63*(4), 568–584.

Dunning, D. (2012). Judgment and decision making. In S. T. Fiske, & C. N. Macrae (Eds.), *The SAGE handbook of social cognition* (pp. 251–272). Sage. https://doi. org/10.4135/9781446247631.

Edwards, W. (1954). The theory of decision making. *Psychological Bulletin, 51*(4), 380–417. https://doi.org/10.1037/h0053870.

Edwards, W. (1968). Conservatism in human information processing. In B. Kleinmuntz, & R. B. Cattell (Eds.), *Formal representation of human judgment* (pp. xii, 273 pp.). Wiley.

Festinger, L. (1957). *A theory of cognitive dissonance*. Stanford University Press.

Firth, J., Torous, J., Stubbs, B., Firth, J. A., Steiner, G. Z., Lee, S., Alvarez-Jimenez, M., Gleeson, J., Vancampfort, D., Armitage, C., & Sarris, J. (2019). The "online brain:" How the internet may be changing our cognition. *World Psychiatry, 18*(2), 119–129. https:// doi.org/10.1002/wps.20617.

Fischer, P., Aydin, N., Julia, F., Frey, D., & Lea, S. E. G. (2012). The cognitive economy model of selective exposure: Integrating motivational and cognitive accounts of confirmatory information search. In J. I. Krueger (Ed.), *Social judgment and decision making* (pp. 21–39). Psychology Press.

Fischer, P., Jonas, E., Frey, D., & Kastenmüller, A. (2008). Selective exposure and decision framing: The impact of gain and loss framing on confirmatory information search after decisions. *Journal of Experimental Social Psychology, 44*(2), 312–320. https://doi. org/10.1016/j.jesp.2007.06.001.

Giddens, A. (1999). *Globalization. Reith Lectures*. http://news.bbc.co.uk/hi/english/static/ events/reith_99/week91/week91.htm.

Gilovich, T., Griffin, D., & Kahneman, D. (Eds.). (2002). *Heuristics and biases: The psychology of intuitive judgment*. Cambridge University Press.

Iyengar, S., & Hahn, K. S. (2009). Red media, blue media: Evidence of ideological selectivity in media use. *Journal of Communication, 59*(1), 19–39. https://doi. org/10.1111/j.1460-2466.2008.01402.x.

Jonas, E., Graupmann, V., & Frey, D. (2006). The influence of mood on the search for supporting versus conflicting information: Dissonance reduction as a means of mood Regulation? *Personality and Social Psychology Bulletin, 32*(1), 3–15. https://doi. org/10.1177/0146167205276118.

Jonas, E., Schulz-Hardt, S., Frey, D., & Thelen, N. (2001). Confirmation bias in sequential information search after preliminary decisions: An expansion of dissonance theoretical research on selective exposure to information. *Journal of Personality and Social Psychology, 80*(4), 557–571. https://doi.org/10.1037//0022-3514.80.4.557.

Messing, S., & Westwood, S. J. (2014). Selective exposure in the age of social media: Endorsements trump partisan source affiliation when selecting news online. *Communication Research*, *41*(8), 1042–1063. https://doi.org/10.1177/0093650212466406.

Moe, W. W., & Schweidel, D. A. (2014). The social effects of strangers. In W. W. Moe, & D. A. Schweidel (Eds.), *The social media intelligence* (pp. 53–66). Cambridge University Press. https://doi.org/10.1017/CBO9781139381338.007.

Nelson, R., Joos, I. M., & Wolf, D. M. (2013). *Social media for nurses: Educating practitioners and patients in a networked world.* Springer.

Olson, J. M., & Stone, J. (2005). The influence of behavior on attitudes. In D. Albarracin, B. T. Johnson, & M. P. Zanna (Eds.), *The handbook of attitude.* Lawrence Erlbaum.

Power, D. J., & Phillips-Wren, G. (2011). Impact of social media and Web 2.0 on decision-making. *Journal of Decision Systems*, *20*(3), 249–261. https://doi.org/10.3166/JDS.20.249-261.

Preece, J., & Maloney-Krichmar, D. (2003). Online communities: Focusing on sociability and usability. In J. A. Jacko & A. Sears (Eds.), *Human–computer interaction handbook: Fundamentals, evolving technologies and emerging applications* (pp. 596–620). Lawrence Erlbaum Associates.

Pyszczynski, T., & Greenberg, J. (1987). Toward an integration of cognitive and motivational perspectives on social inference: A biased hypothesis-testing model. In L. Berkowitz (Ed.), *Advances in experimental social psychology* (Vol. 20, pp. 297–340). Academic Press.

Shearer, E., & Mitchell, A. (2021). News use across social media platforms in 2020. *Pew Research Center – Journalism & Media.* https://www.journalism.org/2021/01/12/news-use-across-social-media-platforms-in-2020.

Simon, H. A. (1957). *Models of man: Social and rational: Mathematical essays on rational human behavior in a social setting.* Wiley.

Small, G. W., Moody, T. D., Siddarth, P., & Bookheimer, S. Y. (2009). Your brain on Google: Patterns of cerebral activation during internet searching. *American Journal of Geriatric Psychiatry*, *17*(2), 116–126. https://doi.org/10.1097/JGP.0b013e3181953a02.

Symister, P., & Friend, R. (2003). The influence of social support and problematic support on optimism and depression in chronic illness: A prospective study evaluating self-esteem as mediator. *Health Psychology*, *22*(2), 123–129. https://doi.org/10.1037/0278-6133.22.2.123.

Thurlow, C., Tomic, A., & Lengel, L. B. (2004). *Computer mediated communication: Social interaction and the internet.* Sage.

Turner, J. W., Grube, J. A., & Meyers, J. (2001). Developing an optimal match within online communities: An exploration of CMC support communities and traditional support. *Journal of Communication Disorders*, *51*(2), 231–251. https://doi.org/10.1111/j.1460-2466.2001.tb02879.x.

van Ginkel, W. P., & van Knippenberg, D. (2008). Group information elaboration and group decision making: The role of shared task representations. *Organizational Behavior and Human Decision Processes*, *105*(1), 82–97. https://doi.org/10.1016/j.obhdp.2007.08.005.

Walker, K. K. (2013). Rare disease-specific social media sites: An opportunity for collaboration. *Journal of Communication in Healthcare*, *6*(1), 71–76. https://doi.org/10.1179/1753807612Y.0000000026.

White, M., & Dorman, S. M. (2001). Receiving social support online: Implications for health education. *Health Education Research*, *16*(6), 693–707. https://doi.org/10.1093/her/16.6.693.

5

Social Media and Behavior

LEARNING GOALS

This chapter will help you understand:

- How do social media change news consumption?
- How do social media alter health behavior?
- What is the culture of sharing?
- How does knowledge collaboration occur in online communities?

KEY CONCEPTS

Knowledge collaboration	Culture of sharing
Metamedium	Online community

THEORY HIGHLIGHT

Social Cognitive Theory

Overview

At almost any tourist spot, some tourists can be seen using smartphones to take photos, which are set, occasionally, on a selfie stick. Then they share the photos instantly through social media, like Facebook, Snapchat, Instagram, or WeChat. Grumbling may be heard if social media does not work well due to a poor cell phone signal. Social media obviously help change their sightseeing behaviors from taking photos to sharing them with families and friends. Part of their sightseeing is sharing "interesting moments" on social media anywhere anytime, adding fresh evidence to the social media impact on human behavior.

On the Web, using social media has become the most popular attraction, overtaking pornography as the No. 1 online activity (Goldsmith, 2008). As social media continue to grow as one of our habits, it is no surprise that using them changes our behavior through affecting cognition and perception. Ample evidence has been found to confirm the impact of social media use on behavior change, ranging from news consumption to health behavior.

By altering behavior, the social media use helps achieve some public agendas in an efficient way, for instance, promoting a healthy lifestyle to fight obesity, educating

Social Media Communication: Trends and Theories, First Edition. Bu Zhong.
© 2022 John Wiley & Sons, Inc. Published 2022 by John Wiley & Sons, Inc.

students to stay away from drugs, and encouraging public involvement in environmental drives or political campaigning. One of the successful examples is that Facebook launched a public health initiative in 2012 that prompted 500,000 people to register as organ donors. The Facebook team did not preach it and no advertisement was run, but simply provided a sharing opportunity on Facebook after people registered to be an organ donor. When people shared the information, their friends were seeing and commenting, resulting in peer influence for more people to do likewise. Other evidence shows that the use of social media enhances patient care, providing new opportunities for patients to participate in supportive communication within a network of individuals dealing with similar symptoms (Coulson, 2005).

Social media increase communication between individuals, groups, and across cultures, fostering a better understanding of crucial issues around the world. The Arab Spring – a series of protests and revolutions in some Arabic countries from 2009 to 2011 – was viewed impossible without using social media. Social media had facilitated political dissent for years, and eventually stimulated local people to express the dissent in ways that have never happened before. The protests and demonstrations are called "Twitter Revolution" or "The YouTube War," illustrating the role of social media in antigovernment protests or acts of dissent (Bandura, 2001; Christensen, 2011).

Social media can also bring about negative effects on human behavior. For instance, users of social media could have decreasing attention spans due to constant exposure to the fast-paced information flow on social media or the average number of sleep hours per night could decrease when they spend more time on social media. (More about the problematic use of social media will be discussed in Chapter 8.) These findings suggest that social media connect people and enable them to share information, and, more importantly, the usage also shapes their behavior.

Social Media and News Consumption

In the social media age, people do not read or watch less news. On the contrary, most of them spend more time in accessing news information than any time in history. However, they no longer wait for morning newspapers for the morning news or sit at a fixed time for the evening news on TV. Traditional news media like newspapers, magazines, radio, and television are still here but are facing a growing competition from online information, which is increasingly transferred through social media. The advent of social media is changing how people access and use news information, and the change is "pulling the rug from under the feet of journalists" (Miller & Ginnis, 2015). (The influence of social media on the news industry will be examined in detail in Chapter 10.)

Do you want to see how the news use habit is being changed? Just take a look at how people around you access their daily news. Nowadays few read newspapers by holding tangible broad sheets or watch TV in front of a TV set, though this did not mean they consume less journalism. In fact, they consume more journalism than ever before but on different platforms and devices. During the shift, social media are fast becoming a major news source in a different way from the websites of news organizations. Unlike visiting a news organization's website, social media users often report that they are not actively seeking news on social media but happen to find it there. The 2014 Pew Research Report on Journalism and Media discovered that most Facebook users did not get news through a journalist or a news organization but incidentally get it as they happen to be on Facebook for another reason (Matsa & Mitchell, 2014). According to the survey, social network sites are not created equally for news consumption, users obtaining news more from certain social network sites, such as Facebook and Twitter, than others, such as Instagram or Pinterest.

On Twitter, groups of people come together around news events they feel passionately about. The opinions expressed on Twitter, however, often differ from broad public opinion. For instance, in the days following the 2012 Sandy Hook Elementary School shootings in Newton, Connecticut, almost two-thirds of the statements on Twitter called for stricter gun control, with 64% supporting stricter gun control and 21% opposing it. The results are in contrast with the more evenly split public opinion found in a survey during the same time period, showing 49% supporting stricter gun control and 42% opposing it (Matsa & Mitchell, 2014).

New trends of consuming the news through social media can be quite different from accessing news on traditional news media like print or broadcast media. Traditional media are famously known as gatekeepers of news information, which often help set the public agenda. Social media, however, do not always facilitate conversation around the important issues of the day. In many cases, people tend to be more likely sharing opinions on certain controversial issues in a face-to-face setting than on Facebook or Twitter, especially as they feel their audiences on social media may disagree with them (Anderson & Caumont, 2014).

TV viewing habits are also shaped by social media, which are increasingly intertwined with the TV viewing experience. A 2015 survey found that about half of the global respondents (49%) say they watch live video programming more if it has a social media tie-in, while over half of them (53%) like to keep up with TV shows so they can join the conversation on social media (Nielsen Global Survey, 2015). Nearly half of the respondents (47%) report that they are using social media while watching video programming.

The Nielson Survey also found that, regionally, Asia-Pacific and Africa/Middle East respondents are particularly engaged in social media while viewing, exceeding the global average use of social media. Compared with the world average of 49%, 65% of Asia-Pacific and 57% of African/Middle Eastern respondents watch live programming if it has a social media content. In addition, 64% of Asia-Pacific and 62% of Africa/Middle East respondents say they like to keep up with shows so they can join the conversation on social media.

While watching TV, many viewers use the second, third, and sometimes fourth screen as a fundamental extension of the viewing experience (Nielsen Global Survey, 2015). Getting ancillary content, researching information about characters, playing mobile games, or reading/watching behind-the-scenes interviews are becoming common practices. Above all, many are getting on social media to chat with friends or discuss the programming they are watching. Other surveys disclose that people are more likely to watch a TV show if they read a post about the show on social media. Thus it is essential to harness the power of social media and social interactivity with TV in order to engage young viewers who experience more changing habits of TV viewing than the elderly.

Thanks to social media, fewer people follow the news by waiting for traditional media to publish or broadcast it at a fixed time, and more are tracking the news in real time on social media like Twitter, Facebook, or WeChat. A 2015 survey conducted by American Press Institute shows that tracking news in real time is one of Americans' primary reasons that they use Twitter (Rosenstiel et al., 2015). The survey also discovers that 80% of those who have followed a breaking story in the past month said they clicked on a story as events were developing in real time. On social media, people do not just follow the news but forward news items to others through the new platforms. In the US, more than half (55%) of Twitter users said they retweeted a story, 53% similarly said they clicked or searched a hashtag, 40% also tweeted their reaction to the story, and 30% said they followed someone new in the past month (Rosenstiel et al., 2015).

Social media can be the first place for people to learn about breaking news, but it is not always accurate, which takes a toll on the credibility of the social media information. While platforms like Twitter allow users to share and receive information from peers, the content can be misleading or completely false. When using social media following news events, students cannot afford not to be vigilant and pay attention to who is the news source, as well as when and where it is posted. In the wake of the 2015 devastating attacks in Paris, France, that left at least 129 people dead and hundreds more injured, social media sites like Twitter, Facebook, and Instagram were flooded with updates on the coordinated attacks. However, some information was incorrect. CNBC reports, for instance, after a series of coordinated terrorist attacks happened in Paris on November 13, 2015, over 10.7 million tweets were posted about Paris on the very day and the day following (Whitten, 2015). More than a few misleading posts began circulating in the aftermath of those Paris attacks, which have now been debunked by various sources (Whitten, 2015). Since then, many people have found that social media can be hubs where false narratives are incubated, reinforced, and cemented.

Social Media and Health Behavior

Health behavior is another area where social media exert a growing impact. Health information and the mediums on which the information have been credited is one factor that has led to a shift in perceptions, attitudes, beliefs, and behavior, including health behavior. One approach to consider when assessing health behavior change is the dynamic interaction among various personal and environmental factors, including media use. The interaction may be best explained by the Social Ecological Model (SEM) (Bronfenbrenner, 1981; McLeroy et al., 1988). The model assumes that human beings are a product of their individual thoughts, interpersonal relationships, organizational entities, and the community structures, systems, and policies to which they are exposed (McLeroy et al., 1988). According to SEM, people live in, and are exposed to, multiple environments and situations that may affect their behavior and beliefs (Vaterlaus et al., 2015).

SEM has been used to describe the complexity of how people make the decisions regarding their health behaviors within concentric ecosystem levels, i.e., individual factors, environmental settings, sectors of influence, and social and cultural norms and values. Scholars agree that health information and the mediums on which the information is shared and communicated are at the sector of the influence level because media use has a direct influence on health behavior as it is a regular part of youth development and psychosocial experience (McHale et al., 2009).

Considering the relevancy of environmental factors on health behaviors, media use should be taken as one of the factors at the individual level of such an ecological system (McHale et al., 2009). Thus, among a variety of factors that influence health behaviors, social media could be a relevant factor (Vaterlaus et al., 2015). Scholars agree that health information and the mediums on which the information is shared and communicated are at the sector of influence level. Thus it is important to examine the relationship between people's social media use and health behaviors.

Other evidence may come from how people use media technology to search for health information. A vast majority of those online adults are searching for health information, which was 80% in 2010 (Fox, 2011), according to a survey by the Pew Research Center. The survey also found that searching for health information is the most popular online activity for adults after e-mail and using search engines (Fox, 2011). Deloitte's 2010 Survey of Health Care Consumers confirms this trend: more than half of consumers said they looked online for health information, including 53% of seniors, 57% of Generation X (born between approximately 1961 and 1981), and 56% of Generation Y (born between 1982 and 2001) (Korda & Itani, 2013).

Evidence about social media's impact on health knowledge, behavior, and outcomes shows that these tools can be effective in meeting individual and population health needs (Korda & Itani, 2013). Healthcare professionals have been quick to recognize social media as an important public engagement platform for reaching and empowering individual needs and interactions in healthcare (Thackeray et al., 2008). A study evaluating the effectiveness of web-based interventions in increasing patient empowerment compared with usual care or face-to-face interventions found significant positive effects on empowerment as measured on self-efficacy scales and mastery scales (Samoocha et al., 2010).

The impact of social media on health behaviors may be tracked down to the interactivity function of social media, which is largely unavailable on traditional media. The interactive nature of social media facilitate more social interaction among users, which eventually leads to behavior change. Some researchers note that the interactive nature of social media may have a unique relationship with health behaviors (Vaterlaus et al., 2015). For instance, social interaction is found to influence food choices and portions among young adults (McFerran et al., 2010).

The social interaction occurring at a school cafeteria may appear on social media due to the shared interactive nature, which has a unique relationship with health behaviors. On social media, people inform others of their healthy lifestyle through posts and pictures about their food and exercises. They love to showcase such a healthy lifestyle on social media because the platform affords the opportunity of controlling how it may be presented to others and what aspects of it may be shared. Rather than presenting their actual selves, users can choose to show the version of themselves that they hope for, which may bring about behavior change eventually.

Finally, social media could be a tool to learn about health behaviors and seek social support. With the ability to share information, social media have become an important health information source, which also empower individuals with healthcare needs. It must be noted that not all the health information on social media is accurate, which also provide opportunities to pseudo professionals, celebrities, and any other individuals to disseminate information about health behavior. Some of the information may be accurate, but the rest could be oversimplified, exaggerated. or completely false.

The Culture of Sharing

Sharing information without a profit motive becomes common among individuals, especially social media users. The practice of sharing is "socially and culturally valuable and will play a key role in the future of our cultures and the creative economies" (Aigrain, 2012, p. 15). Serving as a major platform of information sharing, social media are bringing about a dynamic Web-based sharing culture on a global scale. The sharing culture is triggered largely by the advances of information technology and the pervasive use of social media. The latter also enhances the literacy of social media and encourages nonusers to adopt social media. Without social media, individuals would not engage in sharing so much information on such a large scale as they do today.

Back in the early 1980s, researchers had proposed a model for studying television as a cultural forum (Newcomb & Hirsch, 1983). Television at that time was indeed the most common reference point for public issues and concerns, particularly in American society. Since the 1950s when television became part of mass media in the United States, television has not been merely a source of images and texts impressing information and opinions on viewers, but also a repository and a resource – a forum – articulating and negotiating meanings and world views on behalf of the culture at large (Newcomb & Hirsch, 1983). The significance of the model represents a shift of the predominant focus of mass media studies from questions of transmission and effect (Lasswell, 1948) to questions of culture (Jensen & Helles, 2010). James Carey argues that mass media not just help people communicate with each other by sharing information, communication itself is "a symbolic process whereby reality is produced, maintained, repaired, and transformed" (Carey, 2009, p. 19).

Today, the role of television as a forum of culture is being filled by digital media, in particular social media. For decades, television has been a powerful medium enabling one-to-many communication models. Social media may be more powerful as they enable new models of communication, including one-to-one, many-to-many, or many-to-one communication (Jensen & Helles, 2010). Compared with television, social media penetrate more broadly and profoundly into the fiber of the society due to the extensive usage. As a result, the culture of sharing on social media may bring users more far-reaching implications than the cultural forums created by previous media technologies, including television.

As a direct result of social media use, online communities are created. Here the term of "community" generally refers to groups of people who engage in sustained interaction over time due to their shared goals, concerns, or passion. With the help of social media, various online communities are created, in which, for instance, a team of students learn to do a research project, an alliance of activists promote a political agenda on public affairs, a band of artists seek new forms of expression, a group of programmers design new software, or a network of physicians explore novel treatment plans.

Given the widespread computer-mediated communication and interaction on social media, social media, in a certain sense, are becoming a new type of interactive medium that is similar to the notion of "a metamedium, whose content would be a wide range of already-existing and not-yet-invented media" (Kay & Goldberg, 1977, p. 40).

Knowledge Collaboration

When people get on social media, a growing number of users share not just mundane affairs in everyday life, but offer information that is consequential to others and the community. The latest trend of social media use shows a fast growth of knowledge-intensive activities initiated by both individual users and organizations. A significant part of the information shared becomes knowledge benefiting individuals and communities, and the sharing process contributes to the knowledge collaboration in a computer-mediated environment. Knowledge collaboration is broadly defined as "the sharing, transfer, accumulation, transformation, and co-creation of knowledge" in online (e.g., social network sites) or real-life communities (e.g., schools) (Faraj et al., 2011, p. 1224).

In human history, communities have been an important source of knowledge, like markets and hierarchies (Adler, 2001). The advent of social media is redefining the scope, boundaries, and dynamics of a traditional community, and as a result helps create a virtual form of real-life community – online communities. Online communities are defined as "open collectives of dispersed individuals with members who are not necessarily known or identifiable and who share common interests, and these communities attend to both their individual and their collective welfare" (Faraj et al., 2011, p. 1224). In online communities such as those created by social network sites, human communication and interaction are unconstrained by distance in time and space. As a result, short-term and long-standing coalition, association, or organization can be built and disbanded with minimal cost in an online community (Sproull et al., 2007, p. 1224).).

An online community based on a social media site functions very much like a real-life community, including serving its members as a source of knowledge and innovations. Sharing information online alone does not directly lead to knowledge collaboration. For example, when people get online and send a message, upload a video clip, or write a blog, they do share the information with others in cyberspace. However, their work stands alone, which should not be viewed as collaborative.

Knowledge collaboration is a critical element of the sustainability of online communities as individuals share and combine their knowledge in ways that benefit individuals and contribute to the community's greater worth (Faraj et al., 2011). Knowledge collaboration occurs when people join hands together for a project they share an interest in, such as creating Wikipedia, remixing music, or designing an app or a software application. Knowledge collaboration may occur, for example, when a participant in a health-related support community has a particularly complex problem that members collaborate to help resolve. The participants in such a project do not need to meet face-to-face, and their work is often not organized in a heretical system. In the social media era, much of the knowledge collaboration occurs with no financial incentives involved, for example, people willing to write, verify, or update entries in Wikipedia without being paid.

Since a growing knowledge collaboration is happening on online communities created by social media, individuals who cannot have access to social media have lost an important source of information and knowledge, which is essential to human development and individual well-being. Some governments still block certain social network sites, such as Facebook, Twitter, YouTube, Wikipedia, and even Google Scholar. The freedom of accessing social media is a human right as it belongs to the freedom of speech. It is unfortunate that the right is yet to be universally recognized and respected.

Theory Highlight: Social Cognitive Theory

Social cognitive theory accords a central role to cognitive, vicarious, self-regulatory, and self-reflective processes. An extraordinary capacity for symbolization provides humans with a powerful tool for comprehending their environment and creating and regulating environmental events that touch virtually every aspect of their lives. Most external influences affect behavior through cognitive processes rather than directly. Cognitive factors partly determine which environmental events will be observed, what meaning will be conferred on them, whether they leave any lasting effects, what emotional impact and motivating power they will have, and how the information they convey will be organized for future use. It is with symbols that people process and transform transient experiences into cognitive models that serve as guides for judgment and action. Through symbols, people give meaning, form, and continuity to their experiences (Bandura, 2001, p. 267).

People are self-organizing, proactive, self-reflecting, and self-regulating, not just reactive organisms shaped and shepherded by environmental events or inner forces. Human self-development, adaptation, and change are embedded in social systems. Therefore, a personal agency operates within a broad network of sociostructural influences. In these agentic transactions, people are producers as well as products of social systems. Personal agency and social structure operate as co-determinants in an integrated causal structure rather than as a disembodied duality.

Seen from the sociocognitive perspective, human nature is a vast potentiality that can be fashioned by direct and observational experience into a variety of forms within biological limits. To say that a major distinguishing mark of humans is their endowed plasticity is not to say that they have no nature or that they come structureless. The plasticity, which is intrinsic to the nature of humans, depends upon neurophysiological mechanisms and structures that have evolved over time. These advanced neural systems specialized for processing, retaining, and using coded information provide the capacity for the very capabilities that are distinctly human: generative symbolization, forethought, evaluative self-regulation, reflective self-consciousness, and symbolic communication.

Summary

Social media use is found to affect a wide range of behaviors and habits, which cause both positive and negative changes. Some of the changes may be personal, e.g., taking photos and sharing them during sightseeing, news consumption, or health behaviors, while others may have a profound influence on the society as a whole, e.g., the Arab Spring.

Behavior change is often caused by the dynamic interaction among various personal and environmental factors, including media use. To analyze the inaction, this chapter introduces the Social Ecological Model. The model holds that humans are a product of individual thoughts, interpersonal relationships, organizational entities, and the community structures, systems, and policies to which they are exposed. According to the model, people's behavior can be strongly influenced by multiple environmental and situational factors. Media use, including social media, should be taken as one of the factors at the individual level of the ecological system, which is found to modify health behaviors and knowledge.

The mass use of social media is redefining the scope, boundaries, and dynamics of our traditional community because social media help create a virtual form of real-life community – online communities. In these online communities, the social media use contributes to a Web-based sharing culture that is arising around the world, in which knowledge collaboration at a global scale becomes possible, even without any financial incentives. As the global-scale knowledge collaboration takes shape with the help of social media, the freedom of accessing social media should be viewed as a basic human right as it belongs to the freedom of speech. It is unfortunate that the right is yet to be universally recognized and respected.

Looking Ahead

Chapter 6 will address privacy concerns related to people's social media use in a cross-cultural setting. It will examine the history and current conditions of internet privacy concern and surveillance that are closely related to the use of social media. While we are concerned about the content being leaked in the social media world, we may overlook how the social media use may shape our perceptions, including privacy concerns. Overall, it is essential to treat using social media as a socialization agent that helps create different communication settings and shape different perceptions, including privacy concerns.

Discussion

1. Do you see any major differences in terms of news consumption behaviors between you and your parents' or grandparents' generations?
2. Describe how you and your friends are sharing information through social media. Are there any changes regarding the content and ways of sharing compared to two or three years ago?
3. In addition to personal social media use, like staying connected with others, do you observe that others are using the platforms for knowledge collaboration?

References

Adler, P. S. (2001). Market, hierarchy and trust: The knowledge economy and the future of capitalism. *Organization Science, 12*(2), 215–234. https://doi.org/10.1287/orsc.12.2.215.10117.

Aigrain, P. (2012). *Sharing: Culture and the economy in the internet age.* Amsterdam University Press. http://SK8ES4MC2L.search.serialssolutions.com/?sid=sersol&SS_jc=TC0000630241&title=Sharing%3A%20Culture%20and%20the%20Economy%20in%20the%20Internet%20Age.

Anderson, M., & Caumont, A. (2014). *How social media is reshaping news* [internet]. Pew Reaearch Center. http://www.pewresearch.org/fact-tank/2014/09/24/how-social-media-is-reshaping-news.

Bandura, A. (2001). Social cognitive theory of mass communication. *Media Psychology*, *3*(3), 265–299. https://doi.org/10.1207/S1532785XMEP0303_03.

Bronfenbrenner, U. (1981). *The ecology of human development: Experiments by nature and design.* Harvard University Press.

Carey, J. W. (2009). *Communication as culture: Essays on media and society* (Revised ed.). Routledge.

Christensen, C. (2011). Twitter Revolutions? Addressing social media and dissent. *Communication Review*, *14*(3), 155–157. https://doi.org/10.1080/10714421.2011.597235.

Coulson, N. S. (2005). Receiving social support online: An analysis of a computer-mediated support group for individuals living with irritable bowel syndrome. *CyberPsychology & Behavior*, *8*(6), 580–584. https://doi.org/10.1089/cpb.2005.8.580.

Faraj, S., Jarvenpaa, S. L., & Majchrzak, A. (2011). Knowledge collaboration in online communities. *Organization Science*, *22*(5), 1224–1239. https://doi.org/10.1287/orsc.1100.0614.

Fox, S. (2011). *Health topics* [internet]. Pew Research Center: Internet & Tech. http://www.pewinternet.org/2011/02/01/health-topics-2.

Goldsmith, B. (2008). *Porn passed over as Web users become social: Author* [internet]. Reuters. http://www.reuters.com/article/us-internet-book-life-idUSSP31943720080916.

Jensen, K. B., & Helles, R. (2010). The internet as a cultural forum: Implications for research. *New Media & Society*, *13*(4), 517–533. https://doi.org/10.1177/1461444810373531.

Kay, A., & Goldberg, A. (1977). Personal dynamic media. *Computer*, *10*(3), 31–41. https://doi.org/10.1109/C-M.1977.217672.

Korda, H., & Itani, Z. (2013). Harnessing social media for health promotion and behavior change. *Health Promotion Practice*, *14*(1), 15–23. https://doi.org/10.1177/1524839911405850.

Lasswell, H. D. (1948). The structure and function of communication in society. In L. Bryson (Ed.), *The communication of ideas: A series of addresses* (pp. ix, 296). Harper.

Matsa, K. E., & Mitchell, A. (2014). *8 key takeaways about social media and news* [internet]. Pew Research Center:Journalism & Media. http://www.journalism.org/2014/03/26/8-key-takeaways-about-social-media-and-news.

McFerran, B., Dahl, D. W., Fitzsimons, G. J., & Morales, A. C. (2010). I'll have what she's having: Effects of social influence and body type on the food choices of others. *Journal of Consumer Research*, *36*(6), 915–929. https://doi.org/10.1086/644611.

McHale, S. M., Dotterer, A., & Kim, J.-Y. (2009). An ecological perspective on the media and youth development. *American Behavioral Scientist*, *52*(8), 1186–1203. https://doi.org/10.1177/0002764209331541.

McLeroy, K. R., Bibeau, D., Steckler, A., & Glanz, K. (1988). An ecological perspective on health promotion programs. *Health Education Quarterly*, *15*(4), 351–377. https://doi.org/10.1177/109019818801500401.

Miller, C., & Ginnis, S. (2015, September 10). Separating the truth from the buzz in social media. The Guardian. http://www.theguardian.com/news/datablog/2015/sep/10/separating-truth-from-buzz-social-media-internet-research.

Newcomb, H. M., & Hirsch, P. M. (1983). Television as a cultural forum: Implications for research. *Quarterly Review of Film Studies, 8*(3), 45–55. https://doi.org/10.1080/10509208309361170.

Nielsen Global Survey. (2015). *Live TV + Social Media = Engaged Viewers* [internet]. Nielsen. http://www.nielsen.com/us/en/insights/news/2015/live-tv-social-media-engaged-viewers.html.

Rosenstiel, T., Sonderman, J., Loker, K., Ivancin, M., & Kjarval, N. (2015). *Twitter and breaking news* [internet]. American Press Institute. https://www.americanpressinstitute.org/publications/reports/survey-research/twitter-and-breaking-news.

Samoocha, D., Bruinvels, D. J., Elbers, N. A., Anema, J. R., & van der Beek, A. J. (2010). Effectiveness of Web-based interventions on patient empowerment. *Journal of Medical Internet Research, 12*(2), e23. https://doi.org/10.2196/jmir.1286.

Sproull, L., Dutton, W., & Kiesler, S. (2007). Introduction to the Special Issue: Online Communities. *Organization Science, 28*(3), 277–281. https://doi.org/10.1177/0170840607076013.

Thackeray, R., Neiger Brad, L., Hanson, C. L., & McKenzie, J. F. (2008). Enhancing promotional strategies within social marketing programs: Use of Web 2.0 social media. *Health Promotion Practice, 9*(4), 338–343. https://doi.org/10.1177/1524839908325335.

Vaterlaus, J. M., Patten, E. V., Roche, C., & Young, J. A. (2015). Gettinghealthy: The perceived influence of social media on young adult health behaviors. *Computers in Human Behavior, 45*, 151–157. https://doi.org/10.1016/j.chb.2014.12.013.

Whitten, S. (2015). *Rumors and misinformation circulate on social media following Paris attacks [internet]*.http://www.cnbc.com/2015/11/14/rumors-and-misinformation-circulate-on-social-media-following-paris-attacks.html(CNBC).

6

Social Media and Privacy Concern

LEARNING GOALS

This chapter will help you understand:

- What are privacy concerns on social media in a cross-cultural setting?
- What are the history of surveillance and its new forms involving social media use?
- How is privacy concern affected by media generations and social media power use?
- What cultural factors may affect privacy concern?

KEY CONCEPTS

Privacy concern   Social media surveillance

Generation gap

THEORY HIGHLIGHT

Need for Cognition

Overview

People used to believe they could have good control over their personal data and private information on the internet. As they began to interact with others online, especially through social media, they came to realize that connected activities pose a serious threat to privacy. Thus, the rise of social media has made the concept of internet privacy concern (IPC) increasingly salient since the early 2000s. A Pew Research survey found that about 80% of social media users were concerned about advertisers and businesses accessing the data they shared on social media platforms (Rainie, 2018). As user-generated content and sensitive data are being recorded digitally and stored on the cloud, many users fear a loss of control over personal data, leading to privacy and security concerns few experienced before (Widjaja et al., 2019). When sensitive personal data and information are pushed into the public eye, people feel their privacy is being invaded and, in many cases, develop a sense of surveillance – being watched by unwanted eyes. This chapter will investigate internet privacy concerns and how privacy can be endangered by social media surveillance.

Social Media Communication: Trends and Theories, First Edition. Bu Zhong.
© 2022 John Wiley & Sons, Inc. Published 2022 by John Wiley & Sons, Inc.

Internet Privacy Concern

As more information is shared, accessed, and stored on social media platforms, people have realized that much of their personal information provided in one context could be easily repurposed for other unanticipated settings that could go out of control at any time. The pervasive use of social media has thus led to privacy concerns on the internet. Things get more complicated as personal data are aggressively collected by individuals, organizations, and governments. The practice has become "an organizational logic of virtually every social sphere, including policing, marketing, interpersonal relations and the workplace" (Trottier, 2018, p. 463). Nowadays many social media users are no longer confident that they have control over their own personal data and their social media presence can be distorted in harmful ways. Serious consequences are immanent when personal data end up in the wrong hands. As a result, people tend to feel that the use of social media brings in endless privacy concerns and a sense of surveillance creep, resulting in unwanted forms of exposure on social media. We will first analyze user response toward internet privacy concerns and surveillance on social media. Then we explore the interaction between people's adoption/use of social media and their internet privacy concern. A better understanding of the privacy and surveillance issues on the internet could be achieved in exploring the technological antecedents of social media use.

Internet privacy concern is defined as one's beliefs about the risks and potential negative consequences associated with sharing information online (Baruh et al., 2017). A variety of theoretical perspectives have been applied to the understanding of IPC. Some theories center on socioeconomic factors that influence one's privacy perceptions. Others look at individual factors, such as protection motivation theory, information boundary theory, and privacy calculus theory.

Employing diverse theoretical frameworks, researchers have investigated a range of IPC antecedents, including individual factors (e.g., demographics, psychologic, or ideologic constructs, knowledge of and experience in privacy settings, beliefs/attitudes, perceived harms and risks), social-relational factors (e.g., social norms), organizational and task factors (e.g., privacy policies, corporate reputation, reward offer), macro-environmental factors (e.g., cultural values, governmental regulations), and information contingencies (e.g., information quality or sensitivity). Demographic variables like age, gender, education, and income are often found to influence privacy concerns (Li, 2011). For instance, women generally report to be more concerned about privacy than men (Hoy & Miline, 2010).

Scholarly Perspectives Toward IPC

Age differences in privacy concern have been examined in different countries from various perspectives (e.g., life-cycle theory), but with inconclusive and even contradictory results. A German study showed that age did not affect privacy in a linear way (Taddicken, 2014). A Norwegian study found that young adult users of social media (aged 20–30) had greater privacy concern compared to adolescents (aged 13–19) or adult groups (aged 31–50) (Dhir et al., 2017). On the other hand, a Dutch study found that those aged 40–65 reported the highest privacy concerns, followed by young adults (aged 25–40) and emerging adults (aged 18–25) (Van den Broeck et al., 2015). A study of seven European countries revealed that compared to young people (19–24 years), middle-aged people (45–60 years) tended to have negative views about data disclosure and use, suggesting that young people had less privacy concerns than older adults (Miltgen & Peyrat-Guillard, 2014). A study of Canadian Facebook users reported a higher level of privacy concern among young adult social media users (Nosko et al., 2010).

Two important scholarly perspectives to IPC are technological determinism and its related derivative theory, known as media ecology. According to technological determinism and Marshall McLuhan's media ecology theory, human interactions with information and communication technology (ICT) can shape our culture and daily experiences (Griffin et al., 2019). For instance, more people, young or old, are relying so much on their smartphones that the reliance has become an evolutionary addiction of staying social with others as they need to see others' behavior and be seen by others (Veissière & Stendel, 2018). The smartphone addition could have both personal and social effects, taking a toll on everything from work productivity to emotional and personal well-being (Twenge et al., 2018). Hence, the ICT advances alter the symbolic environment we live in – the socially constructed, sensory world of meanings that in turn shape our perceptions, experiences, attitudes, and behavior experiences (Griffin et al., 2019).

"The effects of technology do not occur at the level of opinions or concepts, but alter sense ratios or patterns of perception steadily and without any resistance" (McLuhan, 1964, p. 25). The forms of media regulate and even dictate what kind of content a given medium form can carry (Postman, 1985), an argument that was preceded by the seemingly perplexing statement – "the medium is the message" – by McLuhan (1964). IPC can be one of such perceptions that are molded by internet-related information technologies. Social media technologies have allowed an unprecedented amount of personal information to be revealed or presented in public, and, in turn, may affect users' privacy perception.

Four Epochs

Analyzing the ICT development, McLuhan (1964) divided human history into four periods, or epochs: tribal age, literate age, print age, and electronic age (Griffin et al., 2019). The tribal age featured a period where most of the important information/communication was acoustic (oral) and needed to be heard instantly. Tribal people acted with more passion/spontaneity, and had less privacy expectation as "(p)rivacy … is unknown in tribal societies" (McLuhan, 1964, p. 134). The literate age led people from a collective communication experience in the tribal age to private detachment, because the act of reading a text, compared to speaking in person, became an individualized (and private) experience. Words no longer had to be alive/immediate. "Perhaps the most significant of the gifts of typography to man is that of detachment and noninvolvement – the power to act without reacting" (McLuhan, 1964, p. 193).

Following the literacy age, the print age made it possible to reproduce the same text over and over again, rendering visual dependence and private detachment even more widespread, as mass-produced books further allowed the masses to read in privacy and to be isolated from others (Griffin et al., 2019). In this period, the development of fixed national languages produced nationalism. Concurring with this new sense of unification was a countering sense of separation and aloneness. "(S)peech lost its magic with writing, and further with printing" (McLuhan, 1964, p. 150).

Later in the electronic age, electronic media are retribalizing humanity as it brought humans back to the tribal village (i.e., global village, as coined by McLuhan, 1964), again with much more instant/spontaneous communication and much less privacy expectation. Then electronic technology "brought US into the age of 'secondary orality'," which has "a striking resemblance to the old in its participatory mystique, its fostering of a communal sense, its concentration on the present moment" (Ong, 1982, p. 133). It seems that human experiences have come full circle due to the advent of ICT. "As the printing press cried out for nationalism, so did the radio cry out for tribalism" (McLuhan, 1964, p. 60).

With the rise of the global village, privacy has become a luxury or a curse of the past. The digital age, which McLuhan did not live to witness, is wholly electric and represents a wireless and more full-fledged global village connected through the information highway (internet) (Griffin et al., 2019). In this sense, privacy is even more difficult to be maintained and protected in the social media age, as ICT allows ordinary users, let alone hackers, to copy, paste, save, forward, or publish private information in no time. Private lives of individuals could instantly become public property. From this perspective, the digital users, particularly social media users, are expected to be less concerned with online privacy as they may be increasingly desensitized by the constant privacy breaches occurring in the social media age.

Social Media Surveillance

Surveillance is a construct related to privacy, which means "watching over others." It can be performed by individuals, organizations, and governments. Surveillance is thus defined as "processes in which special note is taken of certain human behaviors that go well beyond idle curiosity" (Lyon, 2007, p. 13). Trottier (2018) notes that the process of surveillance consists of four major steps:

1. collecting personal data about individuals;
2. processing the data;
3. profiling those individuals or groups of individuals;
4. the social consequences stemming from that assessment.

For example, based on the postings about the restaurants one dined in, more similar restaurants may be recommended that would have a higher chance than other dining places. If monetizing the surveillance data to benefit a catering business seems benign, it could dismay some people if the US government intended to add a citizenship question to the 2020 Census questionnaire, a case that was later reviewed by the Supreme Court.

Researchers have devoted tremendous scholarly effort to surveillance research, which stems from the study of managing one's identity (Goffman, 1959), police activities (Marx, 1988), and media technologies (Lyon, 2007; Norris & Armstrong, 1999). They have discovered that "Surveillance is more than just a strategy for espionage and undercover policing, but rather a broader organizational strategy for knowing and directing a given population" (Trottier, 2018). Collecting personal information is a dominant logic for modern governments, businesses, and organizations (Dandeker, 1990), which is more so in the social media era.

Surveillance activities are so ubiquitous that they should not be simply taken as the result of ubiquity of ICT applications, including social media. The phenomenon is also strongly driven by the fact of watching and assessing private data penetrating "virtually every enduring social relationship" (Rule, 2011, p. 64). Thus, some of the dimensions that render social media "social," including the digitization of pervasive social relations, are precisely what facilitate surveillance practices on platforms like Facebook (Trottier, 2018). In this sense, social media become part of an emerging global virtual community that expands the capacity and persistence of surveillance practices through these platforms.

On the other hand, surveillance on social media primarily concerns users' personal data, in which social media uses play a crucial role in the production and circulation of this information. Social surveillance thus speaks to relationships where those who watch over others on social media are also rendered visible through these very same platforms (Trottier, 2018).

Generation Gap in IPC

Trottier (2018) argues that social media users often voluntarily participate in surveillance, for instance, knowingly sharing information about themselves, and derive some form of empowerment from this sharing (Albrechtslund, 2008). Such practices contract to what many assume that users unknowingly violate their own privacy when sharing the details of their private life on social media. Research shows that users often yield specific pleasures and values from online sharing, such as sharing exercise logs or calorie intake with an online fitness community (O'Hara et al., 2008).

Research confirms that young adults were less concerned with ICT in general, but this does not mean that they do not care about online privacy protection. Younger adults were found to be more likely to share personal information online (an indicator of less privacy concern), but they were generally more likely to use strategies to be less visible online (e.g., changed privacy settings, removed their name from photos in which they were tagged, or took steps to mask their online identities) (Rainie, 2018). Internet privacy protection – the behavioral aspect of privacy – is also a worthwhile topic in future research.

Much of the online privacy studies focus on risk, rather than understanding the necessity of private spaces for young people (Marwick et al., 2010). Privacy concerns are complex and diverse, depending on the applications in question (e.g., email, search engines, social media, or e-commerce) (Bergström, 2008), and on different areas of perceptions (e.g., collection, control, awareness, unauthorized secondary use, improper access, location tracking, trust in mobile advertisers, and attitudes toward mobile commerce) (Eastin et al., 2016).

By saying "the medium is the message," McLuhan (1964) suggested that media, rather than the content, reshape human experience and exert far more change in our world than the sum total of all the messages they contain. In this sense, while we are concerned about the content that is leaked in the social media world, we may overlook the role that social media (as a medium) plays in shaping our perceptions, including privacy concerns. It is important to consider whether a user can fully consent to share personal information on social media due to the ever-changing visibility of platforms, along with other users' unanticipated intentions. Meanwhile, it is critical to treat using social media as a socialization agent that helps create different communication environments and shape different human perceptions.

Privacy Concern at the Workplace

Professionalism has been the umbrella word describing the expected workplace performance of an employee in a traditional business environment. It includes conduct and appearance that demonstrate good judgment, a respectable stature, and the maintenance of competency and a general grasp of the situation. In general, traditional professionalism demands a clear segregation between the employee's professional and private personas (Abril et al., 2012). Nowadays, the diffusion of ICT such as computer use, internet access, and mobile technology has revolutionized the workplace and blurred the traditional boundaries between employees' professional duties and personal activities. For instance, is it acceptable for an employee to use a company-provided laptop to check social media accounts like Facebook or Twitter? Both employers and employees know well that the company-owned laptop is supposed to be used for business use, not personal use. Also, employer-provided mobile devices like smartphones and business email accounts are offered to employees so that they can communicate with others for company-related business affairs. However, is it OK to use them to make personal phone calls or send personal emails?

A more pertinent question is, how much privacy does one have at the workplace if those personal emails and phone calls going through company-provided devices or systems are monitored by employers?

Searching for a widely accepted answer to the above question has been difficult for business leaders and legal experts. Because such privacy issues at the workplace are complex, they involve legal, ethical, and business considerations as well as cultural and social norms. A detailed discussion of them goes beyond the scope of this book, but it is useful to remember that people's expectations of privacy at the workplace are increasingly shaped by the development of information and communication technology, which will keep creating new scenarios and challenges that did not exist in traditional business settings.

What is more germane to social media users is a better understanding of privacy issues related to user-generated data at the workplace. The bottom line is that any time users publish their or others' personal information on social media, they risk exposing privacy, regardless of whether they use a personal or employer-provided device. This helps explain why social media users' concerns about their privacy keep spiking and they feel powerless in the face of the detrimental nature and ineffectiveness of social media companies' self-regulation.

Privacy concerns involving social media use have attracted growing social attention, including that from scholars. Research in this vein examines privacy issues in social media mainly from two different approaches: identification of vulnerabilities and mitigation of privacy risks (Beigi & Liu, 2020). According to data scientists, these are two most frequent types of privacy attacks and are the disclosure of user identity and user attributes. Such attacks could be easily launched by data experts who take advantage of privacy risks associated with user-generated content posted on social media.

Privacy Risks and Coping Strategies

Privacy risks emerge as long as users post information on social media, which becomes digital footprints exposing their identities and attributes. To data experts, such digital footprints contain a rich data pool disclosing users' relationships with others and more personal and private information. The data also make social media users traceable by their employers, businesses, and governments. Consequently, users become vulnerable to a range of privacy breaches, leading to potential risks ranging from exposure of shopping habits to harassment or persecution by employers and governments.

For many sophisticated social media users, it is common sense that they should not share detailed travel plans publicly on Twitter without realizing such information could be used for possible break-ins and thefts against them when they are not at home. However, many users may not realize that their social media content could lead to disclosure of their identity and attributes. Identity disclosure occurs when a user is mapped to an instance in a released dataset, while attribute disclosure happens when the adversary could infer new data points about the user's private life based on the information posted on social media. Of course, attribute disclosure becomes more likely to happen when there is accurate disclosure of people's identities and geographical locations. Researchers also categorize privacy leakage attacks in social media into either identity disclosure or attribute disclosure (Beigi & Liu, 2020).

For example, data experts could decode a social media user's posts by analyzing the geo-location data embedded and accurately infer some attributes of the target user in a given situation. Based on available geo-location data and any additional knowledge about the target user, data experts could precisely, (1) predict the movement patterns of an individual; (2) learn the semantics of the target user mobility behavior; (3) link records of the same individual; and (4) identify points of interest (Gambs et al., 2010). Basically, if you show publicly how you move around, someone can easily figure out who you are. When your published social media content is incorporated into your friends' geo-location data on social media, it becomes even easier to tell who you are. In fact, data science approaches can predict precisely who you are and many of your private attributes based on your friends' social media posts, even when you do not post anything about yourself. Research has discovered that the target users' friends are significant predictors of their location and other attributes due to the strong social ties between them.

To preserve privacy, data scientists recommend several strategies to social media users. First, social media users need to obfuscate their online interactions to hide their actual intentions and prevent accurate profiles on social media platforms, such as age, zip code, and phone number. Users need to consider some tradeoffs when they try to use the obfuscating strategy. In some extreme cases, those tradeoffs could hurt users in unexpected but significant ways. For example, when a user is trapped or highjacked in a dangerous place, it becomes harder to track him down if he does not disclose his geo-location.

That said, data scientists recommend that if social media users follow the obfuscation strategy, they should trust no third parties or external entities to preserve their privacy. Instead, they need to learn to add a large amount of obscure, unclear, and even meaningless information to the social media content, known as "noisy data" in data science. The obfuscation strategy can be performed through numerous techniques and instruments, which are categorized into three major categories: cryptographic-based techniques, differential privacy-based approaches, and perturbation-based techniques.

Another solution to privacy concerns is differential privacy strategy, which requires users to either anonymize user data before posting it on social media or send it to another entity, like a recommendation system collecting personal data, in order to foil the recommendation system from producing accurate outputs. The third strategy is what data scientists call "a perturbation-based technique," which is used to obfuscate users' private data by adding additional random noise to the data. The strategy is based on the concept that the more a user's profile diverges from the general population, the more information a privacy attacker can learn about the user. Then it seeks to find the obfuscation rate for generating forged user profiles so that the privacy risk is minimized. Other strategies include perturbing users' interactions to optimize the privacy risk function.

All of the solutions discussed briefly can be difficult for individual users to adopt in their daily use of social media, but the strategies can be used by businesses to protect their customers' private data with the help of data scientists. To win the trust of the public, the public and governments have no other choice but to do their best to protect the privacy of user information. At the same time, it is important for social media users to know some basics about how data science approaches may infer and secure private data.

Theory Highlight: Need for Cognition

Have you ever complained about a suspense movie/book being too predictable? Have you ever been bored in a class when you have already mastered the course materials? Why do we feel dissatisfaction when we are underchallenged intellectually?

Researchers over time have suggested that we as human beings have the *need for cognition*, that is, the tendency to "engage in and enjoy thinking" (Cacioppo & Petty, 1982, p. 116). As one of the most widely adopted variables in psychology, the *need for cognition* (NFC) is defined as the "need to understand and make reasonable the experiential world" (Cohen et al., 1955, p. 291). If such a need is not met, it would generate a series of negative feelings such as frustration, anxiety, and even low self-esteem. In other words, the need for cognition refers to people's tendency to engage in and enjoy activities that require thinking. Of course, some individuals have relatively little motivation for cognitively complex tasks.

NFC was first proposed by Cohen et al. (1955). During a study at the University of Michigan, the authors first had 57 male undergraduate students read two forms (ambiguous vs.

structured) of the same story and measured their reactions to these stories. What they found was that there seemed to be a certain group of people who were more significantly affected by the ambiguous story in a negative fashion than others. This group of people, as the authors discussed, were those who self-reported high in the need for cognition.

A large number of studies have been conducted since then on NFC. Cacioppo and Petty (1982) developed an NFC scale and claimed such a need can be measured as a stable personal trait in engaging and enjoying effortful thinking. The original scale consists of 34 items with a reliability of 0.91 (Cacioppo et al., 1984). It was later modified by the same group of researchers into the most commonly used 14-item scale with a reliability of 0.90 (Cacioppo et al., 1984). In developing an even shorter form, Wood and Swait (2002) proposed a five-item scale of NFC.

For the past few decades, NFC has been extensively studied and adopted in a variety of domains in communication study, especially in persuasion, as it echoes nicely with the popular dual-process theories (Chaiken & Trope, 1999), for example, the elaboration likelihood model (Petty & Cacioppo, 1981, 1986) and the heuristic systematic model (Chaiken, 1987).

Individuals high in NFC are more likely to engage in systematic processing/elaboration and are thus more likely to be influenced by quality arguments. On the contrary, individuals low in NFC are more likely to engage in heuristic and peripheral processing and thus are more apt to the impact of heuristic cues such as celebrity endorsement in advertising. Profound implications have been produced as a result of persuasion. Advertisers, for example, could target different groups of people strategically by appealing to their different needs for cognition.

Summary

This chapter has examined the history and current conditions of internet privacy concern and surveillance that are closely related to the use of social media. While people are concerned about the content that is leaked in the social media world, some may overlook the role that social media (as a medium) plays in shaping human perceptions, including privacy concerns. Privacy concerns also exist at the workplace. Most of the readers of this book may not be data scientists, but it is helpful to know some basics of data science approaches in the areas of inferring and securing the privacy of user data. Overall, it is essential to treat using social media as a socialization agent that helps create different communication settings and shape different perceptions, including privacy concerns.

Looking Ahead

Chapter 7 is about the impact of cultures on the adoption and usage of social media. It was assumed that cultural unification could emerge to gradually eliminate cultural-based variability in terms of the social media use. However, on the contrary, cultures begin to play a big role in the growing connectedness and interdependence of world economies, populations, and their network societies. Thus, this chapter investigates the cultural differences that influence the social media use. Cultural learning and social learning in the context of cultural evolution will also be reviewed.

Discussion

1. Do you often remind yourself of privacy issues when you are on social media? What are your major privacy concerns, if any?
2. How much do you trust others like government agencies and businesses such as hospitals, tech companies, etc., to keep your information private?
3. How do you think about the development of internet privacy concern in the coming decade? Do you think social media users are better equipped to cope with internet privacy concerns in the near future?

References

Abril, P. S., Levin, A., & Del Riego, A. (2012). Blurred boundaries: Social media privacy and the twenty-first-century employee. *American Business Law Journal*, *49*(1), 63–124. https://doi.org/10.1111/j.1744-1714.2011.01127.x.

Albrechtslund, A. (2008). Online social networking as a participatory surveillance. *First Monday*, *13*(3). https://firstmonday.org/article/view/2142/1949;#author.

Baruh, L., Secinti, E., & Cemalcilar, Z. (2017). Online privacy concerns and privacy management: A meta-analytical review. *Journal of Communication*, *67*(1), 26–53. https://doi.org/10.1111/jcom.12276.

Beigi, G., & Liu, H. (2020). A survey on privacy in social media: Identification, mitigation, and applications. *ACM/IMS Transactions on Data Science*, *1*(1), 1–38. https://doi.org/10.1145/3343038.

Bergström, A. (2008). The reluctant audience: Online participation in the Swedish journalistic context. *Westminster Papers in Communication and Culture*, *5*(2), 60–79. https://doi.org/10.16997/wpcc.67.

Cacioppo, J. T., & Petty, R. E. (1982). The need for cognition. *Journal of Personality and Social Psychology*, *42*(1), 116–131. https://doi.org/10.1037/0022-3514.42.1.116.

Cacioppo, J. T., Petty, R. E., & Kao, C. F. (1984). The efficient assessment of need for cognition. *Journal of Personality Assessment*, *48*(3), 306–307. https://doi.org/10.1207/s15327752jpa4803_13.

Chaiken, S. (1987). The heuristic model of persuasion. In M. P. Zanna, J. M. Olson, & C. P. Herman (Eds.), *Social influence: The Ontario Symposium* (Vol. 5, pp. 3–39). Erlbaum.

Chaiken, S., & Trope, Y. (1999). *Dual-process theories in social psychology*. Guilford Press.

Cohen, A. R., Stotland, E., & Wolf, D. (1955). An experimental investigation of need for cognition. *Journal of Abnormal and Social Psychology, 51*(2), 291–294. https://doi.org/10.1037/h0042761.

Dandeker, C. (1990). *Surveillance, power and modernity: Bureaucracy and discipline from 1700 to the present day*. St. Martin's Press.

Dhir, A., Torsheim, T., Pallesen, S., & Andreassen, C. S. (2017). Do online privacy concerns predict selfie behavior among adolescents, young adults and adults? *Frontiers in Psychology, 8*(815), 1–12. https://doi.org/10.3389/fpsyg.2017.00815.

Eastin, M. S., Brinson, N. H., Doorey, A., & Wilcox, G. (2016). Living in a big data world: Predicting mobile commerce activity through privacy concerns. *Computers in Human Behavior, 58*, 214–220. https://doi.org/10.1016/j.chb.2015.12.050.

Gambs, S., Killijian, M.-O., & Del Prado Cortez, M. N. (2010). Show me how you move and I will tell you who you are. *Transactions on Data Privacy, 4*(2), 34–41. https://doi.org/10.1145/1868470.1868479.

Goffman, E. (1959). *The presentation of self in everyday life*. Anchor Book.

Griffin, E. A., Ledbetter, A., & Sparks, G. G. (2019). *A first look at communication theory* (10th ed.). McGraw-Hill.

Hoy, M. G., & Miline, G. (2010). Gender differences in privacy-related measures for young adult Facebook users. *Journal of Interactive Advertising, 10*(2), 28–45. https://doi.org/10.1080/15252019.2010.10722168.

Li, Y. (2011). Empirical studies on online information privacy concerns: Literature review and an integrative framework. *CAIS, 28*, 1–43. https://doi.org/10.17705/1CAIS.02828.

Lyon, D. (2007). *Surveillance studies: An overview*. Polity Press.

Marwick, A. E., Murgia-Diaz, D., & Palfrey, J. G. (2010). Youth, privacy and reputation. Berkman Center Research Publication No. 2010-5, Harvard Public Law Working Paper No. 10-29. https://papers.ssrn.com/sol3/papers.cfm?abstract_id=1588163.

Marx, G. T. (1988). *Undercover police surveillance in America*. University of California Press. http://SK8ES4MC2L.search.serialssolutions.com/?sid=sersol&SS_jc=TC0000443727&title=Undercover%20%3A%20police%20surveillance%20in%20America.

McLuhan, M. (1964). *Understanding media: The extensions of man*. McGraw-Hill.

Miltgen, C. L., & Peyrat-Guillard, D. (2014). Cultural and generational influences on privacy concerns: A qualitative study in seven European countries. *European Journal of Information Systems, 23*(2), 103–125. https://doi.org/10.1057/ejis.2013.17.

Norris, C., & Armstrong, G. (1999). *The maximum surveillance society: The rise of CCTV*. Berg.

Nosko, A., Wood, E., & Molema, S. (2010). All about me: Disclosure in online social networking profiles: The case of Facebook. *Computers in Human Behavior, 26*(3), 406–418. https://doi.org/10.1016/j.chb.2009.11.012.

O'Hara, K., Tuffield, M. M., & Shadbolt, N. (2008). Lifelogging: Privacy and empowerment with memories for life. *Identity in the Information Society, 1*(1), 155–172. https://doi.org/10.1007/s12394-009-0008-4.

Ong, W. J. (1982). *Orality and literacy: The technologizing of the word*. Routledge.

Petty, R. E., & Cacioppo, J. T. (1981). *Attitudes and persuasion: Classic and contemporary approaches*. W.C. Brown.

Petty, R. E., & Cacioppo, J. T. (1986). *Communication and persuasion: Central and peripheral routes to attitude change*. Springer-Verlag.

Postman, N. (1985). *Amusing ourselves to death: Public discourse in the age of show business*. Viking.

Rainie, L. (2018). *Americans' complicated feelings about social media in an era of privacy concerns*. Pew Research Center. https://www.pewresearch.org/fact-tank/2018/03/27/americans-complicated-feelings-about-social-media-in-an-era-of-privacy-concerns.

Rule, J. (2011). "Needs" for surveillance and the movement to protect privacy. In K. Ball, K. D. Haggerty, & D. Lyon (Eds.), *Routledge handbook of surveillance studies* (pp. 64–71). Routledge. http://ezaccess.libraries.psu.edu/login?url=http://ebookcentral.proquest.com/lib/pensu/detail.action?docID=957182.

Taddicken, M. (2014). The "privacy paradox" in the social web: The impact of privacy concerns, individual characteristics, and the perceived social relevance on different forms of self-disclosure. *Journal of Computer-Mediated Communication, 19*(2), 248–273. https://doi.org/10.1111/jcc4.12052.

Trottier, D. (2018). Privacy and surveillance. In J. Burgess (Ed.), *The Sage handbook of social media* (pp. 463–478). Sage.

Twenge, J. M., Martin, G. N., & Campbell, W. K. (2018). Decreases in psychological well-being among American adolescents after 2012 and links to screen time during the rise of smartphone technology. *Emotion, 18* (6), 765–780. https://doi.org/10.1037/emo0000403.

Van den Broeck, E., Poels, K., & Walrave, M. (2015). Older and wiser? Facebook use, privacy concern, and privacy protection in the life stages of emerging, young, and middle adulthood. *Social Media + Society, 1*(2), 2056305115616149. https://doi.org/10.1177/2056305115616149.

Veissière, S. P. L., & Stendel, M. (2018). Hypernatural monitoring: A social rehearsal account of smartphone addiction. *Frontiers in Psychology, 9*(A141), 1–10. https://doi.org/10.3389/fpsyg.2018.00141.

Widjaja, A. E., Chen, J. V., Sukoco, B. M., & Ha, Q.-A. (2019). Understanding users' willingness to put their personal information on the personal cloud-based storage applications: An empirical study. *Computers in Human Behavior, 91*, 167–185. https://doi.org/10.1016/j.chb.2018.09.034.

Wood, S. L., & Swait, J. (2002). Psychological indicators of innovation adoption: Cross-classification based on need for cognition and need for change. *Journal of Consumer Psychology, 12*(1), 1–12. https://doi.org/10.1207/S15327663JCP1201_01.

7

Social Media and Culture

LEARNING GOALS

This chapter will help you understand:

- How do cultural backgrounds affect adoption of social media?
- What role does culture play in growing connectedness and interdependence?
- How does social media use help cultural learning and social learning?

KEY CONCEPTS

Cultural difference	Cultural learning
Social learning	Cultural evolution

THEORY HIGHLIGHT

Cultivation Theory

Overview

Culture has a significant influence over the adoption and usage of social media around the world. The diffusion of information and communication technologies (ICT) has demonstrated that social media adoption and usage could vary dramatically from culture to culture. Thanks to centuries of the diffusion of media technology and international cooperation, culture begins to play a big role in the growing connectedness and interdependence of world economies, populations, and their networked societies, which is also known as the process of globalization. Hence, culture, as a source of acceptable norms and behaviors, influences social media communication, including communication expectations, preferences, and experiences (Gevorgyan & Manucharova, 2009).

Cultural Diversity

Culture helps determine human perceptions about themselves and the ways they behave toward others, including communication habits and preferences (Sheldon et al., 2017). Effective communication in the globalized world requires us to understand the complexities of target audiences' cultural backgrounds and to embrace cultural diversity. Acknowledging cultural differences is the first step in examining how culture may affect human behavior, attitudes, and perceptions (Naylor, 1996), including social media usage.

Different "cultures collectively construct individuals in different ways" (Kanagawa et al., 2001, p. 90). People from different cultures tend to process information differently, even when they may share common values and perceptions of ethical problems (Armstrong, 1996). For instance, Westerners living in an individualist culture hold an independent self-concept that is not affected much by social contexts and others and drives individuals to attend to self-related information. In contrast, East Asians who live in a collectivist culture hold an interdependent view of the self that is sensitive to information related to significant others and attend to intimate others as much as they do to the self (Markus & Kitayama, 2010).

Culture is defined as the "collective mental programming" (Hofstede, 1983, p. 74), which is shared by individuals with other members of their group or nation, but not with members of other groups or nations (Zhong, 2008). Culture contains a set of specific messages that could be fully understood and interpreted by those who know the culture well. Thus, culture is about learned knowledge, beliefs, and behaviors that are collectively shared by the members of a group or a nation, rather than being inherited from others. Simply, cultural values are shared beliefs and behaviors, not unique to one or two persons.

Hofstede (1980) divides cultural differences representing cultural values into five dimensions: (1) individualism–collectivism; (2) uncertainty avoidance; (3) power distance; (4) masculinity–femininity; and (5) long-term orientation. Among them, the individualism–collectivism dimension has been mostly studied by scholars and viewed as the most important dimension identifying cultural differences between nations (Hofstede, 1991; Srite & Karahanna, 2006). In individualistic societies like Western cultures, individual needs, duties, and rights are predominant. In Western cultures like the United States, people often value self more than family, friends, and their groups. They are more likely to engage in self-promotion than self-effacement, and value pride over modesty. Members of Western cultures tend to have more friends but looser connections to them and friendships are less enduring. These values are rooted in the rugged individualism and freedom of choice that are the foundations of Western cultures.

By contrast, collectivistic societies like Eastern cultures stress the priority of group goals and identity, and members must adopt group-based duties toward a common good (Hofstede, 1991). Living in a collective culture, people tend to value family, friends, and their groups over self. They are more likely to engage in self-effacement than self-promotion, and value modesty over pride. Thus, they may have fewer, closer, and more enduring friendships than members of Western cultures. Eastern values and friendship patterns are rooted in the historical, political, and religious foundations of Confucianism, Buddhism, and Taoism (Jackson & Wang, 2013). Hofstede's model of cultural values has been extensively verified and widely accepted by other scholars due to the model's ability of reducing the complexities of culture by breaking it into specific, fundamental dimensions.

According to uses and gratifications theory (Katz et al., 1973), individual differences influence motivations for engaging with different media. Uses and gratifications theory has been used in a number of studies to understand why people use particular media. Kim et al. (2011) applied the theory to examine how culture influences the motives and usage of social media among college students in the United States and Korea. They found that American students' online social networks were almost five times larger on average than their Korean counterparts, even though American and Korean students spent almost the same amount of time on average on social media platforms. There were also differences in the motives underlying thesocial media use. American students focused more on making new friends through social media, while Korean students tended to focus on nurturing existing relationships with socially close others for informational utility and social support.

In general, individualists tend to derive greater pleasure through emotional release than collectivists because they generally tend to favor self-stimulation and self-satisfaction. Kim et al. (2011) found that American students reported higher entertainment motivation than Korean students. Similarly, Hsu's et al. (2015) study of the 493 active Facebook users in five countries (Australia, Austria, Japan, Taiwan, and the USA) revealed that whereas information-seeking was a stronger predictor of continuance intention among those hailing from individualistic cultures, socialization had a stronger influence on continuance intention for collectivist users.

Five Dimensions of Cultural Differences

Geert H. Hofstede (1980) identifies five cultural dimensions (Figure 7.1), which assign mathematical scores designating a particular country's beliefs about each of the dimensions. The five cultural dimensions are power distance, individualism, masculinity, uncertainty avoidance index, and long-term orientation. Among them, the

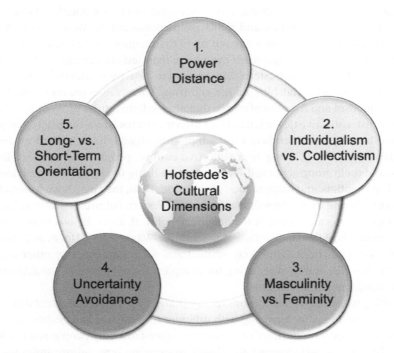

Figure 7.1 Hofstede's five cultural dimensions (Illustration by Moxin Qian).

dimension of long-term orientation was seldom adopted by other scholars. Thus, the remaining four dimensions became a classic model facilitating a large number of studies on cultural differences around the globe because the dimensions are standardized in order to allow multiple and easy comparisons between countries. The five key dimensions are:

1. Power distance index: reflects the perception that members of society have about unequal distribution of power and the extent to which it is accepted in a society. In other words, the less powerful members of groups or organizations accept and expect that power is distributed unequally. This represents inequality (more versus less), but defined from below, not from above. It suggests that a society's level of inequality is endorsed by the followers as much as by the leaders. Power and inequality may be normal and everywhere. Still, all societies are unequal, but some are more unequal than others.

2. Individualism vs. collectivism: the level at which the individuals of a country tend to see themselves as self-sufficient (individualism) as compared to a tendency to see themselves, above all, as part of a social group (collectivism). In an individualist culture, social ties between individuals are loose, whereas in a collectivist culture, people are more closely integrated into strong, cohesive in-groups, often extended families that continue protecting them in exchange for unquestioning loyalty. Those in an individualist culture hold an independent self-concept, while living in a collectivist culture, people tend to hold an interdependent view of the self that is more likely to be influenced by others, especially those in power or with a high social status.

3. Masculinity vs. femininity: the level at which values, such as assertiveness, performance, success and competitiveness, prevail among people in a culture over values such as kindness, quality of life, maintaining warm personal relationships, services, caring for the weak, etc. This dimension refers to the distribution of roles between the genders that is another fundamental issue for any society to which a range of solutions are found. It is found that (a) women's values differ less among societies than men's values and (b) men's values from one country to another contain a dimension from very assertive and competitive and maximally different from women's values, on the one side, to modest and caring and similar to women's values, on the other. The assertive pole has been called "masculine" and the modest, caring pole "feminine." The women in feminine countries have the same modest, caring values as the men; in the masculine countries they are somewhat assertive and competitive, but not as much as the men, so these countries show a gap between men's values and women's values.

4. Uncertainty avoidance: the level at which the individuals in a given culture feel uncomfortable with uncertainty and ambiguity. The fourth dimension deals with a society's tolerance for uncertainty and ambiguity. It indicates to what extent a culture programs its members to feel either uncomfortable or comfortable in unstructured situations. Unstructured situations are novel, unknown, surprising, and different from usual. Uncertainty-avoiding cultures try to minimize the possibility of such situations by strict laws and rules, safety and security measures. People in uncertainty-avoiding countries are also more emotional, and motivated by inner nervous energy. The opposite, uncertainty-accepting cultures, are more tolerant of opinions different from what they are used to; they try to have as few rules as

possible, and on the philosophical and religious level they are relativist and allow many currents to flow side by side. People within these cultures are more phlegmatic and contemplative, and are not expected by their environment to express emotions (Moskowitz, 2009).

5. Long-term orientation: this dimension is also called long-term versus short-term orientation, which originated from a study based on the Chinese Value Survey comparing students from 23 countries (Hofstede & Bond, 1988). This index was initially labeled as "Confucian Work Dynamism," but it was not included in Hofstede's four basic value dimensions identified in his initial research on cultural differences. Long-term orientation indicates a culture's time-orientation values. Living in a society with a culture of long-term orientation, people tend to value more of those virtues oriented toward future reward, especially perseverance, thrift, seniority, and other orders of relation by status. In contrast, societies located at the short-term pole prefer virtues related to the past and present, in particular respecting for tradition, protecting one's "face," and fulfilling social obligations (Guo et al., 2018). According to Hofstede and colleagues, East Asian countries mostly have a long-term orientation, while Australia, the United States, some Latin American, African, and Muslim countries can be identified as short-term orientated societies (Hofstede, 2001).

Cultural Evolution

When examining the role of culture in social media usage, it is beneficial to consider culture as an evolutionary process (Lewens, 2015). To Henrich and McElreath (2003), culture is, in essence, the information acquired by individuals via social learning. Thus, culture can be defined as behavior transmitted through social learning, as opposed to individual learning or genetic inheritance.

Cultural messages are learned through the process of social learning as these messages are not hard-wired in human DNAs. Acquiring cultural messages is the process of "cultural learning," which is "the subset of social learning capacities that allow for cumulative cultural evolution" (Henrich & McElreath, 2003, p. 124). Thus, understanding of technology adaptation, including social media, requires exploring the cultural learning process that shapes our usage and behavioral repertoires.

As part of social learning, cultural learning enables users to respond quickly to cultural setting changes in technology domains, which is much faster than self-learning via exploiting a body of adaptive knowledge stored in their learned behavioral repertoire. Cultural learning allows users to learn technology selectively (boyd et al., 2013), rather than simply accepting the experience of others or following observations. Overall, "the ability to learn culturally can also raise the average fitness of a population by allowing acquired improvements to accumulate from one generation to the next (boyd et al., 2013, p. 135).

To cultural evolutionists, culture refers to "an inheritance system that evolves by mechanisms broadly analogous to the evolution of genes" (Richerson, 2016, p. 1). Thus, a cultural phenomenon may be viewed as "a population-level aggregate of individual-level interactions" (Acerbi, 2016, p. 2). This approach has developed mathematical models generating empirical evidence to linking micro-processes of transmission to macro-processes of cultural change. As a result, numerous cultural patterns may be explained by analyzing cultural behaviors, in particular, the individual cognition behind those behaviors, suggesting that the success of some widespread cultural beliefs may be due to the fact of them being generally attractive to human minds (Acerbi, 2016; Lewens, 2015). Accumulated cultural skills and knowledge are characteristics of all human societies, but cultural learning alone does not increase adaptability (Henrich & McElreath, 2003).

Cultural Influence on Social Media Usage

Social media users' cultural backgrounds are found to be associated with different perspectives toward the use of social media. Those living in individualist and collectivist cultures show differences in terms of users' communication and behavioral styles. For instance, Rosen et al. (2010) found that people from individualist cultures used social media to meet new people and be seen by others, but not so much to maintain their existing relationships in social network sites. On the other hand, people from collectivist cultures utilize social media to maintain relationships with close relatives or friends instead of developing new relationships with others.

Researchers also discovered that the motives for using Instagram vary dramatically between the users from Croatia, a highly collectivistic culture, and from the United States, a typically individualist culture (Sheldon et al., 2017). The gratification in using Instagram – consisting of self-promotion, social interaction, diversion, documenting, and creativity – followed the same cultural line between Croatian and American users. Specifically, American users were more likely to use Instagram for self-promotion than Croatian users. Croatian self-promoters tended to use more hashtags, which American self-promoters did not.

These findings demonstrate that individualism and collectivism have a significant influence on Instagram gratifications. Users living in an individualist culture tended to be associated with self-promotion and documentation in Instagram usage while those in a collectivistic culture centered more on social interaction. Overall, Instagram users seeking different modes of gratifications tend to use Instagram in different ways, and cultural backgrounds moderate the relationship between gratifications and Instagram usage. Thus, cultural differences are evident in Instagram usage, such as uploading, sharing, and tagging personal images. The results are consistent with the literature of cultural studies, which posit that culture determines individuals' perceptions about themselves and others, the ways in which they behave toward one another, including communication habits and preferences (Hsu et al., 2015; Sheldon et al., 2017).

Although globalization, immigration, and other social processes can potentially initiate a trend toward cultural unification, this could potentially eliminate cultural-based variability. Other scholars argue that culture has great inertia and cultural change is slow. Researchers tend to agree that human beings have demonstrated a remarkable capacity to create cultures and then to be shaped by them (Markus & Kitayama, 2010). In the process of creating cultures and being influenced by them, humans are at the center of adopting ICT applications, which have been developing a sense of self-awareness. The sense of self-awareness is important in guiding one's adoptive behaviors, in particular cultural environments. Engaging with their sociocultural contexts, people "reinforce and sometimes change the ideas, practices, and institutions of these environments" (Markus & Kitayama, 2010, p. 420).

Cultural Differences in Social Media Activities

Several major cultural differences concerning social media use have been identified. First, users in a collectivist culture might spend less time using social media and consider social media less important than those in an individualistic culture due the differences of how they view family, friends, and their groups (Jackson & Wang, 2013). For example, people in East Asian countries like China were found to be more restrained in social media use and posted less information about themselves, as Chinese culture values modesty over self-promotion. With a greater investment in real-world relationships, those in collectivist cultures were less likely to invest too much in online relationships compared to those in individualistic cultures. The reverse may be true of members of individualistic cultures like the United States. They values individuals' values over group values and social media serve as an important platform for self-expression and self-realization. They could have more online friends and spend more time with them on social media, which made them think the role of social media in their lives was more important than members of collectivist cultures.

Second, due to the influence of Eastern cultures, social media use for recreational purposes is not encouraged as hard work is emphasized as a means to life success. Spending more time using social media alone goes against traditional cultural values of attaching importance to family or group time over private time. Eastern cultures expect members to give more time to others and their families or groups. For example, Chinese parents were less likely to support their children's use of social media and discouraged their children from using social media at a young age. Generally, Chinese parents were more likely to monitor and set limits on their children's social media activities. Many of their children accepted the limits from parents or teachers and consequentially used social media less than their counterparts in the United States (Jackson & Wang, 2013).

Third, the specific use of social media could be different between collectivist and individualistic cultures. For example, a study found that Korean social media users had fewer, but more intimate, friends, tended to keep their public profiles anonymous, exhibited less personal self-disclosure, and used more non-verbal communication (e.g., graphics or icons) than did US social media users (Cho, 2010). According to the same study, US users had more friends online, exhibited more self-disclosure, and relied more on direct text-based communication than did Korean SNS users. The findings are consistent with a comparative study of Chinese and US social media users in regard to their sharing behavior on social media. For example, Chinese users contributed more to in-group sharing than their American counterparts (Qiu et al., 2012). Qiu and colleagues also found that Chinese users who used both a Chinese social media platform (i.e., Renren) and Facebook could easily switch their sharing behavior patterns in response to different cultural contexts.

It is important to note that cultural differences identified in the existing literature may not apply to current situations because cultures are dynamic and complex. Hence, cultural differences are always fluid rather than static. As social media are widely adopted across the world, some cultural differences that were identified before may no longer be as apparent as before. Part of the cultural differences could disappear, like gender differences regarding social media use. Little difference can be detected by scholars between boys/men and girls/women in terms of social media usage, which may be due to the widespread adoption of social media among people, old and young. The same pattern may be true of the cultural differences reviewed here, which merits more scholarly effort in this area.

Theory Highlight: Cultivation Theory

Cultivation theory was developed by George Gerbner, dean of the Annenberg School of Communications at the University of Pennsylvania, in the 1960s. Later, he and his colleagues expanded further on a media effect theory by Gerbner and his colleague Larry Gross (Gerbner & Gross, 1976). Their study focused on how watching television might alter the audience's perception of everyday life and the outside world. Cultivation theory suggests that frequent viewers of television are more susceptible to media messages and the belief that they are real and valid. Heavy viewers are exposed to more violence on TV and therefore perceive the world as far worse and dangerous than it actually is. The theory suggests that television is responsible for shaping viewers' conceptions of social reality.

The combined effect of massive television exposure by viewers over time subtly shapes the perception of social reality for individuals and, ultimately, for our culture as a whole. Gerbner (1969) argues that cultivation theorists distinguish between "first order" effects (general beliefs about the everyday world, such as about the prevalence of violence) and "second order"

effects (specific attitudes, such as toward law and order or personal safety). There is also a distinction between two groups of television viewers: the heavy viewers and the light viewers. The study focus is on heavy viewers. People who watch a lot of television are likely to be more influenced by the ways in which the world is framed by television programs than those who watch less, especially regarding topics with which the viewer has little first-hand experience. Light viewers may have more sources of information than heavy viewers. Cultivation theorists argue that television has long-term effects that are small, gradual, and indirect but cumulative and significant.

Cultivation analysis is not limited to cases when television "facts" vary from real world statistics. One of the most interesting and important issues of cultivation analysis involves the symbolic transformation of message system data into more general issues and assumptions, as opposed to the comparison of television and real world "fact." One example of this is what we have called the "mean world" syndrome.

Although cultivation theory was developed when television in the US meant three national broadcast networks, nowadays there is little evidence that proliferation of channels has led to any substantially greater diversity of content. Also, although viewers have more media choices today, again there is little evidence that any of this has changed viewing habits – or that the content that heavy television viewers consume most often presents world views and values fundamentally different from most network-type programs.

Cultivation research looks at the mass media as a socializing agent and investigates whether television viewers come to believe the television version of reality the more they watch it. It has been especially effective in forming viewers' perception of particular issues in fields like crime, health and mental health, politics, sex roles, and sexual behaviors. Cultivation analysis is also considered to be ideally suited to multinational and cross-cultural comparative studies (Hofstede et al., 2002; Morgan, 1990). These studies are the best test of system-wide similarities and differences across national boundaries and of the actual significance of national cultural policies. Cultivation theory can be a valuable theoretical framework for studying social media effects on heavy or light users.

Summary

This chapter examines the impact of cultures on the adoption and usage of social media. Facing the growing trend of globalization, some may assume that cultural unification could emerge to gradually eliminate cultural-based variability. On the contrary, since cultural changes happen very slowly, scholars found that cultures begin to play a big role in the growing connectedness and interdependence of world economies, populations, and their network societies. For a better understanding of the cultural differences found in using social media, we also review cultural learning and social learning in the context of cultural evolution. In this chapter, we should have achieved the following objectives:

- Define culture and understand how cultural differences construct people in different ways.
- Learn the five dimensions of cultural values, especially the dimension of individualism and collectivism.
- Examine the process of cultural evolution and differentiate social learning from individual learning.
- Study how cultural differences are demonstrated in using social media around the globe.

Looking Ahead

Chapter 8 will be about problematic use of social media (PUSM). Negative outcomes triggered by the excessive use of social media are associated with a long list of detrimental effects on the physical, psychological, and social lives of the users, though most users do not show addictive symptoms even when they have some PUSM symptoms. PUSM involves both individual users and state actors. State actors can set up a cyber troop to launch weaponized informational attacks on their opponents. When social media are misused regardless of the intention, there are serious consequences that could hurt individual users, others, and the communities they are in.

Discussion

1. Do you see that some differences in using social media may be traced back to cultural differences in one way or anther? Provide an example to illustrate your answer.
2. What are individual learning, social learning, and cultural learning? Can you describe any connection among them?
3. What are the five dimensions of cultural values discussed? Do some of them exist within the same cultural environment?
4. Can you design a social media research project based on cultivation theory?

References

Acerbi, A. (2016). A cultural evolution approach to digital media. *Frontiers in Human Neuroscience, 10*(636), 1–12. https://doi.org/10.3389/fnhum.2016.00636.

Armstrong, R. W. (1996). The relationship between culture and perception of ethical problems in international marketing. *Journal of Business Ethics, 15*(11), 1199–1208. https://doi.org/10.1007/BF00412818.

boyd, R., Richerson, P. J., & Henrich, J. (2013). The cultural evolution of technology: Facts and theories. In P. J. Richerson & M. H. Christiansen (Eds.), *Cultural evolution: Society, technology, language, and religion* (pp. 119–142). MIT Press. https://doi.org/10.7551/mitpress/9780262019750.003.0007.

Cho, S. E. (2010). Cross-cultural comparison of Korean and American social network sites [Doctoral dissertation]. Rutgers University.

Gerbner, G. (1969). Toward "Cultural Indicators": The analysis of mass mediated public message systems. *AV Communication Review, 17*(2), 137–148. https://doi.org/10.4135/9781473915299.

Gerbner, G., & Gross, L. (1976). Living with television: The violence profile. *Journal of Communication Disorders, 26*(2), 173–199. https://doi.org/10.1111/j.1460-2466.1976.tb01397.x.

Gevorgyan, G., & Manucharova, N. (2009). Does culturally adapted online communication work? A study of American and Chinese Internet users' attitudes and preferences toward culturally customized web design elements. *Journal of Computer-Mediated Communication, 14*(2), 393–413. https://doi.org/10.1111/j.1083-6101.2009.01446.x.

Guo, Q., Liu, Z., Li, X., & Qiao, X. (2018). Indulgence and long term orientation influence prosocial behavior at national level. *Frontier in Psychology, 9*, 1–10, Article 1798. https://doi.org/10.3389/fpsyg.2018.01798.

Henrich, J., & McElreath, R. (2003). The evolution of cultural evolution. *Evolutionary Anthropology, 12*(3), 123–135. https://doi.org/10.1002/evan.10110.

Hofstede, G., & Bond, M. H. (1988). The confucius connection: From cultural roots to economic growth. *Organizational Dynamics, 16*(4), 5–21. https://doi. org/10.1016/0090-2616(88)90009-5.

Hofstede, G. H. (1980). *Culture's consequences: International differences in work-related values.* Sage Publications.

Hofstede, G. H. (1983). National cultures in four dimensions: A research-based theory of cultural differences among nations. *International Studies of Management & Organization, 13*, 46–74. https://www.jstor.org/stable/40396953.

Hofstede, G. H. (1991). *Cultures and organizations: Software of the mind.* McGraw-Hill.

Hofstede, G. H. (2001). *Culture's consequences: Comparing values, behaviors, institutions, and organizations across nations* (2nd ed.). Sage.

Hofstede, G. J., Pedersen, P., & Hofstede, G. H. (2002). *Exploring culture: Exercises, stories, and synthetic cultures.* Intercultural Press.

Hsu, M.-H., Tien, S.-W., Lin, H.-C., & Chang, C.-M. (2015). Understanding the roles of cultural differences and socio-economic status in social media continuance intention. *Information Technology & People, 28*(1), 224–241. https://doi.org/10.1108/ ITP-01-2014-0007.

Jackson, L. A., & Wang, J. (2013). Cultural differences in social networking site use: A comparative study of China and the United States. *Computers in Human Behavior, 29*(3), 910–921. https://doi.org/10.1016/j.chb.2012.11.024.

Kanagawa, C., Cross, S. E., & Markus, H. R. (2001). "Who am I?" The cultural psychology of the conceptual self. *Personality and Social Psychology Bulletin, 27*(1), 90–104. https:// doi.org/10.1177/0146167201271008.

Katz, E., Gurevitch, M., & Hass, H. (1973). On the use of the media for important things. *American Sociological Review, 38*(2), 164–181. https://doi.org/10.2307/2094393.

Kim, Y., Sohnb, D., & Choi, S. M. (2011). Cultural difference in motivations for using social network sites: A comparative study of American and Korean college students. *Computers in Human Behavior, 27*(1), 365–372. https://doi.org/10.1016/j. chb.2010.08.015.

Lewens, T. (2015). *Cultural evolution: Conceptual challenges.* Oxford University Press.

Markus, H. R., & Kitayama, S. (2010). Cultures and selves: A cycle of mutual constitution. *Perspectives on Psychological Science, 5*(4), 420–430. https://doi. org/10.1177/1745691610375557.

Morgan, M. (1990). International cultivation analysis. In N. Signorielli & M. Morgan (Eds.), *Cultivation analysis: New directions in media effects research* (pp. 225–248). Sage.

Moskowitz, S. (2009). Hofstede's five dimensions of culture. In C. Wankel (Ed.), *Encyclopedia of business in today's world.* Sage Publications. https://doi. org/10.4135/9781412964289.n468.

Naylor, L. L. (1996). *Culture and change: An introduction.* Bergin & Garvey.

Qiu, L., Lin, H., & Leung, A. K.-Y. (2012). Cultural differences and switching of in-group sharing behavior between an American (Facebook) and a Chinese (Renren) social networking site. *Journal of Cross-Cultural Psychology, 44*(1), 106–121. https://doi. org/10.1177/0022022111434597.

Richerson, P. J. (2016). Tim Lewens, Cultural Evolution: Conceptual challenges. *History and Philosophy of the Life Sciences, 38*(15), 1–4.

Rosen, D., Stefanone, M. A., & Lackaff, D. (2010). Online and offline social networks: Investigating culturally-specific behavior and satisfaction. In *Proceedings of the 43rd*

Hawaii International Conference on System Sciences, Institute of Electrical and Electronics Engineers.

Sheldon, P., Rauschnabel, P. A., Antony, M. G., & Car, S. (2017). A cross-cultural comparison of Croatian and American social network sites: Exploring cultural differences in motives for Instagram use. *Computers in Human Behavior, 75*, 643–651. https://doi.org/10.1016/j.chb.2017.06.009.

Srite, M., & Karahanna, E. (2006). The role of espoused national cultural values in technology acceptance. *MIS Quaterly, 30*(3), 679–704. https://doi.org/10.2307/25148745.

Zhong, B. (2008). Thinking along the cultural line: A cross-cultural inquiry of ethical decision making among U.S. and Chinese journalism students. *Journalism and Mass Communication Educator, 63*(2), 110–126. https://doi.org/10.1177/107769580806300202.

8

Problematic Use of Social Media

LEARNING GOALS

This chapter will help you understand:

- How pervasive is the problematic use of social media?
- What is the mechanism of repetitive use of social media?
- What are the major adverse outcomes of the problematic use of social media?

KEY CONCEPTS

Problematic use of social media	Self-control
Reward system	Fear of missing out (FOMO)
Phubbing	Cyber troops

THEORY HIGHLIGHT

Third-Person Effect

Overview

Scientists have reached more consensus about the benefits of social media use than its adverse effects on users. So far research has not detected a widespread addiction of social media among young or old users. In fact, scholars can hardly agree on how to define problematic use of social media (PUSM) due to the conceptual confusion surrounding the classification of normal or problematic usage of these digital platforms. An excessive and problematic use of social media can be treated as part of generalized internet addiction. Internet addiction is an umbrella term depicting a range of specific problematic use, misuse, and addictions in computer-based technologies, include gaming disorder, sexting, online gambling addiction, and social media addiction. Compared to adults, children and adolescents are often more vulnerable to generalized internet addiction, which brings young people more negative outcomes.

Generally, such disorders or addictive behaviors are comparatively sporadic among users. Large nationally representative surveys, based on investigating 8.44 million US adolescents aged 13–19 from 1976 to 2016, found that few American teenagers engaged in adult activities that were linked to increased internet use (Twenge & Park,

2019). Another study analyzed 41 studies involving 42,000 children and young people's smartphone usage around the world. It discovered that less than a quarter of them (23%) exhibited the prevalence of smartphone addiction (Sohn et al., 2019). Other large epidemiological studies reported that the prevalence of internet addiction ranged between 1% of the general population in Germany (Rumpf et al., 2014) to 18.7% of Taiwanese adolescents (Lin et al., 2014), indicating there may be cross-cultural differences in presentation and assessment (Kuss et al., 2021).

The bottom line is that there has been a rising prevalence of internet disorders, including PUSM, since the 2010s. Excessive social media use in both adolescence and emerging adulthood may lead to symptoms traditionally associated with substance-related addictions and behavioral addictions, such as gambling addiction. As a sub-form of internet addiction, PUSM is increasingly associated with poor academic performance, withdrawal, anxiety, narcissism, and personality disorders among young adults. Some contextual factors like sociocultural conditions and digital environments contribute to these problematic behaviors. PUSM is also related to other sub-forms of problematic internet use, like excessive smartphone use, though most of them exhibit no tendency of behavioral addiction.

Warm Feelings in Social Media Use

Social media users tend to experience warm feelings when they see lots of likes from a Facebook or Snapchat post. MRI (magnetic resonance imaging) scans show that the brain's reward system lights up at those moments. When a person's brain reward system is activated, it helps produce dopamine, a chemical that regulates feelings of pleasure and desire. More importantly, the brain will take note that something important is happening and it is worth remembering and repeating. People love warm feelings, but they do not know when the good feelings will come back again. This drives users to repeat what they do on social media, leading to the possible excessive use of social media or even a pathological addiction. By and large, social media use may affect human brains in some unprecedented ways, which could activate a brain's rewarding center by directly involving the concentration of dopamine in the process (Figure 8.1).

Figure 8.1 Social media use may activate users' rewarding system in the brain, causing feelings of pleasure (Illustration by Moxin Qian).

On the other hand, the algorithms embedded in social media sites or apps have lots of features encouraging additive behaviors. Facebook and Snapchat, for example, have lots of these features such as ease of use, notifications of likes and comments, and feelings of missing out or anxiety when not engaging with the content. Facebook constantly re-ranks the posts from a user's friend circle by placing any posts high when its algorithms predict them to elicit higher emotional arousal. For instance, Facebook could rank a photo of a smiling baby or a cute pet higher than another photo of a glass of tap water because the former could be more likely to trigger warm feelings, even when the latter photo was posted more recently. Therefore, exposure to Facebook can affect users' mood by creating emotionally contagious experiences, some of which are heart-warming and may significantly boost their well-being.

Research has identified a slew of benefits in using social media for young and old users. Social media usage opens up new communication pathways to relieve social isolation and loneliness. Social media updates from users and friends can inspire healthy lifestyle changes, such as quitting smoking or exercising more often. Even announcing healthy lifestyle goals via social media and regularly posting about them promotes one's accountability as the content creates positive reinforcement from the user and friends. The content helps stimulate a formal or informal support group online that often leads the aspirant to form or join other offline communities dedicated to similar pursuits. Sharing a goal on social media not only promotes accountability and helps the user stay focused, but also increases one's chance of success, whether it is about weight loss or recovery from addiction.

In these ways, social media help build and strengthen new and existing relationships. They provide the users, especially teens, with opportunities to develop life skills needed to function in society. Above all, social media often let the users experience warm feelings and other positive emotions. However, social media use is rewarding – up to a point. During the COVID-19 pandemic, for instance, people gained tremendous health informational support and peer support by using social media, which helped boost well-being during the global health crisis (Zhong et al., 2020). However, the same study also finds that excessive use of social media led to serious mental health consequences, including depression and vicarious trauma, even when users did not have a social media addiction. These findings suggest the importance of understanding the mechanism of excessive or problematic social media usage.

Mechanism of PUSM

We will first look at a real case of video gaming addition. In 2018, a nine-year-old British girl was urgently admitted to rehab after playing the combat video game Fortnite for 10 hours straight every day and refusing to go outside or go to the bathroom (Kellaway, 2018). Similar incidents rarely happen to users with PUSM, but scientists have found that the brain reward system of adolescents who played video games and used social media showed similar changes to those found in the brains of drug addicts and alcoholics (Turel & Bechara, 2019; Turel & Serenko, 2020).

MRI scans reveal that addictive video gaming behaviors can affect teenagers' brains in a similar way to drug and alcohol abuse. It is remarkable to see that similarities exist between the effects of video gaming addiction and drug use on young people's brains. What the MRI scans show is astonishing given the fact that drugs like cocaine affect the brain by being injected into the bloodstream and directly stimulate the brain and other organs. However, video gaming never sends any materials into a person's blood vessel and it affects the brain through sensory engagement. Gaming can offer a delightful experience of colors and sounds by engaging the visual, auditory, and proprioceptive senses. Numerous studies show that video gaming has beneficial effects on cognition and the brain depending on how the game is played. As long as little addiction is involved, playing video games is associated with better cognitive function, in particular, in terms of visual attention and short-term memory (Brilliant et al., 2019), though the topic is beyond the scope of this chapter.

Few studies are devoted to examining the similarities between PUSM and drug abuse. Some differences may exist between social media addiction and other forms of internet addiction, although addictions to both video gaming and social media use share a behavioral pattern on the spectrum of repeated compulsive online behaviors that can produce addiction-like symptoms, including salience, withdrawal, mood modification, relapse, conflict, and tolerance (He et al., 2017). Other research suggests that children's PUSM can be associated with the risks of drug use and drinking problems later in life.

Like those with a video gaming addiction, research finds that people who exhibit excessive use of social media have a more active brain reward system, and so are more sensitive to the likes, comments, and forwards on Facebook or Instagram than ordinary users. Social media use provides rewarding experiences that generate dopamine in the brain – the same substance produced when people play video games or eat cake. Over time, it trains your brain to maintain the urge of constantly checking for social media updates. Social media use then becomes habitual and compulsory. When it becomes worse, problematic use of social media emerges as the daily mental and behavioral sequences, which occur automatically in the presence of a trigger. PUSM becomes learned automatic responses activated or reinforced by a variety of contextual cues. Due to its non-conscious nature, PUSM requires little thought, effort, or instruction. The mechanism of PUSM also applies to other technology habits and addictions, as they share certain specific features, for instance, repetitive or habitual behaviors.

The good news is that our brains' self-control system remains intact in most users with social media addictive symptoms, unlike drug abusers. The latter group often demonstrate deficits in the self-control system of the brain. When social media users have a strong motivation to control their social media use, they can do it without much difficulty. By comparison, a drug like cocaine impairs self-control, which makes breaking an addictive pattern much harder. Still, overuse of social media is more problematic in children because their developing brain is more malleable. By the time they reach adolescence, their brain reward system begins to be more activated and develops faster. However, the self-control system is not fully developed until the age of 21. When children are exposed to social media, they can overstimulate their reward center and increase their reward responsiveness. This may explain why PUSM has more serious consequences for children and adolescents than adults.

Reward System and Self-Control

One of the major reasons people keep using social media is that they provide highly rewarding experiences to users. The rewarding nature of social media might trigger repetitive exposure to the content circulated on these digital platforms. For some users, overexposure to social media content can develop into problematic use of social media, even to the extent of use patterns adversely affecting various aspects of life. With PUSM, some users demonstrate moderate to severe symptoms, while others are not bothered much. A survey of over 1,100 US teens aged 13 to 17 revealed that social media use made them felt distracted from important things, such as paying attention to the people around them, spending time with them, homework, and sleep (Common Sense Media, 2018). Meanwhile, 72% of the teens were fully aware that tech companies manipulate users to spend more time on their devices or platforms. Another study, based on a nationally representative sample of 1,749 Americans aged 19 to 32, found that PUSM was positively associated with depressive symptoms after controlling for overall time and frequency of social media use (Shensa et al., 2017).

Most users with PUSM face the consequence of unsuccessful struggles between strong impulsions and weak inhibitory abilities (Turel & Qahri-Saremi, 2018). Thanks to limited self-control capabilities, some people will keep on using social media even when they know about major adverse outcomes. One example is when students skip homework to use social media. This indicates a loss of self-control, also known as "loss of agency," reflecting a decrease in one's ability to control relevant actions and consequences associated with PUSM (Turel & Serenko, 2020). Because feeling socially excluded persistently drives users to reach out to others, they become sensitive to social cues and develop a deep concern for social validation. This deep concern can trigger overuse or problematic use of social media and PUSM can push users into a "social-validation feedback loop," causing a long-term change in the brain's reward system and self-control function.

In the context of social media, loss of self-control manifests some users' limited ability to set control of their own social media use. For other users, social media use has become an automatic response, easily activated by certain contextual cues, such as notifications of new Facebook updates popping up on a smartphone screen. People's sense of agency over their behaviors has been positively related to their perceived behavioral control, reflecting the confidence and beliefs of being able to control a target behavior (Ajzen, 1985). The concept of perceived behavioral control is a key element in the theory of planned behavior (Ajzen, 1991), which may strongly influence both behaviors and behavior change. As a related concept, self-efficacy denotes people's beliefs in their capabilities to exercise control over courses of action, providing the foundation for motivation, well-being, and personal accomplishment (Bandura, 1997). Bandura described these beliefs as determinants of how people think, behave, and feel (Bandura, 1986). Both the theory of planned behavior and self-efficacy theory have been used successfully to predict and explain a wide range of health behaviors and intentions, including smoking, substance use, and PUSM.

As for PUSM, some researchers found that regaining a sense of self-control may not be the prime reason for changing one's behavior on social media, which is also shaped by other factors such as information overload, exhaustion, and regret (Cao & Sun, 2018). Fundamentally, exhaustion, regret, and other internal psychological states induced by social media use could motivate users to reduce time spent on digital platforms, functioning like corrective actions. When users do engage in both active and proactive efforts in these corrective actions, they help social media users to gain a sense of control over social media use (Turel & Serenko, 2020). Earlier researchers have found that the mere sense of self-control, even without intending to quit, is appealing and can yield enhanced self-motivation and improve people's well-being, but loss of agency leads to diminished motivation and well-being (Ryan & Deci, 2000). Thus, increasing a sense of control over social media use may help alter undesirable behavioral patterns and mitigate negative consequence of PUSM, such as fear-of-missing-out (FOMO) and phubbing.

FOMO and Phubbing

For millions of years, evolution has taught humans an important lesson: social exclusion is dangerous as it poses a direct threat to survival. Thus, it makes evolutionary sense for people to avoid social exclusion and actively seek out new social connections. To achieve these goals, people make an effort to increase the likelihood of social acceptance, including enhancing social awareness, changing behaviors, and remaining sensitive to social cues. For primitive people, it was important to strengthen existing and new social connections because their survival depended on it. This remains unchanged today, especially for social media users. For them, both social rejection and social exclusion can cause tremendous social pain (Eisenberger et al., 2003).

In a study published in *Science*, researchers assessed how the human brain interprets social exclusion. They used a functional MRI (fMRI) machine to scan people's brains in a lab at the University of California at Los Angles, measuring blood flow to different brain regions to see how brain activities are activated. While lying in the fMRI scanner, the research participants played a video game called Cyberball, a game allowing them to play catch with two other players using a two-button response pad. In the first group of subjects, two players started throwing the ball only to each other, giving the other subject a sense of social exclusion. The researchers then compared these subjects to a second group who were not made to feel excluded. The excluded group experienced increased blood flow to the same parts of the brain that light up when experiencing physical pain. The experiment shows that social pain avoidance is one of the strongest drivers of human behavior (Eisenberger et al., 2003).

Both FOMO and phubbing happening on mobile phones might be primarily driven by the deep fear of social exclusion. FOMO, or feeling of missing out, refers to feelings of anxiety that arise from the realization that an individual may be missing out on rewarding experiences that others are having. Phubbing is a portmanteau derived from the words "phone" and "snubbing." It refers to the practice of snubbing someone around in a social setting by concentrating on a mobile phone rather than talking or interacting with conversation partners.

FOMO and phubbing are part of smartphone problematic use, but they are directly related to social media use. It is a belief that other people experience more interesting events when one is absent. The fear can be taken as an intrapersonal attribute that drives people to stay alert to what other people are doing on social media platforms. Research has linked FOMO with social media addiction because those who worry about being unable to connect to their networks may develop impulsive checking habits. Over time, the tendency develops into a potential behavioral addictive problem.

FOMO appears to be a powerful predictor or possible component of PUSM in children and adolescents. After analyzing 2663 Flemish students in Germany, FOMO was found to be a good predictor of how frequently teenagers use several social media platforms and how many platforms they actively use (Franchina et al., 2018). FOMO was also a stronger predictor of the use of private social media platforms like Facebook and Snapchat than more public social media platforms like Twitter and YouTube (Franchina et al., 2018). FOMO predicted phubbing behavior both directly and indirectly via its relationship with PUSM.

Therefore, FOMO is more complex than a merely unitary phenomenon of online fear of missing out. Rather it is a multidimensional construct that plays a role in mediating the problematic usage between PUSM and other forms of internet addiction. FOMO is found to be associated with higher levels of problematic smartphone and social media use and phubbing. Social media users who experience high FOMO levels present high levels of anxiety, depression, neuroticism, irritability, inadequacy, and low self-esteem (Balta et al., 2020).

Phubbing can interfere with interactional processes by disrupting affiliation and intimacy with partners, as the behavior hurts mutual attentiveness in a face-to-face environment. When social networking takes up a substantial part of smartphone usage time, users are snubbing others more frequently during face-to-face interactions. A 2016 study claimed that phubbing had become a pervasive norm in modern communication and found that 44% of people reported phubbing and 55% of them phubbed multiple times a day (Chotpitayasunondh & Douglas, 2016). The percentages of phubbing and being phubbed could go much higher than that. It can bring more adverse outcomes in diverse social contexts, such as intimate relationships, organizational behaviors, and parenting practices.

In a work environment, boss phubbing is identified as a negative component that undermines perceived closeness, connection, and conversation quality. Boss phubbing is defined as when employees perceive their supervisor as being distracted by a cellphone when they are talking or in close proximity to each other at work (Roberts & David, 2017). Like in a private conversational setting, boss phubbing can reduce employee trust in their supervisors and undermine the important outcomes of job satisfaction and performance in the company (Roberts & David, 2020). Thus, boss phubbing can hinder rather than foster individual performance. Smartphone use by supervisors while in the presence of their subordinates is associated with reduced supervisor trust, which in turn is associated with lower subordinate job satisfaction and performance. The negative outcomes of boss phubbing could impair workplace interactions and business performance.

Cyber Troops and Social Media Manipulation

Organized social media manipulation may be the most destructive form of PUSM and is plotted by cyber troops in order to launch informational attacks on political rivals or manipulate public opinion. Cyber troops refer to government, military, or political party teams committed to manipulating domestic or international public opinion over social media (Bradshaw & Howard, 2017). Cyber troops are set up by state actors to produce weaponized narratives and circulate them on the internet, especially social media platforms. The goal is to subvert an opponent's democracy, political system, and social stability by generating skepticism and confusion as well as political and social schisms (Allenby & Gagrreau, 2017).

Conventional military power is still crucial to maintain the world order, but that is not adequate in the social media age. When a foreign country can interfere and meddle in US elections by spreading weaponized misinformation, making Americans lose faith in their leaders and political systems, such an attack limits or even eliminates the need for armed forces to achieve political and military goals (Allenby & Gagrreau, 2017).

Back in 2011, when hundreds of thousands of demonstrators took to the streets to demand freedom and justice during the Arab Spring, they hoped social media like Facebook could help them (see Figure 8.2). Ten years after the "Arab Spring," many dreams fell due to political chaos and bloody conflicts in most of the Arabic countries. The spirit of the Facebook Revolution did not die and new revolutions took place again, with demands for change echoing the same slogan in Algeria, Sudan, Lebanon and Iraq in 2019. Meanwhile, authoritarian rulers have learned their own lessons and began to ban social media like Facebook and Twitter or use social media to monitor anyone daring to challenge their regions. They tried all means to choke off information flows between activists, and between activists and the rest of the world.

Egyptian President Hosni Mubarak tried to disconnect his citizens from the global information infrastructure in the last week of January 2011. It was a desperate maneuver with a mixed impact. A small group of tech-savvy students and civil society leaders had organized satellite phones and dialup connections to Israel and Europe, so they

Figure 8.2 In February 2011, a demonstrator holds a sign praising Facebook in the Tahrir Square in Cairo, Egypt. The Arabic words on the sign read "Facebook against every oppressor," and the words on his poster hanging on the chest reads, "The era of fear is over" (Photo by Khaled Desouki/AFP/Getty Images). Source: https://arabic.cnn.com/middleeast/2015/04/26/egypt-facebook.

were able to keep up strong links to the rest of the world. Some of the telecommunications engineers acted slowly on the order to choke off internet access. The first large internet service provider was asked to shut down on Friday, January 28, but engineers did not respond until Saturday. Other providers responded quickly, and returned to normal service on Monday. The amount of bandwidth going into Egypt dropped off for four days, but it was not the information blackout Mubarak had asked for. Taking down the nation's information infrastructure also crippled government agencies. Later other authoritarian rulers developed more effectives ways to interfere with the free flow of information by either temporarily suspending access to any international social media platforms or permanently blocking those social media sites. Some even built a growing firewall as the system of information censorship and surveillance aimed at restricting freedom of speech, identifying and locating individuals, and providing immediate access to personal records. More governments now rely on their cyber troops to launch proactive attacks against domestic or foreign opponents.

Since the 2010s, cyber troops have launched weaponized narratives around the world through social media in the forms of fake news, misinformation, and disinformation. In this book, fake news is defined as the false information purposely produced and circulated, in many cases on social media, which can deceive the audience and manipulate public opinion for political or financial gains. Fake news can be categorized into misinformation and disinformation. Misinformation refers to false information that is disseminated on social media regardless of whether there is intent to mislead, while disinformation is deliberately misleading or biased information with the intention of deceiving others and manipulating public opinion.

Researchers from the Oxford Internet Institute report that governments and political parties around the globe have allocated significant resources to build up their cyber troops to manipulate the opinion of foreign and domestic audiences via social media (Bradshaw & Howard, 2018). Each country's cyber troops may have different names, but they share the same nature of state-sponsored organizations tasked with conducting disinformation campaigns on the internet. The key cyber-troop activity involves the purposeful distribution of fake, misleading, fabricated, or manipulated content.

The attacks from cyber troops are more destructive than non-state actors, including lone-wolf coders or hacker groups, because the state-sponsored actors are more powerful. They are publicly funded and have more resources, including a larger arsenal of experts in communication, machine learning, algorithm design, and data analytics. Their data-driven social media attacks can be launched against precise targets to achieve specific political goals. Such disinformation campaigns can inflict devastating damage by eroding opponents' democracy by undermining public trust in leaders, the media, and institutions, in addition to serving as another tool to restrict freedom of expression in repressive regimes (Bradshaw & Howard, 2018).

Another feature of cyber troop activity is that cyber troop teams use a large number of fake social media accounts known as "bots" to hide their identity and interests. These bots are often used to flood social media networks with spam and fake news. A bot is a software application that is specifically programmed to imitate a human user's behavior on social media. They are created and run by cyber troops to do repetitive tasks such as adding likes and forwarding certain posts or tweets. Bots' activities can be detected by tech companies like Facebook and Twitter, which ban such automated software applications on their platforms. Typically, cyber troops create bots and run them only at critical moments of public life, like voting. For example, Russia was found to push Brexit and Trump at the same time by the same trolls and bots (Simon, 2019). The bots can amplify certain voices and ideas by inflating the number of likes, shares, and retweets they receive, creating an artificial sense of popularity, momentum, or relevance. They can do such tasks much faster than human users could. Cyber troop teams seldom simply spread easily identified fake news on social media, but package it with trivial true information to disguise social media users.

Unlike individual users who also use social media to attack others, cyber troops are the only actors who can launch highly organized social media manipulation campaigns. Before they strike, they carefully calculate the timing of attacks and launch them during critical moments of public life, like on election days. The initial success of public opinion manipulation will drive more countries to exploit social media to spread their weaponized information on social media. It is expected that governments and political parties will dedicate more resources toward the use of social media for public opinion manipulation, which is emerging as "a pervasive and global phenomenon" (Bradshaw & Howard, 2017). The nature of cyber troops has made it more destructive than other types of PUSM, but the era of fear will be over and people will prevail eventually.

Relief of PUSM

People tend to share a growing sense of urgency concerning problematic use of social media, though it has not yet bothered a large number of people, like other addictive behaviors. Young users in the United States (Turel, 2021) and Europe (Franchina et al., 2018) reported that the more they were distracted by PUSM, the more deeply they were involved in using social media, including spending more time and checking updates more often. Other studies have linked PUSM with higher anxiety, depression, and lower self-esteem or life satisfaction. Specifically, FOMO is repeatedly found to be associated with negative health outcomes like depressive symptoms, less mindful attention, and more physical symptoms (Baker et al., 2016). Moreover, FOMO reduces people's capacity for self-awareness and mindful attention, while phubbing can negatively affect professional and romantic relationships.

In the coming years, the algorithms embedded in social media apps will not stop trying to hijack users' brains and to control their behaviors. It is promising to see more young users realizing they are being manipulated by tech companies (Common Sense Media, 2018). The awareness itself can empower users to take control of social media use. When dealing with PUSM, this chapter recommends the following coping strategies:

1. **Abstinence**. This requires users to take a social media break until taking back the power of self-control. This approach is the most effective and restrictive solution and some effects will emerge immediately as long as users stop using social media. The feeling of regaining control of social media use could be incredibly healing, boosting one's self-efficacy and self-assurance. Of course, this is the hardest choice for those who are heavily bothered by PUSM, who, ironically, need to use such a

tactic from time to time in order to combat PUSM. In certain extreme cases, abstinence from social media can be the best option.

2. **Harm mitigation**. For those who are not yet severely hurt by PUSM, they may continue most of their social media behaviors, but intentionally put limitations on certain types of behaviors such as FOMO or phubbing. This strategy may not show immediate effects, but, in time, it will reduce the harm PUSM causes. To make it work, each user needs to design his or her own harm mitigation strategy based on individual specifics. A one-size-fits-all design will not work well.

3. **Self-awareness**. Be clear about the goals of using social media. It is fine that after completing some work, one wants to chill out for 10 minutes or so by checking social media for fun. This may help relieve pressure and boost resilience and well-being. In this way, the 10 minutes on social media are well spent and no one should feel guilty. The bottom line is that the more users understand what is driving their behavior, the better they can eliminate unhealthy habits related to social media use. Hence, self-awareness can help them use social media for a clear purpose.

4. **Screen hygiene**. This asks users to set boundaries when using social media. They should never use platforms to launch cyberbullying attacks, share personal information, or invade privacy. They should not spread hate speech or terrorist messages or sext on social media, as these messages have no place in the offline world. Also, when parents check social media updates at the dinner table, their children will be inclined to do the same. Both young and adult users need to understand that curtailing PUSM means more than limiting excessive use of social media. It requires users to maintain screen hygiene and use the platforms appropriately.

5. **Self-responsibility**. This is the most important among the five strategies recommended in this chapter. Self-responsibility requires users to take back self-control of social media use, rather than complaining or blaming others. More importantly, it demands that users take full responsibility for the spectrum of behaviors on social media. As a tool, social media should not be taken as the culprit for all the negative consequences of PUSM. Users are called on to be responsible for the choices they make on social media. PUSM may never get under control if users do not have the courage of being held accountable. Self-responsibility creates new opportunities for nurturing a self-reflective and self-determining mindset, which can sustainably curb lots of problematic behaviors.

Despite the identified benefits of social media use for most users, a small group of people, in particular children and young adults, can encounter a slew of negative consequences due to PUSM. Both FOMO and phubbing make PUSM worse. However, it is difficult for scientists to differentiate PUSM from frequent nonproblematic habitual use of social media by users. They do know that PUSM causes mood modification, withdrawal, relapse, sleep deficit, and poor memory. Previous research focused on the ways to reduce social media time and frequency to alleviate PUSM, but the results were far from effective. In addition to screen time, many factors contribute to PUSM, such as personality traits, environment, social media information, and quality of social life. Moreover, PUSM affects each user in different ways. For one user, certain types of cues might trigger PUSM, but the same cues may not affect another user at all. There is also a generation gap in terms of PUSM perceptions and experiences between younger and older users. Overall, younger generations seem to be more vulnerable to problematic behaviors as a consequence of social media use.

Theory Highlight: Third-Person Effect

The third-person effect, proposed by W. Phillips Davison (1983), predicts that people typically assume that mass communications exert a stronger impact on others than the self. Davison (1983) defines the third-person effect hypothesis as the likelihood that "individuals who are members of an audience that is exposed to a persuasive communication (whether or not this communication is intended to be persuasive) will expect the communication to have a greater effect on others than on themselves" (p. 3).

The third-person effect hypothesizes two aspects: (1) people exposed to persuasive media messages will perceive the messages to have greater influence on people other than themselves (the perceptual hypothesis) and (2) people who exhibit third-person perception will be more likely to support restrictions on these messages (the behavioral hypothesis) (Li, 2008). The perception may not be counted as a theory, but it has the value of theory building. It reveals the self–other discrepancy in perceived media effects on subsequent behavioral consequences.

There is abundant support for the notion that individuals assume that communications exert a stronger influence on others than on the self. However, the third-person effect does not emerge in all circumstances and for all people. The effect appears to be particularly likely to emerge when the message contains recommendations that are not perceived to be personally beneficial, when individuals perceive that the issue is personally important, and when they perceive that the source harbors a negative bias (Perloff, 1993). In other words, when people do not agree with the message or judge its source as negative, the third-person effect becomes even stronger (Perloff, 1993). The effect is also stronger when messages are not directly relevant to people.

The third-person effect manifests itself through an individual's overestimation of the effect of a mass-communicated message on the generalized other, or an underestimation of the effect of a mass-communicated message on themselves. For example, people tend to perceive greater effects of pornography on others than on themselves. Those who show the greatest difference in the two perceptions were the most supportive of restrictions on porn materials (Gunther, 1995). Gunther also found that people with a higher educational background are more prone to the perceptual bias.

In the political arena, the levels of likelihood to vote can be predicted by the third-person effect. When people feel that others who are less knowledgeable or politically sophisticated than they are might be more likely to be persuaded by political advertising, they attempt to compensate for other's perceived ignorance by taking political action like voting (Golan et al., 2008). Thus, each individual reasons: "I will not be influenced, but they (the third persons) may well be persuaded."

Summary

Negative outcomes triggered by the excessive use of social media are associated with a long list of detrimental effects on the physical, psychological, and social lives of the users, though most users do not show addictive symptoms even when they have some PUSM symptoms. Some negative psychological and behavioral consequences related to social media use have increased worries about potential addicted/problematic use of digital platforms. High engagement in social media use is partially linked to FOMO. There is a significant association between problematic social media use and FOMO or phubbing. Generally, PUSM may be traced back to loss of self-control, which can alter the brain's reward system. Some prevention initiatives appear to have promising results for PUSM, including abstinence from social media. However, the most effective strategy to mitigate PUSM is self-responsibility. It requires that users take back self-control of social media use, rather than complaining or blaming others. Most importantly, they must hold themselves accountable in making good use of social media.

Looking Ahead

Chapter 9 examines the business use of social media and their response to ICT applications. There are some obvious benefits of the business use of social media, but it is a challenge to gain sustainable business values by using social media. Social media are also used by businesses to improve their employees' work performance. Employees then create social capital by interacting with each other on social media at the workplace. Finally, the next chapter will analyze how governments use social media to engage citizens at a time when they do not trust elected officials like before.

Discussion

1. What is the mechanism of the problematic use of social media?
2. How do the brain's reward system and self-control influence the problematic use of social media?
3. Do you experience FOMO and phubbing? How do they affect you and your family members or close friends?
4. Why is the organized social media manipulation run by cyber troops considered the most destructive form of PUSM?
5. What is the most effective way for you to get problematic use of social media under control if you show symptoms?

References

Ajzen, I. (1985). From intentions to actions: A Theory of Planned Behavior. In J. Kuhl, & J. Beckmann (Eds.), *Action control: From cognition to behavior* (pp. 11–39). Springer.

Ajzen, I. (1991). The theory of planned behavior. *Organizational Behavior and Human Decision Processes, 50*(2), 179–211. https://doi.org/10.1016/0749-5978(91)90020-T.

Allenby, B., & Garreau, J. (2017). Weaponized narrative is the new battlespace. *Defence One*. https://www.defenseone.com/ideas/2017/01/weaponized-narrative-new-battlespace/134284.

Baker, Z. G., Krieger, H., & LeRoy, A. S. (2016). Fear of missing out: Relationships with depression, mindfulness, and physical symptoms. *Translational Issues in Psychological Science, 2*(3), 275–282. https://doi.org/10.1037/tps0000075.

Balta, S., Emirtekin, E., Kircaburun, K., & Griffiths, M. D. (2020). Neuroticism, trait fear of missing out, and phubbing: The mediating role of state fear of missing out and problematic Instagram use. *International Journal of Mental Health and Addiction, 18*(3), 628–639. https://doi.org/10.1007/s11469-018-9959-8.

Bandura, A. (1986). *Social foundations of thought and action: A social cognitive theory.* Prentice-Hall.

Bandura, A. (1997). *Self-efficacy: The exercise of control.* Freeman.

Bradshaw, S., & Howard, P. N. (2017). *Troops, trolls and troublemakers: A global inventory of organized social media manipulation.* Computational Propaganda Project: Algorithms, Automation and Digital Politics, 1–37. https://blogs.oii.ox.ac.uk/comprop/research/troops-trolls-and-trouble-makers-a-global-inventory-of-organized-social-media-manipulation.

Bradshaw, S., & Howard, P. N. (2018). The global organization of social media disinformation campaigns. *Journal of International Affairs, 71*(1.5), 23–32. https://www.jstor.org/stable/26508115.

Brilliant, D. T., Nouchi, R., & Kawashima, R. (2019). Does video gaming have impacts on the brain? Evidence from a systematic review. *Brain Sciences, 9*(251), 1–20. https://doi.org/10.3390/brainsci9100251.

Cao, X., & Sun, J. (2018). Exploring the effect of overload on the discontinuous intention of social media users: An SOR perspective. *Computers in Human Behavior, 81*, 10–18. https://doi.org/10.1016/j.chb.2017.11.035.

Chotpitayasunondh, V., & Douglas, K. M. (2016). How "phubbing" becomes the norm: The antecedents and consequences of snubbing via smartphone. *Computers in Human Behavior, 63*, 9–18. https://doi.org/10.1016/j.chb.2016.05.018.

Common Sense Media. (2018). *Social media, social life: Teens reveal their experiences.* Common Sense Media. https://www.commonsensemedia.org/social-media-social-life-infographic.

Davison, P. (1983). The third-person effect in communication. *Public Opinion Quarterly, 47*(1). https://doi.org/10.1086/268763.

Eisenberger, N. I., Lieberman, M. D., & Williams, K. D. (2003). Does rejection hurt? An FMRI study of social exclusion. *Science, 302*(5643), 290–292. https://doi.org/10.1126/science.1089134.

Franchina, V., Abeele, M. V., van Rooij, A. J., Coco, G. L., & De Marez, L. (2018). Fear of missing out as a predictor of problematic social media use and phubbing behavior among Flemish adolescents. *International Journal of Environmental Research and Public Health, 15*(10), 1–18. https://doi.org/10.3390/ijerph15102319.

Golan, G. J., Banning, S. A., & Lundy, L. (2008). Likelihood to vote, candidate choice, and the third-person effect: Behavioral implications of political advertising in the 2004 presidential election. *American Behavioral Scientist, 52*(2), 278–290. https://doi.org/10.1177/0002764208321356.

Gunther, A. C. (1995). Overrating the X-rating: The third-person perception and support for censorship of pornography. *Journal of Communication, 45*(1), 27–38. https://doi.org/10.1111/j.1460-2466.1995.tb00712.x.

He, Q., Turel, O., Brevers, D., & Bechara, A. (2017). Excess social media use in normal populations is associated with amygdala-striatal but not with prefrontal morphology. *Psychiatry Research: Neuroimaging, 269*(30), 31–35. https://doi.org/10.1016/j.pscychresns.2017.09.003.

Kellaway, B. (2018, June 12). Addictive video games may change children's brains in the same way as drugs and alcohol, study reveals. The Telegraph. https://www.telegraph.co.uk/news/2018/06/12/addictive-video-games-may-change-childrens-brains-way-drugs.

Kuss, D. J., Kristensen, A. M., & Lopez-Fernandez, O. (2021). Internet addictions outside of Europe: A systematic literature review. *Computers in Human Behavior, 115*, Article 106621. https://doi.org/10.1016/j.chb.2020.106621.

Li, X. (2008). Third-person effect, optimistic bias, and sufficiency resource in Internet use. *Journal of Communication Disorders, 58*(3), 568–587. https://doi.org/10.1111/j.1460-2466.2008.00400.x.

Lin, I.-H., Ko, C.-H., Chang, Y.-P., Liu, T.-L., Wang, P.-W., Lin, H.-C., Huang, M.-F., Yeh, Y.-C., Chou, W.-J., & Yen, C.-F. (2014). The association between suicidality and internet addiction and activities in Taiwanese adolescents. *Comprehensive Psychiatry, 55*(3), 504–510. https://doi.org/10.1016/j.comppsych.2013.11.012.

Perloff, R. M. (1993). Third-person effect research 1983–1992: A review and synthesis. *International Journal of Public Opinion Research, 5*(2), 167–184. https://doi.org/10.1093/ijpor/5.2.167.

Roberts, J. A., & David, M. E. (2017). Put down your phone and listen to me: How boss phubbing undermines the psychological conditions necessary for employee engagement. *Computers in Human Behavior, 75*, 206–217. https://doi.org/10.1016/j.chb.2017.05.021

Roberts, J. A., & David, M. E. (2020). Boss phubbing, trust, job satisfaction and employee performance. *Personality and Individual Differences, 155*, 1–8. https://doi.org/10.1016/j.paid.2019.109702.

Rumpf, H.-J., Vermulst, A. A., Bischof, A., Kastirke, N., Gürtler, D., Bischof, G., Meerkerk, G.-J., John, U., & Meyer, C. (2014). Occurrence of internet addiction in a general population sample: A latent class analysis. *European Addiction Research, 20*(4), 159–166. https://doi.org/10.1159/000354321.

Ryan, R. M., & Deci, E. L. (2000). Self-toation theory and the facilitation of intrinsic motivation, social development, and well-being. *American Psychologist, 55*(1), 68–78. https://doi.org/10.1037/0003-066X.55.1.68.

Shensa, A., Escobar-Viera, A. C. G., Sidani, J. E., Bowman, N. D., Marshal, M. P., & Primack, D. A. (2017). Problematic social media use and depressive symptoms among U.S. young adults: A nationally-representative study. *Social Science and Medicine, 182*(June), 150–157. https://doi.org/10.1016/j.socscimed.2017.03.061.

Simon, S. (2019). Senate finds Russian bots, bucks helped push Brexit vote through. National Public Radio. https://www.npr.org/2019/01/19/686830510/senate-finds-russian-bots-bucks-helped-push-brexit-vote-through.

Sohn, S., Rees, P., Wildridge, B., Kalk, N. J., & Carter, B. (2019). Prevalence of problematic smartphone usage and associated mental health outcomes amongst children and young people: A systematic review, meta-analysis and GRADE of the evidence. *BMC Psychiatry, 19*(1), 1–10, Article 356. https://doi.org/10.1186/s12888-019-2350-x

Turel, O. (2021). Agency over social media use can be enhanced through brief abstinence, but only in users with high cognitive reflection tendencies. *Computers in Human Behavior, 115,* Article 106590. https://doi.org/10.1016/j.chb.2020.106590.

Turel, O., & Bechara, A. (2019). Little video-gaming in adolescents can be protective, but too much is associated with increased substance use. *Substance Use and Misuse, 54*(3), 384–395. https://doi.org/10.1080/10826084.2018.1496455.

Turel, O., & Qahri-Saremi, H. (2018). Explaining unplanned online media behaviors: Dual system theory models of impulsive use and swearing on social networking sites. *New Media & Society, 20,* 3050–3067. https://doi.org/10.1177/1461444817740755.

Turel, O., & Serenko, A. (2020). Cognitive biases and excessive use of social media: The Facebook implicit associations test (FIAT). *Addictive Behaviors, 105*(8), Article 106328. https://doi.org/10.1016/j.addbeh.2020.106328.

Twenge, J. M., & Park, H. (2019). The decline in adult activities among U.S. adolescents, 1976–2016. *Child Development, 90*(2), 638–654. https://doi.org/10.1111/cdev.12930.

Zhong, B., Jiang, Z., Xie, W., & Qin, X. (2020). Association of social media use with mental health conditions of nonpatients during the COVID-19 outbreak: Insights from a national survey study. *Journal of Medical Internet Research, 22*(12), 1–15, Article e23696. https://doi.org/10.2196/23696.

Part II

Social Media for Social Change

9

Business Use of Social Media

LEARNING GOALS

This chapter will help you understand:

- How are social media used for business purposes?
- What are the top benefits of integrating social media into business practices?
- How does business create and make use of virtual customer environments?
- How do governments use social media?

KEY CONCEPTS

Social media policy   Virtual customer environment

Social capital

THEORY HIGHLIGHT

Social Network Theory

Overview

Online travel agencies, like Expedia and Priceline, provide guests with all kinds of hotel choices after they input a city's name and check-in and check-out dates. How travel sites rank the hotels on a guest's search screen is exactly what the hotel business is concerned with. It is common sense that any hotel with a higher sort order will be more likely to be booked. What data do travel sites use to build the algorithm ranking the hotels? In addition to price and commission hotels offers, travel sites, also a form of social media, rely on guests' reviews and comments on specific hotels to rank them. Good comments will boost a hotel's search rank and bad ones lower it (McCartney, 2016).

Some travel sites have incorporated guests' reviews and comments on hotels that are posted on other social network sites like Facebook into the ranking algorithm. A better ranking system will serve guests, travel agencies, and hotels well as it helps make the business sustainable. It also helps guests get a better hotel room at a better price, and travel agencies will pocket more commission and encourage hotels to enhance service. Obviously, the algorithm works best when it weights millions of guests' comments on social media.

More businesses are engaging customers by actively analyzing online reviews. Zappos, an online shoe dealer, went one step further, according to Harvard Professor

Social Media Communication: Trends and Theories, First Edition. Bu Zhong.
© 2022 John Wiley & Sons, Inc. Published 2022 by John Wiley & Sons, Inc.

Jonathan Zittrain (Dahl, 2013). Zappos used the Amazon Mechanical Turk Web "crowd-sourcing" engine to correct grammar and spelling errors in consumer reviews on services as management believed that error-free reviews should boost sales, even if they are negative (Dahl, 2013). Zittrain said the results remained unclear as the practice was not yet convincingly tested. Professor Jonah Berger of the University of Pennsylvania also found even negative book reviews for unknown authors increased book sales by about 40%, based on his analyses of the sales data from hundreds of books that were reviewed by the *New York Times* (Berger, 2013).

For businesses, the power of social media is not so much about the new tool itself, but about user-generated content, like reviews, comments, and complaints about products and services left on social media or business websites. Some customers reported that when they had a hard time to reach out to customer service by phone or email, sending out a tweet may trigger a much quicker response from the customer service team. The growth of social media has taught an important business lesson: few businesses can afford to ignore customer activities on social media, which are intertwined with various aspects of the business world.

Business Adoption of ICT

Information communication technology (ICT), like the telephone, web technology, and social media, has contributed significantly to the growth of the world economy. For example, a World Bank study found that broadband provides the economy with extensive benefits, especially to emerging markets, in which a 10% increase in broadband penetration brought about a 1.21 percentage point increase in per capita GDP growth (Kelly & Rossott, 2012, p. 5). In the twenty-first century, ICT itself became one of the fastest growing industries, creating millions of jobs around the world and, more importantly, helping to innovate and transform businesses, and, at the same time, creating new industries and services.

Businesses' response to media technologies is mixed at their diffusion stages. Both companies and institutes, ranging from government agencies to nongovernment organizations (NGOs), embrace social media as a powerful platform-enhancing communication and interaction with targeted audiences. This is in stark contrast to their adoption of prior media technologies, like toll-free phone numbers or websites.

The 1-800 number, or "automated collect calling" option, was first introduced to corporate America in 1967 by AT&T. At the beginning, AT&T had a hard time convincing businesses of the toll-free number service. Business owners were reluctant to use the service until they saw that earlier adopters of toll-free numbers, like car rental companies and hotels, had received significantly more reservations over the phone from around the United States. By the early 1980s, 800-numbers grew as a business tool for most American businesses, functioning like a necessity for companies operating on a regional level. The demand for 800-numbers grew so high that the remaining 1-800 options were quickly gone and new toll-free numbers like 888, 877, 866, and 855 were added for the convenience of customers.

Similarly, American companies hesitated to launch their own websites after the world's first website went live in 1990, which was created by Sir Tim Berners-Lee, a British computer scientist. It still exists (see Figure 9.1). When the graphical-based web

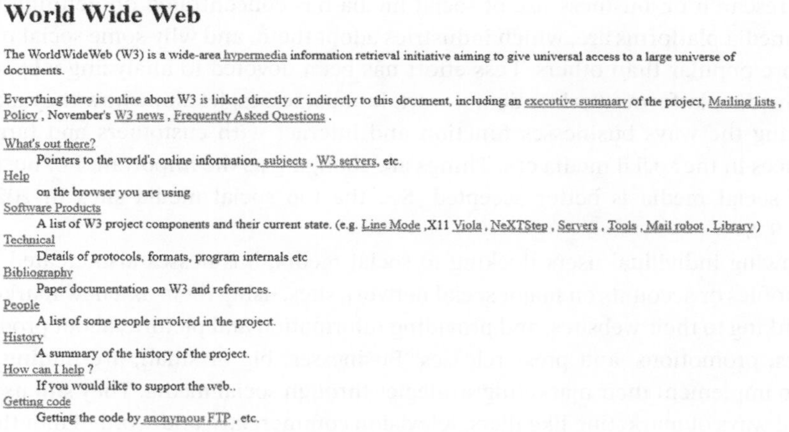

World Wide Web

The WorldWideWeb (W3) is a wide-area hypermedia information retrieval initiative aiming to give universal access to a large universe of documents.

Everything there is online about W3 is linked directly or indirectly to this document, including an executive summary of the project, Mailing lists , Policy , November's W3 news , Frequently Asked Questions .

What's out there?
    Pointers to the world's online information, subjects , W3 servers, etc.
Help
    on the browser you are using
Software Products
    A list of W3 project components and their current state. (e.g. Line Mode ,X11 Viola , NeXTStep , Servers , Tools , Mail robot , Library)
Technical
    Details of protocols, formats, program internals etc
Bibliography
    Paper documentation on W3 and references.
People
    A list of some people involved in the project.
History
    A summary of the history of the project.
How can I help ?
    If you would like to support the web..
Getting code
    Getting the code by anonymous FTP , etc.

Figure 9.1 The screenshot of the world's first website created in 1990.
Source: http://info.cern.ch/hypertext/WWW/TheProject.html.

design debuted in the early 1990s, some American companies started to launch their own websites. It took quite a few years for them to realize that without an online presence, any company and its business or service might not exist to customers in the internet age. The internet and WorldWideWeb, or simply the Web, however, are not the same thing, although the two terms are often used interchangeably. The internet refers to the global network of networks, a networking infrastructure, while the Web, like email, is one of the ways of disseminating information over the medium of the internet.

Businesses' response to the arrival of social media was much more enthusiastic than before. The social media era started with the creation of Six Degrees, the first widely recognizable social network site that was launched in 1997. This time, American companies and government agencies rushed to embrace the new technology by registering social media accounts to engage customers and the public as a whole. The business accounts on social media provided information about companies, organizations, products, brands and services, and, more importantly, improved customer engagement and managed interaction with target audiences. Social media, as a new platform for connecting, organizing, and communicating, are also empowering users by helping bring about social changes.

Business Use of Social Media and Benefits

Social media are not only changing the ways people communicate, interact, and share information, but also how they consume, market, and do business as a whole. Social media are becoming "one of the most transformative impacts of information technology on business, both within and outside firm boundaries" (Aral et al., 2013, p. 3). Social media help create a new world of possibilities and challenges for companies and enterprises, whose transformative power extends beyond marketing and aspects of consumer behavior (Aral et al., 2013).

The research on business use of social media has concentrated on defining what social media platforms are, which industries adopt them, and why some social media are more popular than others. Less effort has been devoted to analyzing why some social media platforms work or do not work for businesses, let alone how they may be reshaping the ways businesses function and interact with customers and targeted audiences in the social media era. Things are changing as the importance of business use of social media is better accepted. See the top social media sites in 2020 in Figure 9.2.

Following individual users flocking to social media, businesses also created their own profiles or accounts on major social network sites, using them as a new marketing tool, linking to their websites, and providing information and pictures about products, services, promotions, and press releases. Businesses, big or small, are finding new ways to implement their marketing strategies through social media. They still use traditional ways of marketing like fliers, television commercials, and word of mouth, but the interactivity and worldwide high penetration of social networking motivate businesses to adopt social media as an instrumental marketing tool to engage, communicate, and interact with customers.

Consumers can also connect with their favorite retailers and brands on social media to stay informed about new developments. Social media serve as alternative (in many

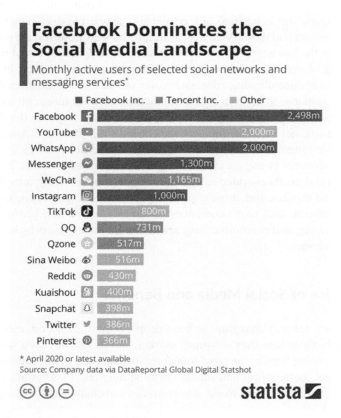

Figure 9.2 Top social media sites in 2020.

cases more convenient) communication channels between businesses and customers. When customers need to contact a business, they increasingly choose to communicate through social media, rather than calling the stores, writing a letter, or sending an email to customer services. When customers discuss a concern involving a business on social media, the issue is more likely to get a response from both the business and other customers. The power of mass media, like newspapers or television, has been well known to businesses. They also fully realize the power of social media, on which any positive or negative feedback or reviews on products or services could affect thousands or millions of customers on social media. Responding quickly on Facebook or Twitter, for example, to resolve a customer problem, can also foster loyalty and improve the company's reputation.

Social media affect the way customers perceive a business's brand. Before social media became popular, most customers considered businesses to be impersonal entities. However, social media opened up a new level of dialogue between a business and its consumers. The type of consumers who connect with a business using social media influences the way other potential consumers perceive the business's brand. For example, if a business that sells sporting goods connects mainly with consumers in their twenties, other consumers are more likely to associate the brand with that particular age demographic.

A survey of 3,700 marketers across the United States (Stelzner, 2015) identified the top five benefits to integrate social media into marketing strategies:

1. *Increased exposure.* The survey shows that 91% of the surveyed marketers reported increased exposure as the top benefit in using social media for business purposes. An increased exposure could be achieved if marketers invested six or more hours in using social media per week, which endowed them with unique opportunities to interact with existing and new customers on their preferred platforms.
2. *Increased traffic.* More than two-thirds of marketers (70%) found that their interaction with customers on social media increased traffic to their websites. The longer marketers used social media, the more traffic went to their business websites. The survey also found that social media users were generally reluctant to leave social media platforms to visit business websites, but "a good mix of engaging content and well-targeted ads with a compelling call to action can help encourage consumers to visit businesses' websites."
3. *Winning loyalty.* The survey found that B2C marketers (73%) were more likely to develop a loyal fan base than B2B marketers (63%). Social platforms help marketers reach their targeted customers more precisely and efficiently based on specific habits, needs, interests, and demographics.
4. *Marketplace insight.* Many marketers (68%) viewed social media as the source of market insight that they did not have access to, or they could hardly obtain elsewhere. Social media enabled them to have a better grasp of their consumers' needs.
5. *Generated leads.* Over 50% of marketers reported that using social media for more than a year helped generate new leads to other businesses that they did not know before. Among all the top five benefits in using social media, new leads to other businesses were the most important factors influencing the bottom line (Zeckman, 2015).

The next five benefits ranked by the survey marketers include: (6) Improved search rankings – 58%; (7) Grown business partnerships – 55%; (8) Established thought leadership – 55%; (9) Improved sales – 51%; and (10) Reduced marketing expenses – 50%

(Stelzner, 2015; Zeckman, 2015). Though the study was conducted quite a few years ago, the top benefits remain almost unchanged so far.

Any company or organization may be viewed as a social network, consisting of employees who are formed into groups based on work relationships. In the social media era, employees are encouraged to adopt certain social media tools to enhance information flows and work performance by connecting them to the new platforms. More importantly, those social media tools have the potential to transform the exchange of knowledge and expertise between employees (Benbya & Van Alstyne, 2011). The trend makes it possible for businesses to co-create value with individual consumers or consumer communities that eventually leads to accelerate innovation and expand the markets for external use of innovation (Zwass, 2010).

Virtual Customer Environment

A wide variety of companies, ranging from the Fortune 500 to small businesses, have adopted social media since the early 2000s, but how to get sustainable value out of using social media continues to pose a challenge to the business world (Culnan et al., 2010). Executives around the globe report that their firms often face a similar challenge in implementing social media applications. They share video clips on YouTube, tweet about products, and engage customers on Facebook, but such applications have yet to deliver benefits and business values in a sustainable fashion (Stelzner, 2015).

Business value and benefits cannot be automatically produced by a business's mere presence on social media. They must be executed based on developing a specific social media policy and strategy. Culnan and colleagues (2010) noted that social media have the potential to provide additional value because they enable the formation of online customer communities, or "virtual customer environments" (VCEs). VCEs can support branding, sales, customer service and support, and product development, and can also create value in each of these areas (Culnan et al., 2010).

Business value can be obtained from VCEs when customers engage with the company on a regular basis, co-creating content and sharing power in conducting business activities. If these relationships are beneficial to both companies and customers, both sides may value the business activities between them, and businesses benefit tremendously when customers act like company insiders and serve as a champion for their products and services. Consequently, customers are more likely to be loyal to the company's products, more willing to try its new offerings, and become resistant to negative information about the company. Business people know the importance of maintaining interaction with customers as it serves at the foundation of developing business relations with customers. A large part of customer engagement can be well managed on social media, which is the foundation for VCEs.

To gain values from VCEs, Business Professor Gerald Kane and colleagues (2009) suggest that a company needs to take the following explicit steps to develop social media strategies and build a social media team to implement them:

1. *Develop a social media policy.* Appropriate standards and guidelines for on-the-job use of social media by employees will make the firm's expectations clear and help govern usage. A good policy is explicit about how employees should interact in communities, giving positive examples and highlighting the possible consequences

of damaging conduct. A survey of companies with formal social media policies reveals the following core guidelines:

Accountability. Employees should take responsibility for their postings, clearly indicating when opinions are their own and not the firm's.

Accuracy and transparency. Posts must be factual, with the poster's identity disclosed.

Lawfulness. Employees must be aware of and respect the legal and professional framework that governs firm behavior.

2. *Monitor external and internal online communities.* Because communities come and go quickly, the team should continually survey the online landscape to identify potential threats and allies.
3. *Engage online communities.* The team should develop your firm's social media presence so that people can talk *to you*, not just *about you*.
4. *Act as first responders.* Some issues require immediate action, but a rapid yet ill-conceived reaction can make matters worse. Therefore, team members, like real-world first responders, should be trained to triage situations, for example, acknowledging mistakes, the first key step in regaining consumer trust; warding off crises, not letting unfounded rumors go out of control; and engaging selectively, avoiding an all-out attack (Kane et al., 2009, pp. 48–49).

Research has shown that business use of social media promotes companies' consumer engagement, such as consumers' identification, participation, and communication in a brand community. Communicating with customers on social media functions, in many ways, like the online version of "word of mouth" marketing strategies. For example, businesses that consistently engage consumers on social media regarding branding often achieve a significant growth in sales, and delivering engaging branding information to consumers through social media may positively affect their purchase behavior (Goh et al., 2013). Interestingly, Goh and colleagues' research discovers that "consumers influence the purchase expenditure of one another through both informative as well as persuasive interactions, whereas marketers influence it only through persuasive communication" (Goh et al., 2013, p. 103). Specifically, the study found that consumers' persuasive effect is 22 times more powerful than that of a marketer (Goh et al., 2013).

It is important to note that maintaining a social media presence cannot guarantee that a firm will gain business values from VCEs. Successful implementation strategies require "mindful adoption, community building, and absorptive capacity," which should enable firms of all sizes to gain business values from interacting with their customers and other stakeholders through social media (Culnan et al., 2010, p. 257).

Work Performance

Research has identified a significant correlation between work performance and social networking (Burt, 1992; Wu, 2013). A company or a business is essentially a type of social network, consisting of employees organized in various groups. In the network, some employees are more capable of linking unconnected groups than others, and act like brokers between the groups in the network. Research has found that the brokers enjoy unique "early exposure to novel information and can act as hubs to facilitate information flow between otherwise disconnected groups" (Wu, 2013, p. 30). As a result, they obtain a competitive advantage over their peers, such as receiving better performance reviews, higher compensation, and earlier promotions (Burt, 1992; Lin et al., 2001; Wu, 2013). Employees in research and development teams, for instance, are found to enjoy "an enhanced capacity for creative problem solving" and their teams have better group productivity when they maintain diverse sets of contacts, skills, information, and experiences (Reagans & Zuckerman, 2001, p. 502).

Researchers have a long history of examining human interactions using social network theory, which is defined as the study of how people, organizations, or groups interact with others inside their network (Scott, 2013). Before the arrival of social media, traditional social networks were embedded into society in the form of a firm, an organization, or a government department, etc. Such a network consists of a set of actors ("nodes") and the relationships ("ties") between the actors, which may be strong or weak (Katz et al., 2004; Wasserman & Faust, 1994). In the network, strong ties may refer to the connection between family members or friends and weak ties to the relationship between acquaintances (Granovetter, 1973).

The advent of social media helps create or move traditional social networks online, in particular, on emerging social media platforms. As in traditional networks, strong ties in an online network are formed between close friends and weak ties are built between other online friends. Regardless of whether it is a traditional or an online network, strong ties are particularly valuable when people seek socioemotional support involving a high level of trust, while weak ties are more beneficial when they seek diverse or unique information from others outside their regular frequent contacts (Katz et al., 2004).

Social Capital

Social networks have value, or social capital, because social resources, including relationships, reputation, trust, contacts, and links, are embedded in the networks of organizational publics (Dodd et al., 2015). When individual actors interact with others, it brings a series of benefits to them, and social capital is accumulated. Everyone has social capital since no one lives outside social networks, but social capital is not equally scattered among people, as some have more of it than others. Social capital is essentially the collective value of social networks. In a business context, social capital is understood as a combination of social and economic approaches that suggests that social resources may be used as a form of exchange to achieve business outcomes (Dodd et al., 2015).

The concept of social capital was first used by Lyda J. Hanifan to describe "tangible substances [that] count for most in the daily lives of people" in rural communities (Hanifan, 1916, p. 130). Pierre Bourdieu (1986) later defined social capital as "the aggregate of the actual or potential resources which are linked to possession of a durable network of more or less institutionalized relationships of mutual acquaintance and recognition" (Bourdieu, 1986, p. 249). James S. Coleman argued that social capital can be defined by its function: "It is not a single entity, but a variety of different entities, having two characteristics in common: they all consist of some aspect of a social structure, and they facilitate certain actions of individuals who are within the structure" (Coleman, 1990, p. 302).

The notion of social capital may be best explained by Harvard Professor Robert Putnam. He said, "Whereas physical capital refers to physical objects and human capital refers to the properties of individuals, social capital refers to connections among individuals – social networks and the norms of reciprocity and trustworthiness that arise from them.... A society of many virtuous but isolated individuals is not necessarily rich in social capital" (Putnam, 2000, p. 19).

Putnam emphasizes that social capital is important to both individuals and their communities because of three major reasons. First, social capital allows citizens to resolve collective problems more easily. Second, social capital greases the wheels that allow communities to advance smoothly. Where people are trusting and trustworthy, and where they are subject to repeated interactions with fellow citizens, everyday business and social transactions are less costly. Third, social capital widens our awareness of the many ways we are linked.

When people lack connection with others, they are unable to test the veracity of their own views, whether in the give or take of casual conversation or in more formal deliberation. Without such an opportunity, people are more likely to be swayed by their worst impulses (Putnam, 2000, pp. 288–290). Thus, when people have social capital, this means that they have the capability to access important resources by virtue of being part of a particular network or social structure. In a business context, social capital plays an important role in marketing strategies at both the individual and firm levels.

Information Benefits in Social Networks

The primary reason companies encourage their employees to engage peers through social networks is that information benefits arise out of communication and interaction. Information benefits enable employees to enjoy unique advantages in productivity, work performance, peer reviews, salary, and promotions (Burt, 1992; Wu, 2013). The rationale is easy to comprehend. Sharing information in a network provides opportunities of mutual learning, cooperation, and collaboration that lead to creation of new knowledge and knowledge transfer. Research has discovered that knowledge transfer in a network stimulates innovation in a company or organization (Tsai, 2001; Tsai & Ghoshal, 1998).

Taking advantage of information benefits requires two conditions: one must have access to the information in a network and have the capability of processing the information in order to absorb knowledge in it. Both information access and information processing capability are essential for businesses to stimulate innovation in a company and improve performance among its employees. Specifically, an information-rich network that is enabled by social media can provide two types of information benefits, information diversity and social communication, both affecting work outcomes and innovation (Wu, 2013).

In a social network, each connection or tie can be critical to knowledge creation and transfer (Levin & Cross, 2004). There are strong or weak ties among the actors in any social network. Strong ties refer to the relationship between individuals and their kinships, close friends, and families (Granovetter, 1982). Maintaining strong ties offers an individual close relations with others in the network (White & Houseman, 2002). Strong ties have relevance to "some key characteristics between the parties of the relationship, such as frequent interaction, extended history, intimacy and sharing, reciprocity in exchanges that allow for mutual confiding, and trust-based interactions" (Jaafar et al., 2009, p. 103). Strong ties thus enable people to access the flow of high-quality information and knowledge resources from the network (Jaafar et al., 2009).

Weak ties, on the other hand, refer to the relations with acquaintances and friends who, as compared to close friends, are more likely to move in different circles (Granovetter, 1982). Weak ties have a special role in a person's opportunity for mobility and are crucial when information is diffused through social interaction, because these ties provide bridges between densely knit clusters of social structure (Granovetter, 1982). However, it is difficult to observe and measure how people make use of the information transmitted through strong or weak ties in a network to turn the information benefits into knowledge. Social media, however, provide an unprecedented opportunity for people to manage their networks, suggesting tremendous values for business processes, human resources, and IT management (Wu, 2013).

Wu (2013) studied how employees adopt and use Expertise-Find, a social media tool that was developed to help users find experts within the firm, how it may change their positions in a social network over time, and what economic benefits were associated with such a change. She found that Expertise-Find provided employees with an opportunity to strategically reach out to different groups of people, and thereby induce their network positions to be more structurally autonomous and information-rich. By examining the network change before and after using this expertise search tool, Wu found that social media tools have the potential to transform and disrupt existing organizational structures. This transformation can have important economic impacts on employees, such as improving their productivity and job security (Wu, 2013, p. 30).

In addition, trust becomes important during the process of building ties in a network because the interaction with others is embedded in a personal relation and structure, which facilitates trust and minimizes distrust (Jaafar et al., 2009). When trust is developed in a network, the actors become more confident in their ties with others, which results in more social interaction in the network. Finally, culture bears a profound impact on the strong or weak ties in a social network. According to Hofstede (1980), culture is defined as a set of shared values and beliefs. In this regard, people are more likely to seek information from the resource providers who share a common cultural bond. These cultural bonds are a major step toward building strong ties on the basis of shared weak ties.

Government Use of Social Media

Government agencies may be half a step behind businesses and organizations in adopting social media, but they seem to catch up quickly in exploring new ways to master the new tool for enhancing the quality of government services and enable greater citizen engagement. Social media, such as Facebook or Twitter, are providing governments with attractive options for meeting these new objectives. Like businesses, most government agencies have Facebook, Twitter, and other social media accounts, but, due to poor management, they are less popular than those social media accounts owned by businesses. Government employees have invested considerable effort in improving their agencies' presence on social media, including posting a wide range of audio, video, and interactive information of public interest. Their effort should be recognized by citizens who can benefit from the e-government services.

While there are many high-profile examples of government agencies engaging in social media tools, for the vast majority of governments across the United States, these tools are still fairly new and relatively unexplored. The process of adopting new tools and managing the related changes in work processes and policies is not easy for any type of organization, but governments at all levels are starting to put more effort into figuring out social media tools that involves exploring new ways of working and shifting communication patterns. It also involves the creation of new policies and guidelines to encourage proper use and to mitigate the risks of social media tools.

Developing a social media policy can be an important first step for those government agencies considering using social media and can ultimately serve as a key enabler for responsibly and effectively leveraging social media tools. Yet, many governments are struggling with what such a policy should encompass and convey. Not surprisingly, given the emergent nature of social media, relatively few US governments actually have a formalized set of policies to guide their own efforts, as well as for others to draw on or learn from. As a consequence, governments are faced with reinterpreting and applying old policies that govern the use of the internet or creating completely new policies.

It is easy for a government agency to create a few social media accounts, but it is difficult to manage those accounts and make them attractive to social media users. To make the best use of social media, a government agency must first develop its own social media policy by answering an eminent question: What are the core elements of a government social media policy? (Hrdinová et al., 2010). While many government agencies and officials have no clear social media policy in mind, some of them have made a serious effort to engage the public on social media, such as the CDC, FDA, TSA, and NASA.

The benefits of government use of social media are self-evident. People want to get more information from government officials, for example, the pandemic situations in local areas during the COVID-19 pandemic in 2020. To meet the information needs of local constituents, government agencies and offices provided real-time updates of pandemic data, which were closely followed by social media users. The official information often serves as an authoritative and reliable source of information. It remains a big challenge for government officials to engage citizens in a time when public trust in government and elected officials is on the decline. It is a civic duty for the government to search innovative ways to engage the citizens who do not trust the government. Social media can serve as an ideal platform of community information. The first step to use government social media effectively is to establish trust within communities. Next, government officials need to learn from businesses' use of social media by publishing content that attracts attention from followers and encourages engagement.

Theory Highlight: Social Network Theory

Social Network Theory studies the connection and relationship in a social network (Katz et al., 2004). A social network is defined as a set of actors (or nodes) and the relations (or ties) between them (Wasserman & Faust, 1994). The actors may be individuals, groups, organizations, or societies. The relationships may refer to the ties between individuals, between individuals and groups, or between groups, and the relations may be based on friendship, kinship, authority, economic or information exchange, etc. Social network theory views individual actors' personality attributes as less important than their connections and ties with others within a social network (Wu, 2013). Simply, "it is not what you know that counts, but who you know," or, more accurately, it is both what and who you know that count (Field, 2008, p. 3).

A network displays how individuals are connected in groups and by what relationship. An employee's network position in a firm, for example, may enhance his or her ability to access and obtain information flowing through the network (Wu, 2013). The novel information the employee obtains becomes the resource for creating a competitive advantage of receiving better pay or a faster promotion (Burt, 1992, 2001, 2004).

Social network approaches have been used to examine how companies interact with each other, characterizing the many informal connections that link executives together, as well as associations and connections between individual employees at different companies. These networks provide ways for companies to gather information, deter competition, and even collude in setting prices or policies.

Research has demonstrated that people are more likely to have innovative ideas if they stand near the nodes of a social structure. Burt argues that opinion and behavior are more homogeneous within than between groups, so people connected across groups are more familiar with alternative ways of thinking and behaving, which gives them more options to select from and synthesize.

New ideas emerge from selection and synthesis across the structural holes between groups. Some fraction of those new ideas are good. "Good" will take on a specific meaning with empirical data, but, for the moment, a good idea broadly will be understood to be one that people praise and value. Figure 9.3 is a diagram displaying a simple social network, in which the nodes are the individual actors and ties are the relationships between the actors. As shown in Figure 9.3, there is a structural hole between Node G and Node D, which means no connection exists between the two nodes. According to the theory, Node A is a strategic position in the network because it functions like a broker to bridge all the nodes in the network. An employee who takes this position may have more opportunities to achieve better productivity, work performance, and peer reviews at a company due to the information benefits arising from the position in the network.

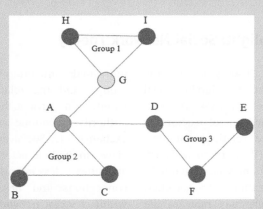

Figure 9.3 Example of a simple social network where nodes (circles) symbolize actors and lines social connections between them. This network comprises nine actors labelled A to I.

Summary

This chapter examines the business use of social media by first introducing how businesses adopted ICT in general. The business response to ICT applications used to be slow and lukewarm until the values were fully appreciated. Unlike previous ICT applications, social media were embraced by businesses almost as soon as they were invented. Benefits for business use of social media emerged after thousands of American marketers were surveyed on the topic. However, it remains a challenge to any business if it intends to gain sustainable business values in using social media. Social media are found to be useful in creating various virtual customer environments, which provide businesses with an interactive platform to engage target customers regarding branding, sales, customer services, and product development. Through a VCE, customers may choose to connect with businesses in conducting business activities and creating business values.

Social media are also used by businesses to improve their employees' work performance. Employees then create social capital by interacting with each other on social media. Social capital functions as a drive to resolve collective problems, "grease the wheels" and allows companies to advance smoothly, and enhance the interaction between businesses and customers, businesses and employees, or among groups of employees. Both businesses and employees have had many information benefits generated in their social networks. Finally, there is a brief discussion of government use of social media. First, it is a challenge for government agencies to engage people on social media at a time when people do not trust elected officials as before. Second, two solutions may help improve the government's social media presence: establishing trust with communities and learning social media strategies from businesses.

Looking Ahead

Chapter 10 will examine how the news industry has been revolutionized by the surge of social media due to changed news consumption habits. In a sense, social media are redefining what news or fake news is. Thus, social media have become part of the force transforming news practices and the news industry. Some lessons social media can offer to journalists and media practitioners will be discussed, which should be helpful to understand the impact of social media on other businesses.

Discussion

1. Among the benefits in the business use of social media, which one do you think will become even more prominent in coming years? Why so?
2. What types of social capital do you obtain from using social media? Is it different from your friends' cases?
3. If you are asked by a government agency about incorporating social media to improve e-government services, what two general strategies would you recommend?

References

Aral, S., Dellarocas, C., & Godes, D. (2013). Social media and business transformation: A framework for research. *Information Systems Research, 24*(1), 3–13. http://doi.org/10.1287/isre.1120.0470.

Benbya, H., & Van Alstyne, M. (2011). How to find answers within your company. *MIT Sloan Management Review, 52*(2), 66–77.

Berger, J. (2013). *Contagious: Why things catch on.* Simon & Schuster.

Bourdieu, P. (1986). The form of capital. In J. G. Richardson (Ed.), *Handbook of theory and research for the sociology of education* (pp. 241–258). Greenwood Press.

Burt, R. S. (1992). The social structure of competition. In N. Nohria & R. G. Eccles (Eds.), *Networks and organizations: Structure, form, and action* (pp. 57–91). Harvard Business Review Press.

Burt, R. S. (2001). Structural holes versus network closure as social capital. In N. Lin, K. S. Cook, & R. S. Burt (Eds.), *Social capital: Theory and research* (pp. 31–56). Aldine de Gruyter. http://alias.libraries.psu.edu/eresources/proxy/login?url=http://www.netLibrary.com/urlapi.asp?action=summary&v=1&bookid=101506.

Burt, R. S. (2004). Structural holes and good ideas. *American Journal of Sociology, 110*(2), 349–399. https://doi.org/10.1086/421787.

Coleman, J. S. (1990). *Foundations of social theory.* Belknap Press.

Culnan, M. J., McHugh, P. J., & Zubillaga, J. I. (2010). How large US companies can use Twitter and other social media to gain business value. *MIS Quarterly Executive, 9*(4), 243–259. https://doi.org/10.1177/1050651920932191.

Dahl, D. (2013). Experts explore how social networks can influence behavior and decision-making [Internet]. *Harvard Law Today.* http://today.law.harvard.edu/experts-explore-how-social-networks-can-influence-behavior-and-decision-making-video.

Dodd, M. D., Brummette, J., & Hazleton, V. (2015). A social capital approach: An examination of Putnam's civic engagement and public relations roles. *Public Relations Review, 41*(4), 472–479. https://doi.org/10.1016/j.pubrev.2015.05.001.

Field, J. (2008). *Social capital* (2nd ed.). Routledge.

Goh, K.-Y., Heng, C.-S., & Lin, Z. (2013). Social media brand community and consumer behavior: Quantifying the relative impact of user- and marketer-generated content. *Information Systems Research, 24*(1), 88–107. https://doi.org/10.1287/isre.1120.0469.

Granovetter, M. S. (1973). The strength of weak ties. *American Journal of Sociology, 78*(6), 1360–1380.

Granovetter, M. S. (1982). The strength of weak ties: A network theory revisited. In P. V. Marsden & N. Lin (Eds.), *Social structure and network analysis* (pp. 201–233). Sage Publications.

Hanifan, L. J. (1916). The rural school community center. *The Annals of the American Academy of Political and Social Science, 67*, 130–138. https://www.jstor.org/stable/1013498.

Hofstede, G. H. (1980). *Culture's consequences: International differences in work-related values.* Sage Publications.

Hrdinová, J., Helbig, N., & Peters, C. S. (2010). Designing social media policy for government: Eight essential elements [Internet]. https://www.ctg.albany.edu/publications/guides/social_media_policy/social_media_policy.pdf.

Jaafar, M., Abdul-Aziz, A.-R., & Sahari, M.-H. (2009). The use of social network theory on entrepreneur's linkages development. *Theoretical and Empirical Researches in Urban Management, 1S*, 101–119. http://um.ase.ro/No1S/9.pdf.

Kane, G. C., Fichman, R. G., Gallaugher, J., & Glaser, J. (2009). Community relations 2.0: With the rise of real-time social media, the rules about community outreach have changed. *Harvard Business Review*, *87*(11), 45–50. www.sciencedaily.com/releases/2009/10/091031002504.htm.

Katz, N., Lazer, D., Arrow, H., & Contractor, N. (2004). Network theory and small groups. *Small Group Research*, *35*(3), 307–332. https://doi.org/10.1177/1046496404264941.

Kelly, T., & Rossott, C. M. (Eds.). (2012). *Broadband strategies handbook*. The World Bank. http://broadbandtoolkit.org/1.3.

Levin, D. Z., & Cross, R. (2004). The strength of weak ties you can trust: The mediating role of trust in effective knowledge transfer. *Management Science*, *50*(11), 1477–1490. https://doi.org/10.1287/mnsc.1030.0136.

Lin, N., Cook, K. S., & Burt, R. S. (Eds.). (2001). *Social capital: Theory and research*. Aldine de Gruyter. http://alias.libraries.psu.edu/eresources/proxy/login?url=http://www.netLibrary.com/urlapi.asp?action=summary&v=1&bookid=101506.

McCartney, S. (2016, January 28). The secret logic to hotel listing on travel sites. *Wall Street Journal*, D1.

Putnam, R. D. (2000). *Bowling alone: The collapse and revival of American community*. Simon & Schuster.

Reagans, R., & Zuckerman, E. W. (2001). Networks diversity and productivity: The social capital of corporate R&D teams. *Organization Science*, *12*(4), 502–517. https://doi.org/10.1287/orsc.12.4.502.10637.

Scott, J. (2013). *Social network analysis*. Sage Publications.

Stelzner, M. A. (2015). *The 2015 social media marketing industry report: How marketers are using social media to grow their businesses*. Social Media Examiner. http://www.toprankblog.com/2015/05/report-social-media-marketing.

Tsai, W. (2001). Knowledge transfer in intraorganizational networks: Effects of network position and absorptive capacity on business unit innovation and performance. *The Academy of Management Journal*, *44*(5), 996–1004. https://doi.org/10.5465/3069443.

Tsai, W., & Ghoshal, S. (1998). Social capital and value creation: The role of intrafirm networks. *The Academy of Management Journal*, *41*(4), 464–476. https://doi.org/10.2307/257085.

Wasserman, S., & Faust, K. (1994). *Social network analysis: Methods and applications*. Cambridge University Press.

White, D. R., & Houseman, M. (2002). The navigability of strong ties: Small worlds, tie strength and network typology. *Networks and Complexity*, *8*(1), 72–81. https://escholarship.org/uc/item/35m4x39n.

Wu, L. (2013). Social network effects on productivity and job security: Evidence from the adoption of a social networking tool. *Information System Research*, *24*(1), 30–51. https://doi.org/10.1287/isre.1120.0465.

Zeckman, A. (2015). New report reveals the true impact of social media marketing for business [Internet]. TopRank Marketing. http://www.toprankblog.com/2015/05/report-social-media-marketing.

Zwass, V. (2010). Co-creation: Toward a taxonomy and an integrated research perspective. *International Journal of Electronic Commerce*, *15*(1), 11–48. https://doi.org/10.2753/JEC1086-4415150101.

10

Social Media Reshape the News Industry

LEARNING GOALS

This chapter will help you understand:

- How do social media change news consumption habits?
- How do social media redefine what news or fake news is?
- What are the major differences between social media and mass media?
- How do social media transform news practices and the news industry?
- What lessons do social media offer to journalists and media practitioners?

KEY CONCEPTS

Agenda setting   News decision making

Algorithm   Misinformation

THEORY HIGHLIGHT

Agenda Setting Theory

Overview

Although social media create ample new business opportunities, they simultaneously pose endless challenges to the business world. Both the opportunities and challenges have fundamentally altered the ways business is conducted. Some businesses like retail and marketing are heavily disrupted by social media, while others like news and publishing industries are largely redefined. The changes represent "one of the most transformative impacts of information technology on business, both within and outside firm boundaries" (Aral et al., 2013, p. 3). In the business world, many have realized that "We don't have a choice on whether we do social media, the question is how well we do it" (Qualman, 2012, p. 262).

Today's news media started with the world's first newspaper that was published in 1609 by Johann Carolus (1575–1634), a German publisher (Figure 10.1). Since then, it has taken the news media over 300 years to grow into mass media and reach millions of users. Nowadays, a story or a video clip can instantly go viral on Facebook or YouTube, and can be shared a million times and reach even more users through social media. Social media communication like this comes with tradeoffs. On the one hand, few take the effort to

Figure 10.1   The title page from the *Relation* in 1609, the first Western newspaper.
Source: University Library of Heidelberg, Germany. https://en.wikipedia.org/wiki/Johann_Carolus#/
media/File:Relation_Aller_Fuernemmen_und_gedenckwuerdigen_Historien_(1609).jpg.

verify the information on Facebook as true or false, unlike an editor who routinely verifies the news information for a newspaper. Facebook engineers and data scientists cannot play gatekeepers, deciding for news consumers what is news and what is not. On the other hand, news consumers can be overwhelmed by the sheer quantity of information with wildly varying quality. They do not have the time or cognitive effort to process so much information, and thus do not know what to believe. Put simply, in the social media age, the conditions are ripe for bogus information to go viral without a check.

This chapter will first examine how people's news consumption habits are changing – in particular, those related to social media use. Then it explores the impacts of social media on the news industry and the fake news circulated through social media. Therefore, this chapter tries to answer two key questions: (1) How do social media transform news consumption and the news industry? and (2) What lessons do social media offer to journalists and media practitioners? After reviewing the major differences between social media and mass media, we should have a deeper understanding of the information flows on social media and gain insight into possible future directions of social media communication.

News Consumption Habit Change

Perhaps no industry has been more deeply transformed by social media than traditional mass media. One of the prominent changes is that the relationship between news media and news consumers is revolutionized in the social media era. First, social media are becoming one of the leading information sources for the public. News consumers are more likely to go to social media for their daily news by using a computer or a phone than holding tangible newspapers in hand, watching TV news at a fixed time, or visiting the websites of traditional news media. Pew Research Center reported that more than half of Americans (53%) got news from social media "often" or "sometimes" and Facebook was the top political news source for 36% of US adults (Shearer & Mitchell, 2021).

Pew Research Center also found that those who rely on social media for accessing political news are less likely to have a good understanding of major political events in the United States (Figure 10.2). This indicates that Facebook and other

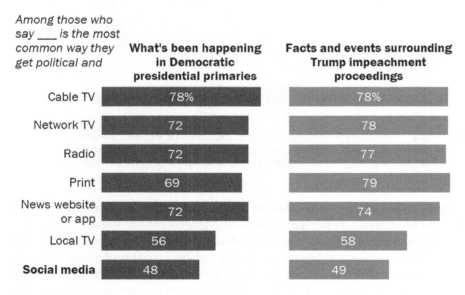

People who get political news most on social media are less likely to understand major political events

% of U.S. adults who said they understood ____ very or somewhat well

Among those who say ___ is the most common way they get political and

	What's been happening in Democratic presidential primaries	Facts and events surrounding Trump impeachment proceedings
Cable TV	78%	78%
Network TV	72	78
Radio	72	77
Print	69	79
News website or app	72	74
Local TV	56	58
Social media	48	49

Source: Survey of U.S. adults conducted Feb. 18-March 2, 2020.
"Americans Who Get Their News on Social Media Are Less Engaged, Less Knowledgeable"

PEW RESEARCH CENTER

Figure 10.2 The social media use affects users' understanding of major political events. (Source: https://www.journalism.org/2020/07/30/u-s-adults-who-mostly-rely-on-social-media-for-political-news-are-often-less-knowledgeable-about-current-events/pj_2020-07-30_social-media-news_03-05.)

social network sites are exerting a large influence on the ways people consume journalism because most users now get the news by first going to social media and search engines. The Facebook News Feed, for example, offers nearly 2 billion users news stories, among other information, based on the users' connections and activities on Facebook. News Feed enables news organizations to reach hundreds of millions of consumers and wields enormous power that few news outlets can achieve alone.

Second, given users' altered news consumption behaviors and habits, social media are reshaping the overall news media landscape and push journalists to change how they report the news and deliver content to the audience. For some journalists, many of the changes are perilous, while others view them as a fascinating part of today's journalism. Daniel Victor, a *New York Times* reporter, is one of the latter. In a guest lecture at his alma mater, Penn State, Victor told a group of journalism majors: "If you're a thrill-seeker, you have to love the idea that we have no idea what you all will be expected to do when you graduate from college, and that you'll be part of the generation to determine that."

The development of ICT applications, including social media, is central to the changes in the world of journalism, ranging from newsgathering and content production to presentation platforms. Because of these changes, most news organizations can no longer rely on their previous business models to win audiences, such as offering free news content supplemented by paid advertisements. Instead it seems, all of a sudden, every big question about journalism and the news business is in play. Whatever all this means, it is a heck of a good story.

The Power of News Media

Researchers have long been intrigued by the role of the news media in shaping people's minds and various public agendas. In his classic book *Public Opinion*, Walter Lippmann (1922) argued that the news media are the principal connection between events in the world and the images of these events in our minds. Bernard Cohen observed that the press "may not be successful much of the time in telling people *what to think*, but it is stunningly successful in telling its readers *what to think about*. The world will look different to different people, depending on the map that is drawn for them by writers, editors, and publishers of the paper they read" (Cohen, 1963, p. 13). Cohen thus expressed the metaphor that led to agenda-setting research that explores the impact of news media on people's daily life.

The theory of agenda setting was formally proposed by Maxwell McCombs and Donald Shaw (1972) in their classic study of the media's role in the 1968 presidential election campaign in Chapel Hill, North Carolina. They compared the media agenda in Chapel Hill through a content analysis of the mainstream news media that were reporting the presidential campaign, and measured public agenda by surveying 100 undecided voters. The media agenda correlated almost perfectly with public agenda. The voters ranked most issues like foreign policy, law and order, and fiscal policy similarly on both agendas, which led to a conclusion that news media are so powerful that they can set people's public agenda.

The 1972 study set off a stream of communication studies for decades by comparing media agenda to public agenda, confirming the agenda-setting power of the news media. Some scholars in political science, sociology, and other social sciences also discovered the agenda-setting effect of news media on policy making. Put simply, news media also have the power of setting policy makers' agenda, which is, of course, one of various influences on policy agenda (see more in the Theory Highlight at the end of this chapter).

Today, traditional news media around the world are experiencing the unprecedented difficulty of engaging the audience. News media's readership and advertisement revenue keeps dropping, and few experts envision a turnaround. Many experts predict that traditional news media, possibly, may never win back the readers or viewers they lost. So far, few good solutions have been found. Perhaps there is no perfect solution at all as young news users are so different from their parents and grandparents when accessing news information. Some journalists seemed to place most of the blame on the pervasive use of social media. Social media, indeed, provide alternative venues for people to obtain the news. Traditional news media, which often forced people to consume news and information at set times from select sources, face an unprecedented challenge of surviving the market. They may still set the public agenda in one way or another, but the influence is not nearly as powerful as before.

Even before the era of social media, some scholars began to ask, "If news media sets public agenda, who is going to set the agenda of the news media?" A better question in today's networked society is, "How much is the agenda-setting power news media held diluted in the social media era?" The latter question is relevant because journalists working for traditional news media cannot decide for news consumers what is news and what is not. As fewer people go to newspapers or TV newscasts for daily news needs, journalists are losing a big chunk of their agenda-setting power. The consequences are clear: during the 2020 pandemic, Americans who turn to social media for political news are less likely to be following coverage of the COVID-19 pandemic and political candidates for the 2020 US presidential election (Mitchell et al., 2020) (see Figure 10.3).

Those who turn to social media for political news are less likely to be following coverage of the coronavirus, 2020 candidates very closely

% of U.S. adults who say they have been following news about the ___ very closely

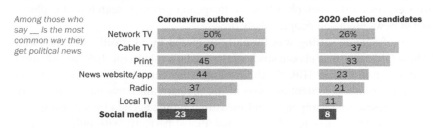

Among those who say ___ is the most common way they get political news	Coronavirus outbreak	2020 election candidates
Network TV	50%	26%
Cable TV	50	37
Print	45	33
News website/app	44	23
Radio	37	21
Local TV	32	11
Social media	23	8

Source: Survey of U.S. adults conducted June 4-10, 2020.

Pew Research Center

Figure 10.3   The social media use affects users' knowledge of COVID-19 and political candidates.

News Decision Making

In the past, journalists often worked like gatekeepers of news information for the public, and decided which news stories should be printed in the newspaper or aired on television or radio. Simply put, journalists functioned like a news decision maker for society and the public relied on them to see the world. Hence, journalists and the news media play a vital role in society due to their gatekeeping function of filtering information on behalf of the public. Part of their power lies in the authorities to decide what information should be included or avoided in the news. Journalists define what is news and what is not, and they will then decide what is fit to be delivered to the public.

Of course, news decisions are not randomly made. Journalists usually follow a set of news media ethical principles, journalism canons, or routine approaches to cope with various external and internal constraints on news production (Zhong & Newhagen, 2009). Different news media organizations in different social systems or cultural environments may choose to follow different social, legal, and societal principles, upon which editorial policies and journalistic practices are built. In some cases, certain news items are rejected by an editor because he or she personally believes there is "not much news there."

Journalism researchers proposed a model of news decision making by studying how journalists make decisions hierarchically from the cognitive system level (e.g., selecting facts for a news report), the cultural system level (e.g., a subtle, cultural influence on news writing) and the rational system level (e.g., ideological discourses) (Zhong & Newhagen, 2009). The model shows that journalists often use the most effort to populate stories about news facts. The process of their news decision-making model allows the application of a more or less coherent set of professional canons that are able to transmit information called "news," even in the face of a great deal of cultural and ideological pressures (Zhong & Newhagen, 2009). A transcultural examination of journalistic practice supports the notion of seeing journalism as an occupational ideology that "presumes the corresponding ideas and values are carried by journalists" across cultural boundaries and "thus suggests a certain kind of similarity or even universality in the characteristics of media practitioners" (Deuze, 2004, p. 278).

The Power of Facebook Algorithms

Journalists play a powerful role in our society as they set the agenda for the public. The power, however, is significantly weakened by the digital power of new media, including that of social media. As social media become an important news aggregation platform, they start to set our agenda like journalists. Such an observation, however, is not completely accurate. A close examination of how social media are programmed shows that the algorithms embedded are setting our agenda as they organize and filter the social media information users share and are exposed to.

In computer science, algorithms refer to a set of steps computers are coded to follow to accomplish tasks. As an integral element of our digital environment, algorithms help run not only social media, but also search engines, apps, personalized news, and shopping websites, etc. Algorithms help track and remember users' online behaviors and habits, which may help make decisions in selecting news stories. As we rely more on social media for news needs, we begin to see the world through the lens of algorithms embedded in social media. In other words, our worldviews are growingly mediated by those algorithms.

The algorithms in social media are constantly programmed by using thousands of factors so that they can better engage users by tracking their online behaviors. Facebook, for example, employs algorithms to populate its users' News Feeds by ranking the posts based on the users' social interactions, engagement cues (e.g., clicks, likes, shares, and comments), and thousands of other factors. Facebook product manager Jacob Frantz said, "The goal of News Feed is to show you the stories that matter most to you. To do this, we use ranking to order stories based on how interesting we believe they are to you: specifically, whom you tend to interact with, and what kinds of content you tend to like and comment on" (Frantz, 2015). The ranking is compiled through the Facebook algorithm. Hence, the posts you see on Facebook are based on relevance, not on chronology, and are ranked or filtered by the algorithm. Similar algorithms can be found in other popular social media platforms like Instagram, LinkedIn, and Twitter. As the algorithms become more advanced, the feeds or posts on all social media will be more intelligently ranked to make them more engaging and relevant to users.

Lars Backstrom, engineering manager for News Feed Ranking at Facebook, could not tell exactly how many factors were coded into the algorithm that powered the News Feed, but estimated that it could be close to 100,000 factors (McGee, 2013). Facebook data scientists are constantly updating and modifying the algorithm for better performance and efficiency. Most of those 100,000 factors in the Facebook algorithm come from the data gathered in the following four areas (see Figure 10.4):

1. **Who posts it?** The more you have interacted with a post's author in the past, the more interested Facebook thinks you will be in their future posts. This interaction could be engagement such as Liking or commenting, but also clicking or slowing down to read their posts, visiting their Page or profile, tagging them or being tagged together in posts or photos, and many other actions on Facebook. This is why you do not see post from old friends or Pages you have not interacted with in years.
2. **How do other people engage with the post?** The more that other people have engaged with a particular post, the more likely that Facebook will also show it to you.

Figure 10.4 The four data sources for the Facebook algorithm.

Sometimes people and Pages post boring things few interact with, so it lets them sink into obscurity. However, if a high percentage of people who do see a post at first do engage, Facebook knows it is interesting and keeps showing it to more people.

3. **What type of post is it?** The more that you typically engage with a certain kind of post (status, link, photo, video, event, job change, content from another app), the more Facebook will show you posts of that type. Different people enjoy different kinds of posts. I might love reading news articles, you might love watching videos. Facebook matches people to post types, so if you never watch videos, you will not see as many.

4. **When is it posted?** The more recently a story is posted, the more likely you are to see it. However, Facebook also detects when you last check the News Feed, and will rank older, good posts higher if you have not logged in since they were posted and have not seen them. If you check every few minutes or hours, Facebook will prioritize very recent posts. Go offline for a week and Facebook might surface a big story like your best friend having a baby even if it was posted five days ago (Constine, 2016).

Facebook also lets its users control what appears on their News Feeds by introducing the "See First" tool, which allows users to prioritize posts from select friends and Pages they follow or like. The "See First" tool, however, is not widely used by Facebook users, though it was added back in 2015. Many users do not know the tool or care about it. That lukewarm response was clear to Facebook. In fact, the Facebook algorithm, on behalf of users, selects the most relevant and engaging posts and pages, and shows them in the News Feed.

Why does Facebook work so hard to rank several thousand posts and pages that appear in a typical News Feed each day and put the most relevant posts into the first few dozen slots that one may actually see? One reason is that Facebook enables a better user experience. Make no mistake, the algorithm can study your initial interaction and make your next interaction better. Algorithms also make business sense because it helps keep users hooked on Facebook. The more engaging the content is, the more time users spend on the platform. In this sense, the algorithm in News Feed has turned Facebook into "the most valuable billboard on Earth – for brands, for publishers, for celebrities and for the rest of us" (Luckerson, 2015).

The success of Facebook and other social network sites also leads to a growing concern about how much they know us and how much our agenda is set by the filtered information we encounter on a daily basis. Social media then could influence, at least indirectly, how we vote, what we buy, and even how we view ourselves and others. Hence, some inherent biases in the algorithms embedded in social media can lead to unintentional consequences. As algorithms become even more complex and involve more factors, concerns continue to grow over their lack of transparency. The power of algorithms in social media are shaping our worldviews, but our understanding of the power is still at its initial stage.

There is little doubt that the algorithms in social media are partially replacing journalists to make news decisions for the public, suggesting that the media's agenda-setting power is switching from traditional news media to social media. How to hold the algorithms accountable deserves more of our attention as we get news on social media. Fake news that is often easily shared millions of times on Facebook and other social media platforms sounds another alarm to the news industry. When fake news goes viral on social media, it does not just mislead a number of gullible people, but hurts the public as a whole. The phenomena of fake news on social media may also raise hopes of a great journalistic awakening to the importance of journalism. The public's trust and confidence in journalists and news media may go up, bringing hope to the future of the news media, and eventually attract more talented young men and women to become journalists, similar to what happened after the Watergate scandal was reported in the 1970s.

Fake News and Misinformation

Gene Foreman, a former managing editor at *The Philadelphia Inquirer*, observes that in the digital media age, journalists cannot play gatekeeper, deciding for the consumers what is news and what is not. As more people turn to social media for their daily news consumption, rather than reading newspapers or watching TV news, fake news and other bogus information follow their steps to find a new home in social media.

Fake news hurts. It can manipulate public opinion, causing the public to lose confidence in others, the news media, governments, and democratic systems. The best example may be the "fake news" phenomenon displayed in social media during the bitter 2016 presidential campaign (Foreman, 2016). During the last three months of the campaign, BuzzFeed reported that more Facebook members shared, "liked," or commented on the top 20 fake news stories than engaged with the 20 most important news stories on real news websites. Sadly, fake news had won over real news in social media. Bogus information like this has posed a serious threat to a democratic society, dependent as it is on an informed citizenry (Foreman, 2016).

Fake news, however, is not new on the internet. The internet has never been short of misinformation, ranging from rumors and fraud to scams and slander. Perhaps due to the fact that the algorithms in social media are not being designed to check against fake news, false stories can easily go viral on social media platforms if they cover what users want to see and like to believe. During the 2016 campaign, the fake news industry – a crop of Web sites dedicated solely to passing off fact as fiction, for the resulting ad revenue – became particularly prosperous and problematic. Some Americans, including both voters and fake news writers, believe Donald Trump's victory in the presidential election was at least partly fueled by a mess of fake news that went viral on social media sites like Facebook, Reddit, and Twitter in 2016 (Sloane, 2016) (see the screenshot in Figure 10.5). History is like a patient teacher, who does not hesitate to teach the lesson again if people do not learn it. During the US presidential election in 2020,

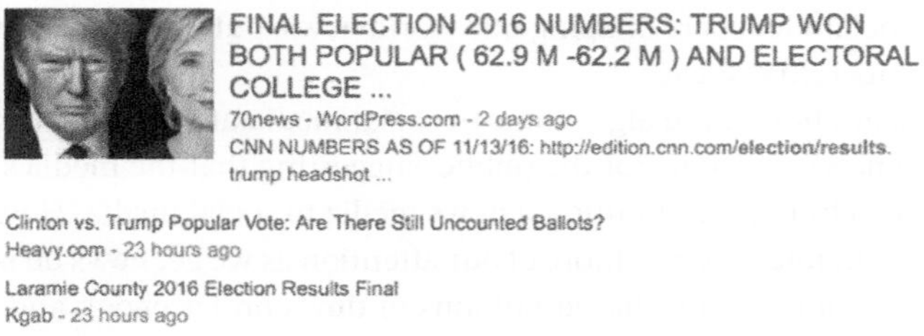

In the news

FINAL ELECTION 2016 NUMBERS: TRUMP WON BOTH POPULAR (62.9 M -62.2 M) AND ELECTORAL COLLEGE ...
70news - WordPress.com - 2 days ago
CNN NUMBERS AS OF 11/13/16: http://edition.cnn.com/election/results. trump headshot ...

Clinton vs. Trump Popular Vote: Are There Still Uncounted Ballots?
Heavy.com - 23 hours ago

Laramie County 2016 Election Results Final
Kgab - 23 hours ago

Figure 10.5 The screenshot of a fake news going viral in 2016.

history repeated itself again with waves of false claims and fake news about vote fraud saturating social media platforms from Twitter and Facebook to Parler and Gab.

In addition to individual fakers, fraudulent "news" sites also used Facebook for circulation by posting headlines that were shared widely, driving web traffic and generating ad dollars. However, why did they spread so much fake news on social media? Some fakers did not mean to produce fake news to support one candidate over another. A lot of fake news was also financially motivated. In 2016, fakers indeed made a lot of ad dollars when millions of users shared and commented on the misinformation. During the election, BuzzFeed uncovered overseas schemes with people making money by hosting websites filled with outrageous stories and driving traffic to them through Facebook. As the 2016 lesson was so harmful to social media companies, those fakers did not cash in much in 2020 even though they produced more fake news.

After all, it is not technologically difficult for social media sites to go after the ad money that funds fake news. Facebook later planned to cut off phony sites masquerading as news sources and to clearly label fake news. In the process, it might help restore programmatic ad revenue to legitimate publishers that have seen bogus sites siphon off marketing dollars. Facebook asks its everyday users to report any posts they consider suspicious. Third-party fact-checkers will determine whether the posts deserve a "disputed" label, a warning to appear prominently in the Facebook feed and pop up when someone tries to share the tagged posts. Fact-checkers include Snopes, FactCheck.org, and Politifact, and are part of Poynter's International Fact Checking Network.

"We believe providing more context can help people decide for themselves what to trust and what to share," Adam Mosseri, Facebook's VP-product for news feed, said in a blog post. "It will still be possible to share these stories, but you will see a warning that the story has been disputed as you share." Meanwhile, Facebook shuts down links to bogus websites, which often use spoof domain names that sound like reputable news sources. When people click on the spoof domains, they mistakenly go to sites that are covered in ads and fake news.

Facebook said it would advocate for what it determines "good journalism" and forge closer ties with news organizations, a sign of it taking a more active role in managing the content on its site. Since 2016, US mainstream media have devoted more space to uncover fake news (see Figure 10.6). The social network outlined a new initiative that includes investing in research and projects that promote "news literacy," building on its efforts in recent months to stamp out misinformation on the main news feed. Facebook also promised to include publishers earlier in its product-development process and help them generate revenue from videos posted on Facebook.

Declining Trust in News Media

It is troublesome to see that certain types of fake news could easily go viral among social media users. One of the reasons behind the upsurge of fake news can be attributed to the public's declining trust in traditional media in recent years. When people no longer trust a news organization, they will stop reading or watching the news it produces as trust is the cornerstone of all human relations. The credibility of traditional media is directly related to their social influence and lack of faith in them contributes to the slump in news media's profits.

The Intersect

Facebook fake-news writer: 'I think Donald Trump is in the White House because of me'

By Caitlin Dewey November 17, 2016

Twitter, Google, Facebook are changing their policies to prevent bullying and improve accuracy. (Reuters)

Figure 10.6 A screenshot of a *Washington Post* article on November 17, 2016.

In 2021, fewer than half of all Americans (46%) were found to have trust in traditional media, according to Edelman's annual trust barometer data (Salmon, 2021). This was the lowest number documented for the first time ever in the history of US media (Figure 10.7). Meanwhile, the same data revealed that Americans' trust in social media also hit an all-time low of 27%.

What is more troublesome was that 56% of Americans agreed with the statement that "Journalists and reporters are purposely trying to mislead people by saying things they know are false or gross exaggerations." Moreover, 58% think that "most news organizations are more concerned with supporting an ideology or political position than with informing the public." After the 2020 US general election, Edelman's poll revealed that 57% of Democrats trusted American news media and only 18% of Republicans did the same (Salmon, 2021). The mistrust of traditional news media was also found in many other countries including those in Asia and Europe. Facing the challenges of fake news and declining trust, news media around the globe must regain the trust of news consumers, who urgently need fact-based news to fight misinformation and disinformation. Thus, how much the public will accept the news content as trustful information will be crucial to the survival and resurgence of the news industry.

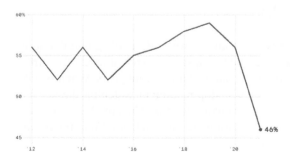

Figure 10.7 Percentage of Americans who trust traditional media (2012 – 2021). Data source: Edelman; Chart by Axios Visuals. Source: https://www.axios.com/media-trust-crisis-2bf0ec1c-00c0-4901-9069-e26b21c283a9.html.

News Media and Social Media Giants

US news media have worked very hard to maintain newsroom's independence so that their news decision making is not influenced by powerful players in society like big businesses and governments. There has always been tension between the news industry and other businesses, including social media giants. The tension centers on competing needs. The US news industry needs to be viewed as credible and trustworthy by its audience members. Thus, its news decision making on how to cover the news should not be influenced or colored by others. On the other hand, the news media, like other businesses, need to make a profit to survive in the market. As the revenues of the news industry fall, news executives face the challenge of survival – how long they can keep their media outlets going in the market.

Despite the public's rising interest in news, the news media must cut back its expenses and lay off part of its staff after the drop in advertising surpassed the rise in digital subscription sign-ups. Some print media outlets like weekly magazines laid off as many as three-quarters of their employees. Before news executives find a solution to let increased traffic and subscriptions make up advertising shortfalls, more journalists will have to accept pay cuts or furloughs.

Some solutions seem rosier than others. One of them is to revisit the relationship between the news media and social media giants like Facebook. In 2020, Facebook announced that it would provide $100 million to support news media outlets across the United States. Among the investment, $25 million was an emergency grant funding local news through the Facebook Journalism Project, and $75 million in additional marketing was spent to move money over to news organizations around the world. This could be a timely help as most news media outlets' advertising plummeted so deeply that the loss threatened media industry revenues. The COVID-19 Community Network grant program funded journalists to continue covering important stories during the global health crisis. The first round of these Facebook grants went to 50 local newsrooms in the United States and Canada.

More collaboration between the news media and social media giants or other profitable technology companies can be expected as access to objective news information is essential to the health of democracy. Citizens need news information to make responsible and informed decisions, rather than acting out of ignorance or misinformation. News information also serves a "checking function" by ensuring that elected officials uphold their oaths of office and carry out the wishes of those who elected them. Supporting local news media in difficult times like the COVID-19 pandemic may be part of corporate social responsibility for big businesses that share the primary responsibility of contributing to the well-being of the society they serve and depend on. It is likely that the news media may team up with other businesses, including social media companies, to find innovative solutions to make news business profitable again in the near future.

That said, the news industry should not solely rely on others' bailout. In the twenty-first century, people consume more journalism than at any time in history, calling for high-quality journalism as it is part of any democracy. Journalists around the world are working hard to embrace social media and integrate it into the process of news production. They have to become multitaskers with a package of skills, like shooting video through drone cameras, and then deliver their products to not only the platforms of their news organizations but also to multiple social media networks. No one can predict the future of the news industry in the coming decades, but it is certain that the transition of the news industry will be continuing along with the advances of information and communication technology, including the evolving nature of social media. During the process, making good use of social media should help journalists gather, produce, and present news information to the public.

Theory Highlight: Agenda-Setting Theory

Agenda setting describes a very powerful influence of the media – the ability to tell audiences what issues are important. Bernard Cohen (1963) stated: "The press may not be successful much of the time in telling people what to think, but it is stunningly successful in telling its readers what to think about." Agenda setting is the creation of public awareness and concern of salient issues by the news media. Two base assumptions underlie most research on agenda setting: (1) the press and the media do not reflect reality – they filter and shape it; and (2) media concentration on a few issues and subjects leads the public to perceive those issues as more important than other issues. One of the most critical aspects is the concept of agenda setting and the role of mass media.

Back in 1922, newspaper columnist Walter Lippman was concerned that the media had the power to present images to the public. Later, American scholars Maxwell McCombs and Donald Shaw investigated the country's presidential campaigns in 1968, 1972, and 1976. In their research done in 1968, they focused on two elements: awareness and information. Investigating the agenda-setting function of the mass media, they attempted to assess the relationship between what voters in one community said were important issues and the actual content of the media messages used during the campaign. McCombs and Shaw concluded that the mass media exerted a significant influence on what voters considered to be the major issues of the campaign.

Most of the research studies on agenda setting have measured the effect of media agendas on public opinion, but some intriguing findings suggest that media priorities also affect people's behavior. For example, prominent stories of airplane crashes and hijacking in the newspaper would both lower airplane ticket sales and increase the purchase of insurance the following week (McCombs & Shaw, 1972). Such a behavioral effect of the media agenda is more apparent in the business of professional sports, as well as politics. For example, by analyzing multiple presidential elections, it has been found that the cumulative effect of long-term attribute salience could alter viewers' attitudes and behavior (Son & Weaver, 2006).

Summary

As people consume more news content than at any time in history, the news industry, ironically, is facing a daunting challenge of winning its audiences back in the social media age. After reviewing how news consumption habits are being changed in social media, this chapter explores the role of news media in our society, introduces the process of traditional news decision making and explains how algorithms assist in news decision making, which are developed by social media platforms like Facebook and news organizations. It also addresses why fake news could go viral on social media. Given so much fake news people had encountered since 2016 and ongoing distrust in mainstream news media, we are expecting a great journalistic awakening as more people need professional journalists to help them in assessing true and false information. The public's trust and confidence in journalists and news media could go up as a result. As long as social media enable lies to travel farther and faster than the truth, news media will have a long way to go before they can build Americans' trust in them. Overall, the new media landscape has been changed by the advent of social media for good and their relations can be more complex and difficult in the coming years.

Looking Ahead

In Chapter 11, we will examine how social media are used in the healthcare industry. Social media are helping medical organizations to engage with target audiences, boost patient engagement, and improve health outcomes. During the process, health communication is playing a growing role in improving medical decisions for both healthcare professionals and patients. It is important to understand how social media users process health information. Health information obtained through social media platforms offers strong social support to patients, which may function like a type of alternative medical intervention.

Discussion

1. How different do you see the news consumption habits between your generation and those who are older or younger than you?
2. What changes may happen to younger generations' news use habits?
3. What is news decision making? How does it affect how you see others and the world?
4. How likely do you think the news industry is to team up with other businesses and make news business models more profitable?

References

Anderson, M., & Caumont, A. (2014). How social media is reshaping news. http://www.pewresearch.org/fact-tank/2014/2009/2024/how-social-media-is-reshaping-news.

Aral, S., Dellarocas, C., & Godes, D. (2013). Social media and business transformation: A framework for research. *Information Systems Research*, *24*(1), 3–13. http://doi.org/10.1287/isre.1120.0470.

Cohen, B. C. (1963). *The press and foreign policy*. Princeton University Press.

Constine, J. (2016). How Facebook News Feed works. https://techcrunch.com/2016/09/06/ultimate-guide-to-the-news-feed.

Deuze, M. (2004). Journalism studies beyond media: On ideology and identity. *Ecquid Novi*, *25*(2), 275–293. https://doi.org/10.1080/02560054.2004.9653298.

Foreman, G. (2016). What is driving the rise of "fake news," and news literacy lessons to spot it? http://www.thenewsliteracyproject.org/news/teachable-moments/what-driving-rise-%E2%80%98fake-news%E2%80%99-and-news-literacy-lessons-spot-it.

Frantz, J. (2015). Updated controls for News Feed. http://newsroom.fb.com/news/2015/07/updated-controls-for-news-feed.

Lippmann, W. (1922). *Public opinion*. Allen & Unwin.

Luckerson, V. (2015). Here's how Facebook's News Feed actually works. *Time*. http://time.com/3950525/facebook-news-feed-algorithm.

McCombs, M., & Shaw, D. L. (1972). The agenda-setting function of mass media. *Public Opinion Quarterly*, *36*(2), 176–185. https://doi.org/10.1086/267990.

McGee, M. (2013). EdgeRank is dead: Facebook's News Feed algorithm now has close to 100K weight factors. http://marketingland.com/edgerank-is-dead-facebooks-news-feed-algorithm-now-has-close-to-100k-weight-factors-55908.

Mitchell, A., Jurkowitz, M., Oliphant, J. B., & Shearer, E. (2020). Americans who mainly get their news on social media are less engaged, less knowledgeable. *Pew Research Center: Journalism & Media*. https://www.journalism.org/2020/07/30/americans-who-mainly-get-their-news-on-social-media-are-less-engaged-less-knowledgeable.

Qualman, E. (2012). *Socialnomics: How social media transforms the way we live and do business*. Wiley.

Salmon, F. (2021). Media trust hits new low. *Axios*. https://www.axios.com/media-trust-crisis-2bf0ec1c-00c0-4901-9069-e26b21c283a9.html.

Shearer, E., & Mitchell, A. (2021). News use across social media platforms in 2020. *Pew Research Center - Journalism & Media*. https://www.journalism.org/2021/01/12/news-use-across-social-media-platforms-in-2020/

Sloane, G. (2016). Inside the plan to combat fake news. *Advertising Age*, *87*(24), 6. https://facebookads2017.files.wordpress.com/2017/01/inside-the-plan-to-combat-fake-news-ebscohost.pdf.

Son, Y. J., & Weaver, D. H. (2006). Another look at what moves public opinion: Media agenda setting and polls in the 2000 US election. *International Journal of Public Opinion Research*, *18* (2), 174–197. https://doi.org/10.1093/ijpor/edh090.

Zhong, B., & Newhagen, J. E. (2009). How journalists think while they write: A transcultural model of news decision making. *Journal of Communication*, *59*(3), 587–608. https://doi.org/10.1111/j.1460-2466.2009.01439.x.

11

Social Media and Healthcare

LEARNING GOALS

This chapter will help you understand:

- How are social media used in healthcare practices?
- What are the trends of searching health information through social media?
- What social support do patients obtain in interacting with online peers?
- Why can health information function like a medical intervention?

KEY CONCEPTS

Social support   Health information support

Emotional support   Peer support

THEORY HIGHLIGHTS

Health Behavior Model and Crisis and Emergency Risk Communication Model

---

Overview

People are increasingly seeking online health information by using social media, healthcare websites, and search engines, especially when they have medical concerns or even before and after seeing a doctor. Among the online sources of health information, social media play a pivotal role in receiving and sharing health information with others on a daily basis. Most people have several social media apps in their smartphones and they carry them wherever they go. Checking social media information has become the most frequent activity on a typical smartphone, making the content conveniently available anywhere and any time. Therefore, it comes as no surprise that one of the most effective ways to deliver health information is circulating it through various social media venues.

On the other hand, the health information that people obtain through social media was found to help reduce health concerns and enhance symptom management, leading to improved health literacy. This may explain, at least partially, why people keep using social media to access health information. The trend of using social media for accessing health information was particularly manifest in 2020 after the COVID-19

Social Media Communication: Trends and Theories, First Edition. Bu Zhong.
© 2022 John Wiley & Sons, Inc. Published 2022 by John Wiley & Sons, Inc.

pandemic spiraled into a global disaster and killed hundreds of thousands of people and infected millions more around the world. Living through an unprecedented health crisis was extremely stressful for everyone, including non-patients. They had difficulty in making life function like before as the stresses and uncertainty induced by health risks could be too much to handle. When people encounter a panic attack due to health risks, a natural reaction is to check what is going on in social media and see how others are responding to the imminent dangers.

Health Information on Social Media

Social media start to play a role in disseminating health information that was once solely reserved for traditional mass media. This does not mean that social media are replacing traditional mass media's function in delivering health information. Rather they become useful alternative media channels for accessing health information, in which considerable health misinformation exists. Health information disseminated through traditional media channels remains critical to increase awareness and knowledge of particular health risks and diseases. For example, although physicians' advice plays a key role in women's decisions to have mammograms, media coverage of mammography screenings contributes to women's decisions to participate in mammography utilization, which is particularly effective for the women who do not have regular access to physicians (Yanovitzky et al., 2000). Research finds that traditional news media are effective in spreading doctors' advice in persuading individuals to change health behaviors like receiving flu shots and cancer screenings and adopt other health behaviors (Yoo et al., 2013).

As for disseminating health information, social media can complement traditional news media as a powerful information platform for the public. After initial exposure to an important health issue in life or via the news media, social media users often seek more information through their interpersonal communication networks online and offline. Increasingly, social media has become an attractive option for accessing health information. Social media use also helps people to have a better understanding of the information thanks to the platforms' interactive features. After people post health information on social media, others may forward, like, or comment on it. Some will ask questions or contribute more related information to the same topic.

Online interaction and discussion among users benefit the whole group by exposing a range of viewpoints on the same health issue from various sources, including healthcare providers, patients, and care givers. What is more, users can easily go into greater depth about issues of importance by providing feedback and asking more questions on social media platforms. The feedback function might not seem particularly exciting to social media users, but it has fundamentally changed the one-way flow of information of traditional media into multiple-way flows of information on social media. Health information on social media, plus feedback from various sources, could strongly influence people's decision-making in healthcare contexts and persuade them to take actions on specific health issues.

As more people rely on social media to seek and share health information, social media usage becomes a welcome relief from a health disaster like the COVID-19 pandemic. Google search results show that Americans' social media activities roughly matched their search results for the COVID-19 vaccine from the 2020 US election day (November 3, 2020) to January 4, 2021, when the first COVID-19 vaccine shots were

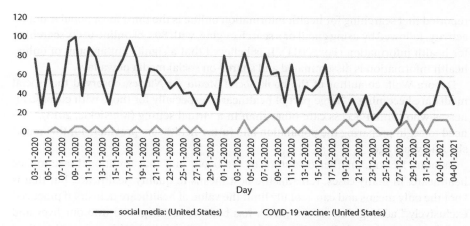

Figure 11.1 Google search results of "social media" and "COVID-19 vaccine" in the United States from November 3, 2020 to January 4, 2021 (created by the author via Google Trends on January 10, 2021).

given in the American mass vaccination campaign. As Figure 11.1 indicates, Americans followed vaccine information closely on social media platforms, with both the black line (representing search results for "social media") and gray line (representing the search results for "COVID-19 vaccine") generally following a similar pattern. This suggests that social media activities may reveal how much the public cared about vaccine information, which used to be a social function of traditional news media.

Patients' Use of Social Media

Overall, information on social media has a substantial effect on people's medical decision-making and health behavior. The information created and shared in a social media community is transmitted among members in a way that can be different from traditional media content. Unlike traditional media, social media enable users to provide feedback for information, turning one-way information flow among users into two-way or even multiple ways. Thus, it is not always the influential power of a few that leads to the diffusion of information. An alternative path for the diffusion of information exists if there is a critical mass of easily influenced individuals who can fuel the viral takeoff of a health topic, a treatment plan, or diagnosis. Such an effect would not be possible if the process did not happen in a social context with interactive features.

Attention to health information, in general, is associated with one's education level, health status, gender, age, and income (Ramanadhan & Viswanath, 2006; Rooks et al., 2012). Differences in race and ethnicity alter health information-seeking patterns. In the United States, for instance, little difference was found between African Americans and whites in terms of seeking health information and using it when they talked with doctors, but Latinos were significantly less likely to seek health information before clinic visits (Rooks et al., 2012). The trend of using social media for consuming health information indicates that health information may function like medical intervention for users.

Social media have become the primary source of information for health issues like the flu shot, cancer screenings, or specific treatment plans. The Pew Research Center reported that searching for health information online is the third most popular online activity, followed by using email or a search engine, with 80% of online users searching for health information (Fox, 2011). It is believed that a significant amount of online health information is disseminated and shared on social media nowadays.

Debora Wolf, co-author of the book *Social Media for Nurses*, observed that social media are becoming a "large part of healthcare," especially for those with chronic illnesses who cannot access care other than in a virtual setting (McNickle, 2013). "We need to begin preparing the population and future healthcare providers for this road," she said years ago.

Ramona Nelson, another co-author of the book, said that traditional face-to-face healthcare, in many cases, remains the best means to quality healthcare, but that is "not the only means and can actually limit the value of healthcare delivery if practiced exclusively," adding that "social media has become so integrated into our lives and health care, and we believe it must be incorporated into health care and policy" (McNickle, 2013).

A study analyzed the information processing among urban adolescents from elementary, middle, and high schools and discovered that the health information they gained through social media helped them manage depressive symptoms, but the health information from traditional media did not show the same effects (Zhong & Chen, 2021). It is interesting to note that these teenagers reported that they trusted traditional media more than social media and other online media. The discrepancy indicates that sometimes people might not fully realized the benefits they harvested in social media. The teenagers in this study did not lie but might truly believe, as their teachers and parents told them, that they should use more traditional media but less social media. What this research uncovered was that only social media content helped mitigate depression, not that from traditional media.

Health Professionals' Use of Social Media

US medical organizations are integrating social media into medical practice as they recognize the importance of the emerging communication platforms in marketing campaigns. In order to engage with patients on the platforms they use, health professionals can no longer view social media as an optional channel to reach out, but part of the overarching physician–patient communication strategy, which centers on building trust. Health professionals can learn significantly more about their patients by reading their posts on social media, a big part of which may not be accessible at a doctor's appointment or during inpatient care. Thus, it is clear to health professionals that social media open up many opportunities for health systems that were hardly available before.

The platforms also provide caregivers with new means of building connections, exchanging ideas, sharing health information, and developing credibility, leading to better compliance to doctors' orders and better symptom management. On the other hand, patients are using social media to obtain health information to make informed medical decisions. A report found that between 70 and 75% of US consumers look to the internet for healthcare advice; 40% rely on responses from social media (Evariant, 2015).

In addition to health forums (e.g., IBSgroup.org) founded by patients or caregivers, a new trend in using social media in healthcare is that medical organizations are starting social media support groups to engage with targeted patients. For example, a large number of Facebook support groups have been set up for patients with chronic medical conditions like diabetes or Crohn's disease. Some are managed by patients themselves and others are run by health professionals, or both patients and doctors. In these support groups, patients can explore care methods, learn from each other, and share their symptom management strategies and recovery experiences with health systems. Moreover, patients may seek help from medical professionals in managing symptoms or other medical conditions.

The new trend is that there are a growing number of patient support groups that are routinely managed by doctors and their nurses. For example, a group of Chinese gastroenterologists in Guangzhou had set up two social media groups for their patients with Crohn's disease (CD) (Zhao et al., 2021). Thanks to the support groups, both the patients and physicians have benefited from better communication. The physicians and patients could leave text or audio messages and reply to them, ask questions, or share CD-related health messages in these social media groups. What the patients loved the most about the support groups was that one gastroenterologist was designated to answer questions from patients for two hours, every other Friday, since 2012. Such support groups on social media became popular in China with the help of China Crohn's & Colitis Foundation (CCCF), providing rapport between clinicians and IBD patients (Chen, 2018).

The trend of setting up social media support groups has attracted more physicians and nurses to go beyond exchanging emails with their patients to interacting with them more frequently in their shared social media support groups. The quality of patient–caregiver communication has been an integral part of effective healthcare. In regards to colorectal cancer screening, for instance, the quality of physician–patient communication was found to be the most important determinant of patients' engagement with cancer screening (Yoo et al., 2013). In this sense, when people had good communication with their healthcare providers, like physicians and nurses, they were more likely to be screened than those with only poor communication.

Healthcare organizations' active participation in using social media may be attributed to their effectiveness in helping educate patients since the 2010s. Frequent social media posting, including live tweets, provides numerous opportunities for education on innovative medical cases and patient engagement. Despite misinformation circulated through social media groups, the increased accessibility of health information on social media has the potential to improve patient care and change the perception of medicine as cryptic or esoteric (Pershad et al., 2018).

Values of Social Media Support Groups

Social media support groups are of great value to those with chronic medical conditions who need long-term patient care, but the benefits can be limited for anyone with merely mild symptoms like having a runny nose or a sore throat. Such influenza symptoms without any infection will go away in a few days and people having the symptoms may not need much support, but for patients with complex chronic diseases, using social media support groups to connect with others who share similar experiences is an invaluable part of patient care. Social integration through social media brings remarkable benefits to those with disabilities and chronic or mental illness, who constantly feel isolated or marginalized. On the other hand, social isolation causes feelings of loneliness, low self-esteem, and hopelessness. The support patients gain by using social media groups as it offers them a positive mood and optimism, boosts self-esteem, and decreases anxiety and depression.

Online patient support communities often provide social support in ways the physical world may not be able to. Such communities provide patients with access to others who are willing to share experiences and insights with a level of empathy. Strong bonds could thus be built between patients and clinicians that were unimaginable before the advent of social media. Online health communities are particularly valuable to anyone who is isolated or lacks mobility. Patients could ask difficult questions and gain support and wisdom from others.

Another benefit of social media support groups is that they provide new opportunities to patients who may not be able to ask questions or do not have the desire to attend face-to-face sessions. Their presence may help them to gain valuable information from others in the support groups even when they do not ask any questions at all. A study compared online and offline support groups to cancer support communities and found little difference between cancer patients' perceptions of the listserv and their perceptions of their face-to-face partner regarding support for their specific illness (Turner et al., 2001). With concerns of sensitive private data, patients often feel reluctant or embarrassed to disclose their medical conditions via face-to-face interaction. Members of social media support groups are less concerned with their medical conditions and thus disclose more information about them. More information can certainly improve patient care outcomes.

Despite the identified benefits, social media support groups pose potential challenges to some patients who lack the skills of making the best use of social media. Some older patients, for instance, could easily get lost in online communities. Other barriers for those seeking help in social media can be technical skills, the digital divide, or lack of resources. As health systems positively respond to patients' requests for better communication with caregivers, they should identify potential strengths and weaknesses of social media support groups and find innovative solutions rapidly.

Health Information Support

One of the major benefits of using social media to access health information is that the content provides tremendous social support, resulting in a series of benefits that improve symptom management, disease recovery, life safety, and well-being. Here, social support is defined as "the individual feeling valued and cared for by their social network as well as how well the person is embedded into a network of communication and social obligation" (Stephens & Petrie, 2015, p. 735). Social support involves an exchange of resources among individuals who perceive it as intended to enhance the recipient's well-being (Tengku Mohd et al., 2019). However, the effect of health information support depends on the characteristic of medical concerns and the match between the type of support offered and patients' medical needs (Petrie, 2001). Social support, as a multidimensional concept, can be best analyzed by examining its three major dimensions: informational, emotional, and peer support (Zhong et al., 2021).

1. Informational Support

People are motivated to seek health information on social media because of the benefits of social support that comes in the form of information that aids in health decision-making (Uchino et al., 2018). Informational support obtained through social media offers higher self-esteem and increased perception of social capital (Selkie et al., 2020). With strong informational support, patients gain more medical knowledge and build up enhanced health literacy. All of these can help people to achieve positive health outcomes. Meanwhile, informational support decreases people's perceived health risks and improves coping strategies, consequentially leading to more support for physical and psychological well-being.

2. Emotional Support

Emotional support is closely related to people's quality of life and health outcomes, but it is difficult to define what emotional support is in a healthcare context. Some researchers define it to include the provision of care, empathy, love, and trust (Langford et al., 1997), while others emphasize expressions of encouragement, active listening, reflection, and reassurance (Dale et al., 2012). In this book, emotional support is defined as support in the form of caring, trust, and empathy the health information carries to social media users, which usually comes from other users in the same social media groups. High emotional support has a lot of benefits, for example, reducing stress and preventing detrimental effects of depression or post-traumatic stress disorder (Mehnert et al., 2010). Overall, the general benefits of emotional support to people's well-being and health outcomes have been well documented.

3. Peer Support

Peer support refers to the support from others who share their experiences by providing health information related to one's medical conditions or concerns on social media. The most effective peer support is the type of support matching the needs of social media users, who are eager to stay connected with others and share a sense of belonging to the same groups. Peer support obtained on social media could increase self-esteem and self-efficacy, and reduce uncertainty about one's self (McKenna & Bargh, 1998). Seeking support and social connection is a critical point in the lives of people with health concerns and medical conditions. Thus, peer support complements communication needs for retaining social connection and reduces social isolation, which is necessary for managing medical disorders.

The three types of support above can be viewed as different aspects of health information support. Health information support gained via social media also promotes health behavior change. After COVID-19 hit the world, for example, many Americans actively sought health information about the virus and its risks. Soon they began to change their health behaviors, including wearing masks, using sanitizers, and washing their hands. The same health information, however, failed to change other people's heath behavior, as some intentionally refused wearing masks and even took the extreme actions of "inhaling and ingesting" disinfectants and cleaners in an effort to kill COVID-19 (Joseph, 2020). Of course, many factors contribute to health behavior change in the context of a health crisis, but the role social media plays in behavior change should not be ignored. In addition to behavior change, health information on social media could also alter patients' trust in medical professionals and health systems.

Trust in Doctors

"Trust me, I am a doctor" is a 39-episode BBC-produced TV show that was first aired in 1996. The title is quite well-known among Americans even though many of them never watched the show, which combines factual reporting and satire. That is because doctors are generally trusted by the public in the United States, Britain, and many other countries. As people increasingly turn toward social media to access information on healthcare and self-diagnose, we should ask: Do patients still trust health professionals like they did before? How is the doctor–patient relationship changed by social media content? Research finds that patients' relationships with their clinicians have been dramatically changed following the rise of social media use (Nelson et al., 2013). The first step in this change came when patients gained access to medical information online. Now they are taking advantage of social media's power, like crowd sourcing, collaboration, and online health forums, which turned them into more educated patients. As a result, they are able to interpret medical information and diagnoses, and, more importantly, they are essentially empowered to become a member of their own healthcare team (Nelson et al., 2013).

Trust is a cornerstone in all human relationships, including the effective physician–patient relationship. The trust relationship is "characterized by one party, the trustor, having positive expectations regarding both the competence of the other party, the trustor, and that they will work in their best interests" (Rowe & Calnan, 2006, p. 4). In the context of healthcare, trust in clinicians is a critical part of having informed patients who are more willing to participate in medical decision-making, as it helps patients save time and effort in seeking and verifying relevant health information. Trust in doctors promotes compliance to doctors, continuity of care, improved health outcomes, and quality of life (Petrocchi et al., 2019; Rotenberg & Petrocchi, 2018). It is important to differentiate patients' trust from their satisfaction in medical services. Both can be highly correlated, but they are conceptually distinct. Trust is forward-looking and reflects a commitment to an ongoing relationship, whereas patient satisfaction tends to be based on past experience and refers to assessment of performance (Rowe & Calnan, 2006).

Patient non-compliance, or non-adherence, is one of the most common causes of treatment failure in the US health system. The World Health Organization reports adherence at approximately 50% among patients taking medications for chronic illnesses (Bentley & Potts, 2019). Poor adherence has been associated with reduced quality of life, disease progression, mortality, and increased healthcare costs in the United States. Hospitalization due to poor medication adherence is linked to approximately 125,000 deaths per year and an estimated healthcare cost of $100 billion annually (St. Peter, 2015). Trust in doctors was found to be a significant predictor in patients' compliance. Those who trust more in their doctors and nurses are more likely to adhere to the treatment plans and medications prescribed by their doctors.

One study finds that patients with Crohn's disease reported less trust in their physicians when they spent more time using social media support groups that were not managed by their doctors (Zhao et al., 2021). The finding indicates that social media usage, in general, could undermine trust in medical professionals. The same study also reveals that health information shared and obtained by patients on social media could function like a type of medical intervention, assisting them in managing symptoms by improving their treatment understanding and trust in doctors.

An improved patient–physician relationship increases adherence to doctors and treatment plans, leading to better patient satisfaction and health outcomes. Good communication between patients and their doctors in social media groups could promote trust in doctors, treatment understanding, and symptom management. Thus, both physicians and patients are encouraged to take advantage of the benefits of using social media, as they provide ample positive effects in patient care. Meanwhile, they must guard against health misinformation circulated through social media, which could quickly go viral and cause tremendous harm to patients and their online support communities.

Theory Highlights: Health Belief Model and Crisis and Emergency Risk Communication Model

The Health Belief Model (HBM) (Rosenstock, 1966) was developed to explain why people fail to adopt disease prevention measures or screening tests for the early detection of disease (Carpenter, 2010). The model helps us understand strategies to improve health behaviors, like adherence to treatment (Jones et al., 2014). According to the model, people start to engage in a health-related behavior when they perceive susceptibility to a disease that has severe consequences and when the benefits of health-related behavior outweigh the barriers (Castonguay et al., 2016).

The initiation of health behavior changes can be motivated by cues to actions, like perceived personal relevance of a health risk (Jones et al., 2015), or social and environmental cues, like hospitals being overwhelmed by infected patients or a growing number of people getting sick (Champion & Skinner, 2008). Informed by HBM, individual characteristics are studied as modifying variables that influence perceptions and indirectly affect health behaviors (Carpenter, 2010; Jones et al., 2014).

The Health Belief Model includes six constructs: perceived susceptibility, perceived severity, perceived threat, benefits to actions, barriers to actions, and cues to action. Rosenstock used the six constructs and some demographic factors to predict and explain why people will take certain preventive health behaviors. Research shows that when people perceive susceptibility to a disease that might result in serious consequences, and the benefits to take action outweigh the barriers, they are likely to take preventative health actions. Moreover, some related factors were identified to influence health behavior change, such as a perceived threat to the disease, cues to action (e.g., health campaigns, others' advice), demographics, and sociopsychological variables. Later, self-efficacy was added to the model, which suggests that they have enough confidence in successfully changing their health behaviors.

HBM has been widely used in health communication research. In examining the relationship between social media use and harm to mental health, a study revealed that some demographic variables predicted depression or trauma among those who first experienced the COVID-19 outbreak in Wuhan, China (Zhong et al., 2021). The model helps us understand not only people's health behavior change, but also their health concerns and health outcomes.

A related model, the Crisis and Emergency Risk Communication Model (CERC), was first proposed by Reynolds and Seeger (2015). This model outlines five stages of public crises (e.g., an infectious disease outbreak): (a) precrisis, (b) initial event, (c) maintenance, (d) resolution, and (e) evaluation. This model can be used to anticipate and prepare for subsequent communication needs. It also helps analyze how ordinary people communicate during different stages of a public health crisis (Zhong et al., 2021). Compared to HBM, the CERC model is relatively new, but both of them can conjunctively lead to a better understanding of health communication on social media.

Summary

Social media have become a necessity for the healthcare industry as they help medical organizations to engage with target audiences, boost patient engagement, and improve health outcomes (Evariant, 2015). As cost and access to healthcare and social support is already challenging for millions of individuals around the globe, access to online support through social network sites has become popular. A growing number of groups and organizations are providing online support, which is viewed as a tremendous help for patients and their families. Meanwhile, vigilant attention should be paid to the negative impact of false health information that may go viral on social media. The trend also calls for a better understanding of the long-term implications of social media use for healthcare purposes. Health information obtained through social media platforms offers strong support to patients as a type of alternative medical intervention.

Looking Ahead

Chapter 12 will dive deep into the mechanism of social media by examining the role artificial intelligence and mobile apps plays in the surge of social media usage. Both AI and apps are directly related to social media usage. A big part of social media popularity is powered by artificial intelligence. In a similar fashion, social media would not be so popular and easy to use without countless mobile apps developed for smartphone users. To engage social media users, developers are designing millions of mobile apps to serve target customers and, at the same time, are trying to monetize services in innovative ways. A smartphone without apps would not be smart at all.

Discussion

1. How is social media use shaping health information processing and medical decision-making?
2. Are there any differences between patients' and doctors' use of social media?
3. Why do social media support groups play such an important role in patient care?
4. In general, do you think social media use will further improve or reduce patients' trust in doctors in the coming years?

References

Bentley, D., & Potts, J. W. (2019). Medication adherence and compliance. *Fresenius Medical Care*. https://fmcna.com/insights/education/medication-adherence-and-compliance.

Carpenter, C. J. (2010). A meta-analysis of the effectiveness of Health Belief Model variables in pedicting behavior. *Health Communication*, *25*(8), 661–669. https://doi.org/10.1080/10410236.2010.521906.

Castonguay, J., Filer, C. R., & Pittsb, M. J. (2016). Seeking help for depression: Applying the Health Belief Model to illness. *Southern Communication Journal*, *81*(5), 289–303. https://doi.org/10.1080/1041794X.2016.1165729.

Champion, V. L., & Skinner, C. S. (2008). The health belief model. In K. Glanz, B. K. Rimer, K. Viswanath, & C. T. Orleans (Eds.), *Health behavior and health education theory, research, and practice* (4th ed., pp. 45–66). Jossey-Bass. http://ezaccess.libraries. psu.edu/login?url=http://ebookcentral.proquest.com/lib/pensu/detail. action?docID=353367.

Chen, Y. (2018). Perspectives of IBD China: Is Crohn's and Colitis Foundation model a solution to health care issues for the country? *Inflammatory Bowel Diseases*, *24*(5), 925–929. https://doi.org/10.1093/ibd/izy056.

Dale, J. R., Williams, S. M., & Bowyer, V. (2012). What is the effect of peer support on diabetes outcomes in adults? A systematic review. *Diabetic Medicine*, *29*(11), 1361–1377. https://doi.org/10.1111/j.1464-5491.2012.03749.x.

Evariant. (2015). The evolving role of social media in healthcare: Benefits & tactics. *Evariant – Moving healthcare ahead*. https://www.evariant.com/blog/the-evolving-role-of-social-media-in-healthcare.

Fox, S. (2011). *Health topics*. Pew Research Center: Internet & Technology. https://www.pewresearch.org/internet/2011/02/01/health-topics-2.

Jones, C. J., Smith, H., & Llewellyn, C. (2014). Evaluating the effectiveness of health belief model interventions in improving adherence: A systematic review. *Health Psychology Review*, *8*(3), 253–269. https://doi.org/10.1080/17437199.2013.802623.

Jones, C. L., Jensen, J. D., Scherr, C. L., Brown, N. R., Christy, K., & Weaver, J. (2015). The Health Belief Model as an explanatory framework in communication research: Exploring parallel, serial, and moderated mediation. *Health Communication*, *30*(6), 566–576. https://doi.org/10.1080/10410236.2013.873363.

Joseph, A. (2020). CDC: Some Americans are misusing cleaning products – Including drinking them – In an effort to kill coronavirus. *Stat: Bulletin of the Wisconsin Nurses*

Association. https://www.statnews.com/2020/06/05/cdc-misusing-bleach-try-kill-coronavirus.

Langford, C. P. H., Bowsher, J., Maloney, J. P., & Lillis, P. P. (1997). Social support: A conceptual analysis. *Journal of Advanced Nursing, 25*(1), 95–100. https://doi.org/10.1046/j.1365-2648.1997.1997025095.x.

McKenna, K. Y. A., & Bargh, J. A. (1998). Coming out in the age of the internet: Identity "demarginalization" through virtual group participation. *Journal of Personality and Social Psychology, 75*(3), 681–694. https://doi.org/10.1037/0022-3514.75.3.681.

McNickle, M. (2013). Social media changes healthcare landscape. *Information Week.* http://www.informationweek.com/mobile/social-media-changes-healthcare-landscape/d/d-id/1108296?

Mehnert, A., Lehmann, C., Graefen, M., Huland, H., & Koch, U. (2010). Depression, anxiety, post-traumatic stress disorder and health-related quality of life and its association with social support in ambulatory prostate cancer patients. *European Journal of Cancer Care, 19*(6), 736–745. https://doi.org/10.1111/j.1365-2354.2009.01117.x.

Nelson, R., Joos, I. M., & Wolf, D. M. (2013). *Social media for nurses: Educating practitioners and patients in a networked world.* Springer.

Pershad, Y., Hangge, P. T., Albadawi, H., & Oklu, R. (2018). Social medicine: Twitter in healthcare. *Journal of Clinical Medicine, 7*(121), 1–9. https://doi.org/10.3390/jcm7060121.

Petrie, K. J. (2001). Social support and recovery from disease and medical procedures. In J. D. Wright (Ed.), *International encyclopedia of the social and behavioral sciences* (pp. 14458–14461). Elsevier.

Petrocchi, S., Iannello, P., Lecciso, F., Levante, A., Antonietti, A., & Schulz, P. (2019). Interpersonal trust in doctor–patient relation: Evidence from dyadic analysis and association with quality of dyadic communication. *Social Science and Medicine, 235,* Article 112391, 1–8. https://doi.org/10.1016/j.socscimed.2019.112391.

Ramanadhan, S., & Viswanath, K. (2006). Health and the information nonseeker: A profile. *Health Communication, 20*(2), 131–139. https://doi.org/10.1207/s15327027hc2002_4.

Reynolds, B., & Seeger, M. W. (2015). Crisis and emergency risk communication as an integrative model. *Journal of Health Communication, 10*(1), 43–55. https://doi.org/10.1080/10810730590904571.

Rooks, R. N., Wiltshire, J. C., Elder, K., BeLue, R., & Gary, L. C. (2012). Health information seeking and use outside of the medical encounter: Is it associated with race and ethnicity? *Social Science and Medicine, 74*(2), 176–184. https://doi.org/10.1016/j.socscimed.2011.09.040.

Rosenstock, I. M. (1966). Why people use health services. *The Milbank Memorial Fund Quarterly, 44*(3), 94–124. https://doi.org/10.1111/j.1468-0009.2005.00425.x.

Rotenberg, K. J., & Petrocchi, S. (2018). A longitudinal investigation of trust beliefs in physicians by children with asthma and their mothers: Relations with children's adherence to medical regimes and quality of life. *Child: Care, Health and Development, 44*(6), 879–884. https://doi.org/10.1111/cch.12604.

Rowe, R., & Calnan, M. (2006). Trust relations in health care – The new agenda. *European Journal of Public Health, 16*(1), 4–6. https://doi.org/10.1093/eurpub/ckl004.

Selkie, E., Adkins, V., Masters, E., Bajpai, A., & Shumer, D. (2020). Transgender adolescents' uses of social media for social support. *Journal of Adolescent Health, 66*(3), 275–280. https://doi.org/10.1016/j.jadohealth.2019.08.011.

St. Peter, W. L. (2015). Management of polypharmacy in dialysis patients. *Seminars in Dialysis*, *28*(4), 427–432. https://doi.org/10.1111/sdi.12377.

Stephens, M. H., & Petrie, K. J. (2015). Social support and recovery from disease and medical procedures. In J. D. Wright (Ed.), *International encyclopedia of the social & behavioral sciences* (pp. 735–740). Elsevier. https://doi.org/10.1016/B978-0-08-097086-8.14129-7.

Tengku Mohd, T. A. M., Yunus, R. M., Hairi, F., Hairi, N. N., & Choo, W. Y. (2019). Social support and depression among community dwelling older adults in Asia: A systematic review. *BMJ Open*, *9*(7), 1–12. https://doi.org/10.1136/bmjopen-2018-026667.

Turner, J. W., Grube, J. A., & Meyers, J. (2001). Developing an optimal match within online communities: An exploration of CMC support communities and traditional support. *Journal of Communication*, *51*(2), 231–251. https://doi.org/10.1111/j.1460-2466.2001.tb02879.x.

Uchino, B. N., Bowen, K., de Grey, R. K., Mikel, J., & Fisher, E. B. (2018). Social support and physical health: Models, mechanisms, and opportunities. In E. B. Fisher, L. D. Cameron, A. J. Christensen, U. Ehlert, Y. Guo, B. Oldenburg, & F. J. Snoek (Eds.), *Principles and concepts of behavioral medicine: A global handbook* (pp. 341–372). Springer. https://doi.org/10.1007/978-0-387-93826-4_12.

Yanovitzky, I., Blitz, C. L., Yanovitzky, I., & Blitz, C. L. (2000). Effect of media coverage and physician advice on utilization of breast cancer screening by women 40 years and older. *Journal of Health Communication*, *5*(2), 117–134. https://doi.org/10.1080/108107300406857.

Yoo, W., Kwon, M.-W., & Pfeiffer, L. J. (2013). Influence of communication on colorectal cancer screening: Revisiting the Health Belief Model. *Journal of Communication in Healthcare*, *6*(1), 35–43. https://doi.org/10.1179/1753807612Y.0000000023.

Zhao, J., Han, H., Zhong, B., Xie, W., Chen, Y., & Zhi, M. (2021). Health information on social media helps mitigate Crohn's disease symptoms and improves patients' clinical course. *Computers in Human Behavior*, *115*, 1–10, Article 106588. https://doi.org/10.1016/j.chb.2020.106588.

Zhong, B., & Chen, J. (2021). Health information helps mitigate adolescent depression: A multivariate analysis of the links between health information use and depression management. *Child: Care, Health, and Development*, *47*(2), 201–207. https://doi.org/10.1111/cch.12831.

Zhong, B., Huang, Y., & Liu, Q. (2021). Mental health toll from the coronavirus: Social media usage reveals Wuhan residents' depression and secondary trauma in the COVID-19 outbreak. *Computers in Human Behavior*, *114*, 1–10, Article 106524. https://doi.org/10.1016/j.chb.2020.106524.

12

The App Economy and Artificial Intelligence

LEARNING GOALS

This chapter will help you understand:

- What are the major factors behind the boom of the app economy?
- How are the apps used to promote business?
- How does AI differ from machine learning, deep learning, and algorithm?
- How can users evaluate the algorithm experience on social media?
- How is AI shaping the social media use in business settings?

KEY CONCEPTS

Mobile app	App intelligence
Artificial intelligence	Algorithm

THEORY HIGHLIGHT

Knowledge Gap Hypothesis

Overview

This chapter has two topics. The first one is about mobile apps and the second about artificial intelligence that powers social media functions and user experience. The two topics may seem not to be directly related to each other but both of them are closely associated with the mechanism of social media usage. At the end of this chapter, we will discuss the knowledge gap hypothesis, a theoretical approach to analyze how people with a high or low socioeconomic status may be different in terms of absorbing information presented by mass media. The former can take in the information much faster than the latter, resulting in an increased gap in knowledge between these two segments of society. First, let us discuss the rising app economy.

1. The App Economy

Without mobile apps, our smartphones may look like a brick. As social media users keep downloading new apps on to their smartphones for various purposes, like searching for a

Social Media Communication: Trends and Theories, First Edition. Bu Zhong.
© 2022 John Wiley & Sons, Inc. Published 2022 by John Wiley & Sons, Inc.

takeout eatery or hiring a plumber, we all know that the business of the mobile app industry is booming. The apps have come to play a huge role in the virtual world no one can part with. With the help of these apps, we can enjoy music from every corner of the world, meet foodies or romantic partners, manage our diet, exercises, pay bills, and connect with friends, of course. Augmented reality apps are changing the way we watch football games and play video games with friends or algorithms. In sum, the mobile app industry has been growing so fast that it has been one of the most profitable segments in the world's new economy in the late 2010s (Kumar, 2016). In 2020, apps became even more important for people to survive the COVID-19 pandemic. They helped people to stay in touch with distant friends, family, and colleagues. Moreover, they shaped people's lockdown lives by helping to facilitate social distancing and contact tracing. Without those apps, living through the global pandemic could be more traumatic for people around the world.

The first common use of "app" as shorthand for "software application" may be traced back to 1985 (Goldsmith, 2014). The first apps emerged in 2008 when Apple's App Store opened its doors to Apple users with its first iteration of 500 apps. In 2020, there were over 1.85 million apps in the Apple Store. Android users have even more to choose from Google Play Store, which had 2.56 million apps in 2020. The number of apps from Google and Apple grows rapidly every day, making it hard and pointless to track the exact total number.

According to MobileAction, a mobile data and analytics provider, global users downloaded 205.4 billion apps in 2018 and were predicted to download 258.2 billion apps in 2022 (MobileAction, 2018). For using these apps, they paid US$101 billion in 2018, up 75% from 2016. Few industries have taken off as fast as the mobile app industry in the history of modern business. Experts claimed that the mobile app industry may be the fastest growing business ever and will continue its current momentum for decades as it shows no sign of slowing down in the near future (Space-O Technologies, 2019).

Nowadays, it makes little sense to ask how many apps are available for mobile phone users because there were over US$3.8 billion smartphone users around the world in 2021 (Iqbal, 2020) (see Figure 12.1). Each user can have dozens of apps or more in his

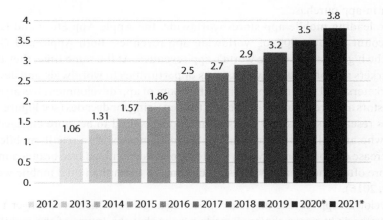

Figure 12.1   The number of smartphone users worldwide from 2012 to 2021 (in billions).
Note. This chart was created by the authors based on the data from Statista (Data source: https://www.statista.com/statistics/330695/number-of-smartphone-users-worldwide).

or her mobile phone. There is little doubt that app users have become the world's largest consumer base and are using countless apps every day. Overall, without apps in a smartphone, it is just like a brick that can make phone calls. For social media users, making phone calls is far less important than using apps on their mobile devices.

The fast growth of apps clearly demonstrates their importance to users. For example, apps had played a part during the COVID-19 pandemic that shaped people's lockdown lives in 2020. They helped facilitate social distancing and contact tracing, in addition to the crucial role they played in enabling people to keep in touch with distant friends, family, and colleagues.

Apps Promote Business

As mobile devices have become a big part of our digital lives, using mobile apps to connect with old and new customers is ideally suited for small and large businesses. The apps can help engage target customers more easily at a lower cost than traditional communication channels. Research shows that as long as users find values in using apps, they often choose paid apps over free ones and more users have installed paid apps, especially gaming apps. While mobile users are using apps to play games, order food, get weather updates, and check updates in social media, companies are increasingly using mobile apps to reach their customers and increase their sales and revenues.

The jump in sales and revenues after using apps is mainly powered by much better understanding of customer needs and behaviors. App developers and marketers have gathered and analyzed big volumes of in-application data. Most of the data contain valuable information about the trends of customer behavior and attitudes toward products or services. Small apps are producing big data in real time. After gaining the insights from in-app data, businesses can optimize their products and service, and launch data-driven marketing strategies. The success in business use of apps has fostered app marketers' confidence and belief in their capacity to achieve bigger success in winning customers and target markets. This may also explain why app users have seen more app-based advertising and received more push notifications for in-app purchase.

As the leading mobile app stores worldwide, the Apple App Store and Google Play account for over 90% of worldwide app revenues. Both Apple and Google pocket the biggest share of the world's app revenues. At the same time, they create new markets and offer lucrative business opportunities to worldwide app developers, marketers, and advertisers. Hence, the boom of app development has attracted big investors as its revenues are expected to keep rising for decades (see Figure 12.2). Business research shows that users of mobile apps tend to be more engaged customers who are willing to communicate with businesses. As a result, mobile apps help increase customer loyalty and loyal customers download free branded mobile apps more often and spend twice as much time on them than on a mobile website (Kumar, 2016).

To develop an app for reaching and connecting target customers is no longer a novel idea but a basic business choice. Experts predict that the future of the mobile app industry will be very bright and profitable in coming decades. So far, gaming apps are the most popular app category, accounting for 25% of all active apps downloaded on

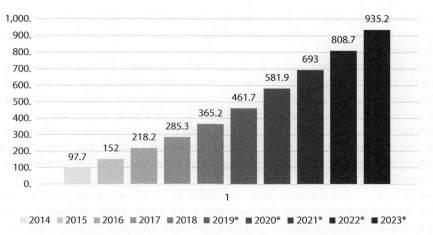

Figure 12.2 Worldwide mobile app revenues from 2014 to 2023 (in billion US dollars). Note. This chart was created by the authors based on the data from Statista (https://www.statista .com/statistics/269025/worldwide-mobile-app-revenue-forecast).

smartphones (MobileAction, 2018). Next to gaming, business apps are the second most popular apps, with a share of 10% of active apps. It is easy to create an app, but it is very hard to gain insights by analyzing the in-app data. What is more difficult and important is how to let more customers download it and keep using it, leaving it to make profits and achieve other business goals through the app.

A new app trend shows that app developers are not the only ones to show an intense interest in the app economy. The importance of app use is well accepted by powerful social players, ranging from charities and nonprofit organizations to government agencies like the Centers for Disease Control and Prevention and National Park Service. Creating an app makes perfect business sense in the social media age.

The App Intelligence

After an app is created and published, how to let it be discovered by target customers remains a challenge. A fancy app with "amazing features and ground-breaking design" may not automatically be accepted by customers. In fact, it is almost a daily nerve-racking experience for app developers and publishers to boost their apps' downloads. They know first hand that it is so hard to make an app stand out from millions of similar ones already available on the market. The Apple App Store and Google Play Store are two of the most popular and largest app systems around the world. Both systems use self-developed algorithms to display and rank apps in their search results.

Like internet search engines, both app systems keep pushing app developers and businesses to pay to rank their apps high in users' search results. Since 2016, for example, the App Store has let developers use a tool called "Apple Search Ads" to place their specific app at the top of App Store search results. According to the data provided by Apple Search Ads, 70% of App Store visitors use a search to find apps, 65% of downloads that occur directly after a search on App Store, and Apple Search Ads' average conversion rate is 50%. The idea behind the three numbers is simple. No matter how fancy your app is, it will not be a success if no one sees it in the App Store or Google Play Store.

The App Store service functions like most pay-per-click (PPC) networks, meaning that developers who paid for ads were charged for every ad click or tap on a mobile device by an app user (Cavaness, 2019). On the App Store, the Apple Search Ads operate like a traditional PPC approach, in which app developers pay for taps. They can also choose keywords and target customers based on user demographics like age, gender, and geographic locations, device type, and purchase history. Developers can also manage app campaigns based on revenue metrics and track improvements over time for specific business goals.

To be successful in app marketing, developers and marketers must create an action plan of app strategies based on app intelligence. A big part of app intelligence requires an in-depth knowledge of App Store Optimization (ASO). ASO helps answer the toughest questions in the process of app marketing, such as "How do I increase the downloads of my app?" "How can I get the first million downloads for my app?" "How do I get more people to discover my app?" and "How can I keep my customers after they download my app?"

App Store Optimization

App Store Optimization (ASO) is a three-step process of optimizing mobile apps to maximize their exposure to app users. The first step is placing it high on the search results page of the App Store. The second step is increasing the conversion rate by converting any potential users who have discovered the app to maximize the download number. The third step is maintaining the customer base and encouraging them to spend more time in using the app in various situations, which is mainly based on analyzing the in-app data concerning customer behavior. The ASO process and mechanism are similar to those used in search engine optimization (SEO). The goal of ASO is making effort to let more people discover your app and encourage more organic downloads and spend more time in using it.

All the factors affecting ASO can be divided into two categories: those can be changed by app developers and those that cannot. The first group of factors under the full control of the app developers may be changed through App Store Connect or Google Play Console. These factors include any app title and subtitle, short and long descriptions, keyword field and promo text (App Store only), app icon, category, URL/Package, video previews, and screenshots (MobileAction, 2020). In reality, these factors are constantly monitored by app designers. They change the app elements to boost keyword rankings, visibility, and user conversion about the app in the Apple App Store and Google Play Store.

The second group of factors are out of control of app developers. The uncontrollable factors include rating and reviews, download number or speed, the size of the app, etc. These app elements are generally the result of optimization efforts and cannot be affected directly. ASO requires constantly monitoring the app performance and identifying elements that may alter its performance right now or in the future. Therefore, the ASO process can be time-consuming and the effects may not match how much effort is invested.

One of the solutions is to improve the analysis skills of the in-app data for revealing more business insights. For example, using review mining to obtain valuable user feedback on new app features that they wish to have but do not yet exist. For app features, the users have the best ideas. Review mining may be used to find new ASO keywords, understand which features to kill or develop further, or generate new marketing ideas based on analyzing the user reviews left in the App Store or Google Play. Machine learning approaches including the latent Dirichlet allocation topic modeling and graph neural network analysis can be good tools in decoding user reviews. All these efforts will contribute to cultivating app intelligence.

In coming decades, the app economy will further develop in the two main areas: (1) adopting more digital technologies such as beacon technology, the augmented and virtual reality; and (2) applying in more business settings, ranging from hospitality business to digital health. Thus, we expect four technology trends of app development and four app trends in the area of mobile commerce.

Trends of App Development

As foldable smartphones are introduced to the markets, many existing and new apps must be re-designed to display properly on the new devices. Thus the first tech trend of app development is more apps are developed for foldable smartphones that are being used on 5G networks. As a game-changing technology, 5G is offering high-speed mobile internet connectivity that is more stable, allows faster downloads, and supports the transfer of vast amounts of data in real-time from scores of connected devices. As a result, users required their apps to have improved performance and responsiveness due to better connectivity and decreased load times thanks to 5G networks. The first groups of apps will be substantially improved and should be video apps, which have better visual clarity due to higher resolution and decreased latency. The first trend will lead to significant changes to enhanced app functionalities and, more importantly, will improve such apps' user interface and user experience as a whole. In the long run, better app performance can drive more downloads and reduce app abandonment.

The second tech trend is that more apps are being developed for smart wearable devices, not just Apple Watch or Fitbit. New apps for wearable devices will not just monitor heart rate, electromyography (EMG), or blood glucose levels that are already available on Apple Watch or Fitbit. They can track electrical signals from people's leg muscles as they walk or run. Mbody Live 3, an app from the Myontec, for example, can track muscle load, muscle balance, muscular fatigue threshold, heart rate, and cadence when it is connected with the wearable devices from the same company. Mbody Live 3 records the data about muscle performance that are used by athletes to analyze and improve performance. Collecting such data could be extremely difficult and expensive if used without an app.

The third trend is that more apps will have AR and VR features. Video gaming apps have had these features for years and nongaming apps have started to adopt AR or VR. For example, the virtual makeup app by L'Oreal allows users to see how their faces would look with makeup. The fourth trend is that AI and machine learning are embedded into more apps, which become an inherent part of the mobile app industry. Alexa from Amazon and Siri from Apple are two well-known AI-powered apps. The AI-incorporated apps can deliver a new and unique user experience to the user, which will be further discussed in the second section of this chapter.

Trends of Mobile Commerce Apps

Mobile commence apps connecting customers with different service providers will come to users' smartphones in batches. They enable users to order more products or services, which could be delivered in minutes. Currently people use Grubhub or DoorDash to order food delivery or book a car ride with Uber. Such apps are known as "on-demand apps," which are part of the booming on-demand economy. More economic activities accumulate through on-demand apps, which help big or small business owners to offer goods or services to customers. They are attracting not just young and wealthy users but more mainstream customers.

Back in 2016, *Harvard Business Review* reported that the on-demand economy attracted over 22.4 million consumers annually who spend $57.6 billion in using on-demand services, such as transportation like Uber, Lyft, food or grocery delivery, home services, freelancer services, and health and beauty services (Colby & Bell, 2016). A big share of the on-demand services will be increasingly delivered by using an app, which can be the first trend of mobile commerce apps.

The second trend involves using beacon technology, which uses low-energy Bluetooth technology to send signals to other smart devices nearby. For years, some businesses like Starbucks have used beacons to connect and transmit information to users' smart devices, making location-based searching and interaction easier and more accurate. For example, when a smartphone user walks by a Starbucks store, her phone can receive a push notification saying, "A Starbucks store is nearby," even though she may not see the Starbucks located on the ground floor of the mall. More businesses will integrate beacon technology into their apps to launch proximity marketing, for example, tracking customer behavior inside and outside their stores.

The third trend is that businesses invest more in building highly secure and reliable apps that guard against data security and user privacy. The investment makes business sense as customers will stop using any apps that leak private information and violate privacy. Finally, the fourth trend is low-code app development. Developers do not have to spend too much energy in coding an app as they can use some low-code development tools for creating apps, such as Google App Builder, Kissflow, Zoho Creator, and Appian. This indicates that the app technology is lowering barriers to entry. Meanwhile, the app industry with enhanced secured data and personal information will increase barriers to obtain business insights by analyzing in-app data.

Discussion

1. Can you remember or imagine your life before mobile apps? If you cannot use any apps while waiting in a line or taking a bus or subway ride, how do you like to spend the time?
2. Discuss two things about the app industry that you did not know before? Do any of the new knowledge points about the app economy surprise you?
3. One thing this chapter does not cover about the app business is the privacy concern about in-app user data. How much do you like to share your private data with the developers of the app you use, for example, the personal information about your eating routines or exercising habits?

References

Also read: 2018 app industry report and trends to watch for 2019. https://www
.mobileaction.co/blog/app-news-analysis/2018-app-industry-report-trends-to-
watch-for-2019.

Cavaness, K. (2019). Apple Search Ads: 11 things you need to know. *Klient Boost*. https://
klientboost.com/ppc/apple-search-ads.

Goldsmith, B. (2014). The smartphone app economy and app ecosystems. In G. Goggin,
L. Hjorth (Eds.), *The Routledge companion to mobile media* (pp. 171–180). Routledge.
http://hdl.library.upenn.edu/1017.12/1724961.

Iqbal, M. (2020). App download and usage statistics. *Business of Apps*. https://www.
businessofapps.com/data/app-statistics.

Kumar, N. (2016). Mobile app industry is the fast growing segment in the new economy.
NDOT. http://www.ndot.in/blog/mobile-app-industry-fast-growing-segment-economy.
html.

MobileAction. (2018). 2018 app industry report & trends to watch for 2019. *Mobile Action*.
https://www.mobileaction.co/blog/app-news-analysis/2018-app-industry-report-trends-
to-watch-for-2019.

Space-O Technologies. (2019). Mobile app development trends to take over 2019. https://
www.spaceotechnologies.com/mobile-app-development-trends-2019.

Overview

2. Artificial Intelligence

It is important to develop a deep understanding of algorithms, deep learning, machine learning, and artificial intelligence (AI) technologies embedded in social media sites. The pervasive use of AI-powered social media indicates that people are growingly seeing the outside world through the lens of AI. The second part of this chapter will explore one of the main reasons behind the successful penetration of social media sites – using AI to engage users. The power of AI is being growingly integrated into business practices, in particular, searching for and engaging with target customers. AI-powered marketing solutions can also bring out new strategies and expanded capabilities for business optimization across every growth level.

LEARNING GOALS

This section will help you understand:

- How is AI different from machine learning, deep learning, and algorithms?
- How do people evaluate their algorithm experience on social media like Facebook and Twitter?
- How is AI shaping social media use in business settings?
- What lessons can marketers learn from AI-powered solutions in business settings?

KEY CONCEPTS

Algorithm	App intelligence
Artificial intelligence	Algorithm

AI Helps Social Media Penetration

Social media are powerful information platforms that are shaping social life and defining human living, even more so due to integrating artificial intelligence. AI is helping social media to penerate deeper into the fabric of our society. The term "artificial intelligence" was coined in 1956 by John McCarthy, who defines it as "the science and engineering of making intelligent machines, especially intelligent computer programs. It is related to the similar task of using computers to understand human intelligence, but AI does not have to confine itself to methods that are biologically observable" (McCarthy, 2007, p. 2). Simply, AI is the field of study that aims to understand and build intelligent entities, which are fueled by the availability of big data, advanced machine learning approaches, and growth in computational power.

A Brookings Institution report predicted that 25% of US workers, or 36 million jobs, would face so-called "high automation exposure" in the next few decades, meaning such jobs would be highly affected by automation and AI advances (Muro et al., 2019). The report also estimated that another 36%, or 52 million jobs in the United States, would face "medium exposure." The most vulnerable jobs were those with "predictable physical and cognitive tasks," and the most secure jobs tended to require more creativity or require higher interpersonal social skills or higher education (Muro et al., 2019). Basically, the bottom line is that there is really no field that will not be affected by automation and AI.

Experts say the rise of artificial intelligence will make most people better off, but many have concerns about how advances in AI will affect what it means to be human, to be productive, and to exercise free will. In coming decades, we will see the growing role that AI has in our society, which will amplify human effectiveness but also threaten human autonomy, agency, and capabilities. Today's computers can match or even exceed human intelligence and capabilities on tasks such as complex decision making, reasoning and learning, sophisticated analytics, pattern recognition, visual acuity, speech recognition, and language translation.

AI-powered "smart" systems in communities, in vehicles, in buildings and utilities, on farms and in business processes will save time, money, and lives, and offer opportunities for people to enjoy a more-customized future (Anderson & Rainie, 2018). Still, some people feel uneasy with the question, "Will AI-powered robots kill jobs and replace human workers?" The answer is "no" for the moment. In the near future, communication professionals who have a good understanding of AI would certainly replace those who do not.

AI-Powered Business Solutions

When AI is discussed, people often mention other related terms like machine learning, deep learning, and algorithm. It is useful to consider these concepts as a set of Russian dolls nested within each other, beginning with the smallest and working out. An algorithm refers to a set of step-by-step guidelines that a computer follows to solve a problem or perform a task, and complex tasks often require multiple algorithms, for example, deep learning. Deep learning is a subset of machine learning, and machine learning is a subset of AI.

Hence, AI is an umbrella term for technologies that enable machines to mimic human intelligence in the areas of, to name a few, image recognition, natural language processing, decision making, news generation, fraud detection, and purchase prediction. AI research uses tools and insights from many fields, including computer science, psychology, philosophy, neuroscience, cognitive science, linguistics, communication, economics, control theory, probability, optimization, and logic (Russell & Norvig, 2003).

For centuries, businesses have tried to offer customers tailored products and services because they know relevance is the top driver behind the growth of business and revenue, but it is never easy for businesses to create and sustain the "always-on, always-me" experiences for their consumers. The business power of AI can help unlock insights by providing highly customized service at a decreased service-cost per customer. Embedding AI into core business functions has brought excellent customer service and experiences to a next level almost immediately. AI helps businesses cater to millions of customers' unique needs all at once. AI helps predict what customers need before they ever know their own needs, which significantly improves customer satisfaction. These AI-powered new services win millions of customers who are delighted to pay more for the unique experience and makes them feel like they are the only important customer.

AI helps maximize value per customer by pinpointing highly relevant products and services, which strengthens relationships with current customers and wins more prospective customers. AI can reveal a real-time, 360° view of target markets and customers and predict possible trends and outcomes that may not be predicted otherwise. As a result, AI-powered business solutions can bring out new strategies and expanded capabilities for business optimization across every growth level. Such resolutions required us to combine AI with data, analytics, and automation under a strategic vision to scale AI and transform business. Around the world, AI-powered strategies are redefining business possibilities and powering new outcomes in the areas of customer engagement, revenue growth, and other business functions. During the process, more effort is contributing to analyzing how people respond to the algorithm experience they do not see directly but can feel it all the time in using the products, for example, social media platforms.

The Algorithm Experience

Algorithms provide opportunities to utilize user data to predict user behaviors and react to how people behave in cyberspace. Most industries are taking advantage of data insights via algorithms in order to provide a more engaging, tailored and accurate experience for individual users. Algorithms can be used to mediate and assist in human decision making through a wide variety of venues, such as recruiting algorithms, tailored news aggregation services, online machine learning recommender systems, and credit scoring methods (Shi et al., 2020).

Algorithms embedded in social media are progressively transforming business communication, especially interactions with information, target customers, other businesses, and governments. Algorithms are designed to utilize user data to predict user behaviors and to react to how people behave in cyberspace. Most industries will be increasingly driven by data insights in order to provide a more engaging, tailored, and accurate experience for individual users. Algorithms can be used to mediate critical decisions in human contexts through a wide variety of venues, such as recruiting algorithms, tailored news aggregation services, recommendation systems, and credit scoring methods (Willson, 2017).

In the domain of social media, algorithms are designed to help sort posts in a user's feed based on relevancy instead of publish time. Social media prioritize what type of content users encounter by the likelihood they prefer to see first and respond. Before using such algorithms, social media feeds often displayed posts in a reverse chronological order. The way of always displaying the newest posts from the accounts a user followed is less engaging than letting social media algorithms determine which content is displayed first based on relevance and prior behaviors. For example, Facebook or Twitter often put posts from closest friends and family members at the top of daily feeds because those are the accounts people interact with most often and, quite possibly, the ones they also care about most dearly.

The power of social media algorithms also make them controversial, as many algorithms may have bugs due to their imperfect designs. Without social media algorithms, it is cumbersome to sift through the overwhelming amount of social media content flowing across hundreds or thousands of accounts a user follows on social media platforms. In these cases, algorithms do the legwork of delivering what you want and filtering out content that is deemed irrelevant or of low quality. However, algorithms may also hide information that a user needs to stay informed or kick in biased information filters due to the incidentally flawed designs of those algorithms.

By and large, algorithm technologies are increasingly characterized as an ecosystem of complex sociotechnical matters. Considering the ecosystem of algorithms and possible flaws in social media algorithms, it is important to develop a deep understanding of algorithms, deep learning, machine learning, and AI because people are growingly seeing the outside world through the lens of AI.

Social Media and AI

It is often assumed that the user base of social media has been so well established that it did not change much in a year-by-year analysis. That assumption has repeatedly been proven to be inaccurate in recent decades. In 2019, the number of social media users worldwide has risen by 9% over the previous year, reaching 3.484 billion (Chaffey, 2019). Meanwhile, the most popular social media sites vary a lot in terms of their usage and engagement in different social groups, age groups, cultures, and countries. For example, Saudi Arabia has the largest social media penetration at 99%, twice as much as the global average of 45%. Other countries with the largest social media penetration include Taiwan, South Korea, and Singapore, while Ghana, Kenya, and Nigeria have the lowest levels of social media penetration (Chaffey, 2019). Facebook remained the most popular social media platform around the world, but in China the most popular social media site was WeChat, which was seldom used in any other country.

With so many active users on social media, it is important to make good use of social media to reach out to users. The question is not whether we should reach out to those users through social media, where our target customers gather, but how to monetize such a significant number of users and target the right market. For industrial leaders, the answer is simple: artificial intelligence.

As businesses have increasingly adopted artificial intelligence (AI), social media beg not to be different. Seeing the power of social media, more businesses are joining in the race to win customers on social media. Going beyond the initial stage of using AI to acquire new customers, businesses are developing AI solutions based on data of millions of users' behaviors (e.g., viewing webpages, online purchasing) and interactions (e.g., with businesses, products, and other users) on social media. Facebook, for example, has embedded AI to analyze keywords, images, likes, comments, and interactions through its neural network learning system. The AI-powered algorithms help engage Facebook users and make its service more efficient. As a result, Facebook users can hardly get rid of it and become more addicted to it each day.

As more people become online shoppers who often purchase products online rather than offline, companies are motivated to search for new ways to reach out to target markets and sell smarter. One of the new ways of serving online shoppers is analyzing people's searching habits on social media with the help of AI. Based on the results, AI could further recommend products or services tailored to their likes, tastes, and needs.

Twitter is also working on using AI and machine learning to categorize every single tweet. Its AI helps to rank thousands of tweets one specific user receives in a given time based on relevance, relationships, and user habits. The idea is to let AI repackage the content as more relevant and engaging information so that users may pay more attention to it and care about it more. The AI-powered practice could mean a significant shift in the way that people currently view tweets within the chronological timeline format. Another example is that Twitter also uses neural networks to crop photos to maximize their aesthetic output. To do this, machine learning studies eye-tracking. Eye-tracking records what area people look at first in a picture, meaning AI can understand which part of a photograph is most appealing.

AI Empowers Marketers

AI-powered recommendations, in many cases, have shown a stronger influence on people's choices than advice from other people (Montal & Reich, 2017). Companies are better at leveraging social media through artificial intelligence, enabling a better understanding of the customers' buying personas. Better marketing strategies may be worked out to serve customers with more relevant products. Marketers can personalize content for their customers by understanding buying habits, people's everyday environments, and what motivates them to make their decisions (Egorsheva, 2018). AI can learn these habits at a rate much faster than humans.

The ever-changing environment of social media makes it harder for companies to keep on top of trends, which is the main reason why they are turning to AI for solutions (Egorsheva, 2018). Machine learning algorithms analyze everything that is happening on social media in real time and convert the information to tangible data for businesses to utilize. AI studies data and makes recommendations based on its findings. Such vast information would typically take months for a human to cultivate. Deep learning, algorithms, and datasets empower AI, which in turn streamlines the process for marketers.

It is practically impossible to have a brand without a social media presence, yet just being on these platforms is not enough. They need to be utilized correctly to achieve maximum output, generate more customers, and ultimately increase ROI. However, many businesses do not have the resources to hire human staff who can monitor trends, social patterns, and insights. AI is a way of solving such problems and affords marketers the freedom to be creative with their outreach. AI acts as a way for brands to scope the vast pool that is social media. They can cover bases that were once hard to monitor.

In the coming decades, AI is expected to keep evolving at a much faster speed, which makes it hard to predict the future development of AI. Countless new algorithms will be developed to power AI to make our machines more intelligent in solving problems humans face. A new trend is emerging suggesting that AI will be able to solve harder problems better than humans. Moreover, AI-powered intelligent software embedded in social media could bring out more efficient quality communication and interaction between businesses and target customers.

Theory Highlight: Knowledge Gap Hypothesis

The Knowledge Gap Hypothesis explains that knowledge, like other forms of wealth, is often differentially distributed throughout a social system. Specifically, the hypothesis predicts that "as the infusion of mass media information into a social system increases, higher socioeconomic status segments tend to acquire this information faster than lower socioeconomic status population segments so that the gap in knowledge between the two tends to increase rather than decrease" (Tichenor et al., 1970, pp. 159–160). The hypothesis indicates that "information haves" read more and engage more in higher-level conversations, creating greater existing pools of knowledge and using information for fulfilling specific purposes and needs. Greater use enhances speed of information acquisition and develops schemas, which over time is likely to accelerate a knowledge gap between those who have access and those who do not. Therefore, although the "have-nots" gain knowledge, the "haves" gain it faster, and by gaining it faster, they are able to gain more.

Back in the 1920s, mass communication researchers had already begun to examine the influence of individual characteristics on people's media content preferences. For example, Gray and Munroe (1929) identified that education is positively correlated with a person's consumption of serious print content. Lazarsfeld (1940) found that people of lower socioeconomic status were less likely to listen to serious radio content. Results of a number of public opinion polls led Hyman and Sheatsley (1947) to discuss the nature of problems that make it difficult to inform certain segments of the public; they

called for research on these "chronic know-nothings." Later, Phillip J. Tichenor, Associate Professor of Journalism and Mass Communication, George A. Donohue, Professor of Sociology, and Clarice N. Olien, Instructor in Sociology – three University of Minnesota researchers – first proposed the formal knowledge Gap hypothesis in 1970.

Regardless of topic, methodological, or theoretical variations, studies have reported similar demonstrations of the knowledge gap. These differentials tend to be especially severe for those groups during economic downturns and hard times (Gaziano, 1997). Therefore, the knowledge gap deserves greater focus and attention. However, despite numerous findings on knowledge disparities, conditions under which gaps change are not well-documented and some results conflict (Gaziano, 1997). Internal barriers (i.e., motivation, interest, involvement, etc.) and external barriers (i.e., social stratification, distribution of media access, etc.) to knowledge are of high concern by mass communication researchers. Knowledge gap research is also considered to have great policy implications because policy decisions have played a major role in increasing inequality (Fischer et al, 1996). Last but not least, the linkage among gaps in behavior, attitudes, values, and knowledge may improve information campaign results, especially for health and public affairs topics (Gaziano, 1997).

Summary

This chapter covers two topics: the app economy and artificial intelligence that power the social media use. A new trend is emerging that AI will be able to solve harder problems better than humans. Moreover, AI-powered intelligent software embedded in social media could bring out more efficient quality communication and interaction between businesses and target customers. Both AI and apps are directly related to social media usage. A big part of social media popularity is powered by artificial intelligence. In a similar fashion, social media would not be so popular and easy to use without countless mobile apps developed for smartphone users. Most of us may not be an AI expert, but it is essential for us to understand how AI may shape our marketing effort, business campaigns and career development. Let us start by first understanding how apps and AI are adding more power to social media.

Looking Ahead

In Chapter 13, we will learn about social media campaigning in some political and social movements. Social media functions as an important tool connecting people for the purposes of bringing about social changes. The chapter examines how social media speed up social movements around the world, like the Arab Spring and Black Lives Matter movements. Moreover, how social media help mobilization and coalition building in social movements will be analyzed in detail. Three perspectives concerning the relations between social media and democracy will be discussed, which are the optimistic, pessimistic, and neutral perspectives.

Discussion

1. Based on your observation and experience, do you think AI is affecting your daily life and work? If so, in what areas?
2. What are the top benefits and top concerns you have for the AI development in the next decade?
3. What are the top benefits and setbacks of AI-powered solutions?

References

Anderson, J., & Rainie, L. (2018). Artificial intelligence and the future of humans. *Pew Research Center: Internet & Technology*. Retrieved December 10, from https://www.pewresearch.org/internet/2018/12/10/artificial-intelligence-and-the-future-of-humans.

Chaffey, D. (2019). Global social media research summary 2019. *Smart Insights*. smartinsights.com/social-media-marketing/social-media-strategy/new-global-social-media-research.

Colby, C., & Bell, K. (2016). The on-demand economy is growing, and not just for the young and wealthy. *Harvard Business Review*, 1–7. https://hbr.org/2016/04/the-on-demand-economy-is-growing-and-not-just-for-the-young-and-wealthy.

Egorsheva, O. (2018). The impact of artificial intelligence on social media. *Martech Advisor*. https://www.martechadvisor.com/articles/machine-learning-ai/the-impact-of-artificial-intelligence-on-social-media.

Fischer, C. S., Hout, M., Jankowski, M. S., Lucas, S. R., Swidler, A., & Voss, K. (1996). *Inequality by design: Cracking the bell curve myth.* Princeton University Press.

Gaziano, C. (1997). Forecast 2000: Widening knowledge gaps. *Journalism & Mass Communication Quarterly*, 74 (2), 237–264. https://doi.org/10.1177/107769909707 400202.

Gray, W. S., & Munroe, R. L. (1929). *The reading interests and habits of adults: A preliminary report.* Macmillan.

Hyman, H. H., & Sheatsley, P. B. (1949). Some reasons why information campaigns fail. *Public Opinion Quarterly*, 11 (3), 412–423. https://doi.org/10.1086/265867.

Lazarsfeld, P. F. (1940). *Radio and the printed page: An introduction to the study of radio and its role in the communication of ideas.* Duell, Sloan, and Pearce.

McCarthy, J. (2007). What is artificial intelligence? http://www-formal.stanford.edu/jmc/whatisai.pdf.

MobileAction. (2020). Boosting app growth: Power of app intelligence. *MobileAction.* https://www.mobileaction.co/blog/app-analytics/boost-app-growth-app-intelligence.

Montal, T., & Reich, Z. (2017). I, robot. You, journalist. Who is the author? Authorship, bylines and full disclosure in automated journalism. *Digital Journalism, 5* (7), 829–849. https://doi.org/10.1080/21670811.2016.1209083.

Muro, M., Maxim, R., & Whiton, J. (2019). Automation and artificial intelligence: How machines are affecting people and places (pp. 1–12). https://www.brookings.edu/wp-content/uploads/2019/01/ES_2019.01_BrookingsMetro_Automation-AI_Report _Muro-Maxim-Whiton-FINAL.pdf.

Russell, S. J., & Norvig, P. (2003). *Artificial intelligence: A modern approach* (2nd ed.). Prentice Hall.

Shi, D.-H., Zhong, B., & Biocca, F. (2020). Beyond user experience: What constitutes algorithmic experiences? *International Journal of Information Management, 52*(102061), 1–11. https://doi.org/10.1016/j.ijinfomgt.2019.102061.

Tichenor, P. J., Donohue, G. A., & Olien, C. N. (1970). Mass media flow and differential growth in knowledge. *Public Opinion Quarterly, 34*(2), 159–170. https://doi.org/10.1086/267786.

Willson, M. (2017). Algorithms (and the) everyday. *Information, Communication & Society, 20*(1), 137–150. https://doi.org/10.1080/1369118X.2016.1200645.

13

Social Media and Social Movement

LEARNING GOALS

This chapter will help you understand:

- What is the role of social media in social movements?
- How are networked publics related to the use of social media?
- What is the relationship between social media and democracy analyzed?
- What are the three perceptions concerning social media's role in social movements?

KEY CONCEPTS

Social movement Networked publics

Core group Peripheral group

THEORY HIGHLIGHT

Diffusion of Innovation Theory

Overview

Global social movements have spread around the world since the 2010s, such as the Arab Spring (2010–2012), Occupy Wall Street (2011), Umbrella Revolution in Hong Kong (2014), #MeToo Movement (2006–2017), and Black Lives Matter (2013–2020). Most of the movements tended to be leaderless, but all used social media to connect protesters, motivate supporters, and mobilize resources. Significant social changes were generated out of the massive social demonstrations across nations. The Arab Spring, for example, was a series of pro-democracy social movements that enveloped several Arabic countries like Tunisia, Morocco, Syria, Libya, Egypt, and Bahrain. Not all of the movements could be viewed as successful if the political goals were judged by how much democracy and cultural freedom people had won from their governments. Some uprisings had led to regime changes in countries such as Tunisia, Egypt, and Libya, but few significant changes happened in other countries due to the social movements. However, there is little debate on the critical role social media played in the Arab Spring and other social movements around the world, including those happening in the United States.

Social Media Communication: Trends and Theories, First Edition. Bu Zhong.
© 2022 John Wiley & Sons, Inc. Published 2022 by John Wiley & Sons, Inc.

Social Media Speed Up Social Movements

For the first time in history, the world has witnessed the power of social media when their users reached a critical mass. The power was strong enough to transform the societies that had been under tight control of authoritarian regimes for centuries. During the Arab Spring, social media became a vital component that stirred a series of anti-government protests, uprisings, and armed rebellions that spread across much of the Arab world. Some scholars argue that those social movements were inevitable in the region, but few doubt that social media helped speed them into revolutions, which are also known as "Twitter Revolution" or "Facebook Revolution." Some protesters even called Facebook the "PeopleBook" (see Figure 13.1). With the help of social media, it was easy to coordinate millions of Arab people to get on the street to protest against their governments. Scholars rightly pointed out that these social movements might be unavoidable in northern Africa and the Middle East, but they could be notably delayed without the widespread use of social media in those countries.

So, how did social media speed those leaderless political or social uprisings?

Central to the answer is how people make use of social media to reach their political and social goals in massive social demonstrations. A few years after the Arab Spring, waves of anti-government protests swept through Hong Kong from the Umbrella Movement in 2014 to more protests in 2019. The latter caused concerns of possible radical solutions from beleaguered officials in Hong Kong and Beijing. One of the biggest concerns included a partial or complete internet block to cut off protesters from their key organizing social media platforms (Griffiths, 2019). The concern of the internet block indicated the critical role social media played in those social movements, which could bring about unexpected long-term effects on the future of Hong Kong.

On the other hand, social media have radically simplified organizing and coordinating large groups of participants in social movements. Before the advent of social media,

Figure 13.1   Social media were of great importance in the Arab Spring movement in 2011 (Note: The Arabic words on the poster reads "PeopleBook").
Photo by Essam Sharaf, Wikimedia Commons, CC-BY-SA 3.0 (Source: https://politikorange. de/2015/06/mach-ich-revolution-tu-ich-facebook.)

many of them might not be mobilized to join hands because of weak ties or lack of trust among them. These days social media are enabling new kinds of protests with broad reach. Online organizing and coordinating the details of protests help raise consciousness and call attention to the goals of planned social movements, and, at the same time, overcome the barriers of weak ties and lack of trust among participants.

Hong Kong, for instance, has had a long tradition of dissent, but the 2019 protests, with such intensity and characteristics, were new to local residents. This was partially due to the use of social media as the communication channels. The massive demonstrations in Hong Kong displayed several unique changes, which were also seen in several other protest movements worldwide (Pinckney, 2019). One of them was that the Hong Kong protests displayed a significant degree of self-organization, with coordinating groups playing an insignificant role, if any. Those youth-led leaderless movements projected a self-organized united front that was less prone to violence. They are part of a growing global phenomenon of a predominately youthful, largely nonviolent, public resistance.

Scholars have identified three characteristics beyond sheer numbers that tend to help primarily nonviolent movements succeed in bringing about change: unity, strategic planning, and nonviolent discipline (Pinckney, 2019). The three characteristics must be executed coherently in order to achieve the goal of a social movement. The process needs strong leadership, which is, ironically, invisible in numerous protests since the 2010s, for example, Occupy Wall Street in 2011 and the Hong Kong protests in 2019 and 2020.

Social media function like multiple meeting rooms in a conference center. People can always find a room full of people like themselves. Social movements also require a wide participation of people with different backgrounds. Coordinating a social movement through social media has its own challenges, including how to bring people together, rather than sorting them into different echo chambers. On social media, millions of users search, access, and disseminate information through likes, shares, forwards, and retweets. Therefore, it is crucial to examine how social media help launch so many political demonstrations and social movements.

New Path to Social Power

Scholars had a mixed response to the role of social media in social movements after they extensively studied a series of social movements that swept across North Africa, the Middle East, and other regions since the 2010s. Some dismiss or downplay any causal relationship existing between social media use and the success of organizing massive demonstrations for shared goals (Papacharissi, 2013). In the 1960s, they argued that Americans got on the street to protest and launch, to name a few, the Civil Rights movement, the Anti-Vietnam War movement, the Women's movement, the Gay Rights movement, and the Environmental movement. Each, to varying degrees, brought about social changes and removed or revised government policies. Moreover, these movements had significantly changed American society as a whole. In those movements, they argued that social media helped nothing, as they were not yet developed. In this sense, digital technology cannot save the world and social media like Facebook or Twitter are just places where revolutionaries go (Morozov, 2012).

Other scholars maintain that use of social media accelerated the development of social movements around the globe, in ways similar to how the printing press and other mass media facilitated revolutions in the past (Papacharissi, 2013). This does not mean that humans are no longer important. Fundamentally, these social movements were launched, organized, and executed by humans and are "ultimately enabled by human cost and sacrifice" (Papacharissi, 2013, p. 145). In the age of social media, putting large numbers of people on the street has become increasingly easy. It is humans who could turn those numbers into meaningful political and social changes.

At the same time, protesters have little choice, but make good use of media technologies, especially social media, which is helpful in achieving their goals. This has become increasingly evident in recent waves of political and social protests. Meanwhile, the use of social media did not guarantee that protesters would attain the desired movement outcomes. In past years, demonstrations that made use of social media led to a variety of outcomes, such as government upheavals, democratic reforms, violence, or further suppression of political freedoms – some of which are yet to be determined (Papacharissi, 2013). In Egypt, for example, a largely leaderless group succeeded in ousting dictatorial president Hosni Mubarak, but then struggled to consolidate its gains once he was gone. Other spontaneous leaderless protests, such as Occupy Wall Street or the Gezi Park demonstrations in Turkey, have had difficulty turning the momentum of their initial turnout into a series of targeted tactics designed to achieve specific goals.

Social media are so important in empowering individuals and groups of individuals with public exposure that they can not imagine an era without social media. Social media function like a powerful mass media platform that can be used by ordinary people, but used to only be available to those in power or those with tremendous social and economic resources. Hence, social media present a new path to achieve social power, certainly not the only one, through which small groups of individuals may get their voices heard in a bigger world, online and offline. Despite some disagreement, scholars generally agree that social media have brought several fundamental changes to the social movements happening in the twenty-first century, including mobilizing core or peripheral participants and building a coalition among them.

Mobilization and Coalition Building

After studying the Black Lives Matter movement, some scholars argue that the most powerful and instinctive relationship between social media and social movements lies in the potential for mobilizing a wide range of activists and participants (Mundt & Ross, 2018). Because social media are serving users as opinion forums and information channels, it is much easier for social movement leaders and activists to mobilize more people to join them through social media. In the process, social media actually help create new participation opportunities that could hardly be achieved through traditional mass media. In the past, anyone who wanted to reach out to a large audience had to write a letter to the editor of a newspaper. It was up to the editor to publish it in the newspaper or not. So nothing could be guaranteed in those good old days.

In the social media age, activists do not have to rely on traditional media to scale movement endeavors, including boosting protest turnout or launching fundraising campaigns. During the 2011 Tahrir Square protests in Cairo, for instance, Egyptians used Facebook to disseminate information and mobilize activists and other residents in the city to protest against the government without relying on traditional news media that were controlled by the government. Researchers found that Facebook also provided "safe spaces" for protesters to meet and exchange information about their activities (Khamis & Vaughn, 2012). Such online spaces also helped the Black Lives Matter movements in the United States to build a forum for continued involvement and reflection around issues related to race and policing, and highlighted its significance for developing common understandings of ideology and a shared sense of movement identity (Mundt & Ross, 2018).

Research has identified two significant groups of participants in a social movement: a core group and a periphery group (Barberá et al., 2015). The core group are those on the street, actively protesting and spreading their message, and the periphery are low-commitment participants, echoing and sharing that message through social media platforms. Other researchers found that information is most mobilizing when it is coming from acquaintances or a stranger with a common communal background, as opposed to a friend, family member, or loved one (Granillo, 2020). When people see others show up for a protest in their social media feeds, they would be more likely to join the same protest as they think this is what their network is doing. In fact, the best predictor of who would join the demonstrations are the people who are invited, persuaded, or pressured into going (Granillo, 2020). Thus, social media assist in not only bringing awareness and amplifying messages, but also in creating new opportunities of political participation, in particular, for those peripheral sympathizers. The participation of peripheral groups often functions as a game changer for a social movement to go to the next level or become a bigger success.

Central to the success of a social movement are both the recruitment of participants and fundraising for their activities. Social media are an effective and low-cost tool for social movement activists to mobilize necessary resources, especially generating monetary donations and digital crowdfunding campaigns. One of the classic examples is that former President Donald Trump raised over US$495 million between October 15 and November 23, 2020, according to filings released by the Federal Election Commission (Alba & Kamisar, 2021). Nearly half of it, or US$207.5 million, was raised since Election Day (November 3, 2020) as Trump told his followers that he needed money to fight based on his unsubstantiated claims of voter fraud. Trump's tweets and his campaign's fundraising emails and text messages played a major role in mobilizing the windfall of donations.

Another strength of social media in social movements is that they can significantly shape coalition building, which is essential to turn a social movement into social changes. Social media can create new venues to reach out to both core activists and peripheral protesters to combat their mutual enemy. Empirical evidence shows that social media can be used to build up a large scale of coalition in participants with diverse identities, interests, and backgrounds. How strong the coalition is built up by using social media will be inevitably shaped by specific sociopolitical and economic conditions and resources. Global social movements that happened in the past decades have clearly demonstrated that social media use could boost coalition building, participant recruitment, and resource mobilization, including donations and crowdfunding. These elements had become an essential part of the success of past social movements from the Arab Spring and Occupy Wall Street to Black Lives Matter and the pro-Trump riot on Capitol Hill.

Networked Publics

Media technology presents a way to counter powerlessness by allowing individuals to propose and occupy new spaces, online and offline, like Occupy Wall Street. These social spaces, created with the help of social media, represent the sum of human experiences that were seldom achieved in the past when social media or other media technologies were not developed.

Social media, along with mobile devices and other media technologies, enable users to engage in social movements to bring about social changes that were almost impossible in the past. Despite the fact that social movement outcomes vary dramatically, users have been actively seeking to renegotiate the status quo of the existing hierarchy of power to win autonomy. Autonomy, personal and collective, is defined by the way in which the private is balanced against the public, and vice versa.

Greater access to information is enabled by online media, but does not necessarily lead to increases in political participation. On the other hand, social media help facilitate engagement by activating latent ties that may be crucial to the mobilization of social movements. More importantly, social media offer opportunities to build up networked publics around the globe, which are impossible without new communication tools. For example, millions of children and young students poured into the streets for a day of global strike in 2019, protesting about climate change in thousands of cities and towns worldwide (Sengupta, 2019). Without social media, it is hard to imagine how to motivate those young students to participate in such movements. These students are part of the networked publics that have emerged in a range of global social movements.

Networked publics are defined as "(1) publics that are restructured by networked technologies and (2) the imagined collective that emerges as a result of the intersection of people, technology, and practice" (boyd, 2010, p. 39). However, boyd (2010) emphasizes that networked publics are not just "publics networked together, but they are publics that have been transformed by networked media" (p. 42). Networked publics are formed around both actual and virtual communities. The properties of social media lend networked publics particular affordances that can be traced in the ways individuals mobilized during the recent waves of uprisings in the Middle East and North Africa (Papacharissi, 2013). While social media like Facebook or Instagram certainly did not cause the uprisings, they have offered new chances to empower both activists and latent networked publics to engage in social movements. Meanwhile, they become surveillance tools used by governments and other powerful social players to monitor the unfolding of social movements and political uprisings.

Of course, the impact of social media is subject to sociopolitical context.

Social Media and Democracy

Social media are making it easier to organize social movements today, but the relationship between media technology and democracy is complex and dynamic. By comparing the digital origins of democracy and dictatorship across Islamic political regimes, Philip N. Howard (2010) identifies five causal conditions that lead to democratization and individual autonomy: (1) a comparatively active online civil society; (2) a relatively small population; (3) a relatively well-educated population; (4) a state with a comparatively well-developed information infrastructure; and (5) an economy not dominated by fuel exports. He found that different combinations of these causal conditions may yield specific democratizing outcomes and may permit social media to become the supporting infrastructure of social movements.

For Papacharissi (2013), asking the question of whether social media caused social movements or political uprisings misses the point. She argues that it was too early to claim these movements as revolutions as they can only be determined by long-term democratic outcomes. Some fundamental questions regarding the links between social media and democracy remain unanswered, such as whether social media help or hinder social movements, or whether social media can help achieve the goals of social movements. A more meaningful question may be: Can social media create the tipping point that leads to a movement's success? (Kidd & McIntosh, 2016).

Facing this central question of the ties between social media and social movements, Kidd and McIntosh (2016) identified three types of scholarly perception: optimistic, pessimistic, and ambivalent approaches. Now we will review the three approaches in turn.

1. The Optimistic Perception

Scholars holding an optimistic stance emphasize the power of social media technologies to solve social problems. They argue that the revolution can be tweeted or brought to the next level by the pervasive use of social media. These scholars tend to agree with Marshall McLuhan's (1964) media ecology theory, which contends that the use of information and communication technology (ICT) assists in defining historical stages. With a particular historical period being developed around the dominant medium of the day, the specific ICT and media platforms can alter and influence human perceptions, values, attitudes, and behaviors. Thus, they show great faith in the revolutionary power of social media.

One of the leading scholars in this category is Manual Castells. He views the use of Twitter and Facebook as tools for political upheaval as confirmation of theoretical principles that he presents in his trilogy of books: *The Information Age: Economy, society, and culture* (Castells, 1996, 1997, 1998) and in his later work *Communication power* (Castells, 2009). Castells argues that the information age has brought out an information society, or a "network society." In the network society, the real power is in the hands of programmers and switchers as they are the people who, metaphorically, act as programmers and switchers to make connections and collaboration for social movements (Castells, 2012).

For Castells, one notable characteristic of social movements in the network society is that they are leaderless due to the distrust that the movements have for those in power and the ways that the network society has flattened organizational hierarchies (Kidd & McIntosh, 2016). By examining information flows on Twitter – tweets and retweets – during the Tunisian and Egyptian uprisings that were part of the Arab Spring, scholars found that media organizations, journalists, bloggers, and activists played different roles in information distribution in those social movements (Lotan et al., 2011). In the cases of the Egyptian and Tunisia uprisings, journalists and activists "serve primarily as key information sources, while bloggers and activists are more likely to retweet content and, thus, serve as key information routers" (1390). They find that individuals (including journalists and bloggers) are more successful in seeding information – starting a flow – than organizations. However, they also found important differences in the information flows of Egypt and Tunisia, suggesting that culture and context also shape the pattern of these flows. Their main conclusion is that social media really has transformed journalism into a conversation across different types of actors, and that activists and bloggers are significant producers of information, in addition to journalists.

2. The Pessimistic Perception

Those holding a pessimistic stance argue that social media are incapable of ushering in a social revolution or even that social media hinder positive social change. They tend to see others as overstating the potentials of social media in a social movement and views their power as hyperbolic and superficial. When comparing social movements in network society to those in the 1960s, like the Civil Rights Movement, Malcolm Gladwell (2010) argued that the social changes facilitated by social media-based social movements were "small."

Evgeny Morozov also argues that the world has been overwhelmed by cyber-utopians who ignore or exaggerate the benefits of new technology with little use of evidence and a blind-eye to history (Morozov, 2012). Unlike others in this category, Morozov knows well the powerful influence of the internet, social media, and social networking, but he correctly emphasizes that the set of powerful tools may be more effectively used by authoritarian regimes than activists or protesters who launch social movements because the former has the tools and has the most access to powerful new tools. Digital media technologies like social media that were supposed to boost democratic participation could be used to crack down on democratic movements. The internet, he points out, offers excellent tools for authoritarian governments – including ones that claim to be democratic – to track, infiltrate, and undermine counterpolitical movements (Morozov, 2012).

In the social media era, Navid Hassanpour (2013) contends that the public does not lack information, but people are often bothered by the disruption of information. The more access people have to the flow of information, the more they will be disgruntled by its disruption. Christian Christensen (2011) highlights the fact that social media can be just as useful for powerful political leaders who are being protested against as it is for the protestors themselves. He cites the use of social media policing by leaders in Iran during the protests of 2009 as an example. He concludes that we should not place too much stock in the "virtues" of social media.

3. The Ambivalent Perception

Most researchers holding either optimistic, pessimistic, or ambivalent perception tend to agree, to some degree, that the impact of social media use on social movements can be mixed, sometimes powerful, but trivial in other cases (Kidd & McIntosh, 2016). That said, researchers with an ambivalent perception focus more on the role of weak ties in social movements that are mainly induced by social media use. For them, social media are relevant, but they may not be able to start a revolution. Rather, they played certain practical roles in social movements that were unseen before. In the 2011 Egyptian uprising in Cairo, for example, Twitter served three purposes for Egyptian activists: "(1) a real-time information stream maintained by Egyptian citizen journalists; (2) a means for local information and updates to reach an international audience, including international journalists; and (3) a means to organize disparate activist groups on the ground. Perhaps its greatest impact was in the second purpose and its least in the third purpose" (Murthy, 2013, p. 112).

Acknowledging the mixed effects of social media on social movements, researchers in this category insist that people's shared political appeal and collective passion are the main drivers behind those demonstrations, although social media could, indeed, be instrumental as a tool for communication, and even be key to the formation of protests (Kidd & McIntosh, 2016). In other words, what matters the most in social movements are humans, not the media technologies used to connect them to achieve their goals. This had been repeatedly proven and verified in a range of social movements and demonstrations since the late 2000s.

The ambivalent perception toward social media gets more scholarly attention in studying social movements these years. Those who embrace the ambivalent perception have identified multiple major flaws in both the optimistic and pessimistic stances. Three major flaws in the optimistic perspective are: "(1) it overstates the newness of social media; (2) it jumps to prediction without evidence; and (3) it underestimates the capacity of existing hegemonies to adapt to technology." The pessimistic approach also has major flaws: "(1) it falsely romanticizes life before social media; (2) it underestimates the agency of social media users to create new ways of utilizing these communication tools; and (3) it overstates the negative potential of social media, obscuring the balancing effects of positive outcomes" (Kidd & McIntosh, 2016, p. 792).

In sum, social media use by contemporary movements has created new opportunities of broadening the reach of and strengthening connections between social movement participants. Evidence shows that both social changes and social movements rely on social media to achieve theirs goals, but the success of a social movement needs much more than that. Those who believe that social media are empowering citizens should never underestimate how governments, military, and police could make use of social media as effective surveillance tools or even the means of disrupting any challenges to dictatorship. Violent extremist groups, including racists and terrorists, are never hesitant in using social media to embolden their followers and magnify their anti-social goals. An important lesson about the relations between social media and social movements is that social media will keep evolving and their usage can help foster both positive and negative social changes.

Theory Highlight: Diffusion of Innovation Theory

Diffusion of innovations is a process whereby (1) an invention is (2) communicated through certain channels (3) over time (4) within social systems. It has attempted to explain the variables that influence how and why users adopt a new information medium. Rogers (1983) defines five adopter categories: innovators, early adopters (opinion leaders), early majority, late majority, and laggards (Figure 13.2). He noted that diffusion occurs through a four-step process: knowledge, persuasion, decision, and confirmation. Nowadays, the diffusion of technologies is one of the most studied areas,

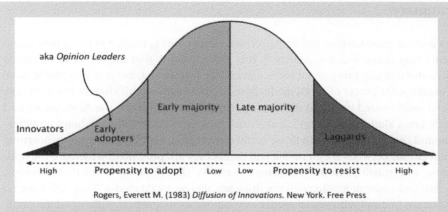

Rogers, Everett M. (1983) *Diffusion of Innovations*. New York. Free Press

Figure 13.2   The diffusion of innovations (Rogers, 1983).

including the radio, television, VCR, cable, flush toilet, clothes washer, refrigerator, telephone, cellular phone, and social media.

In 1890, French sociologist Gabriel de Tarde first brought up the concept of "leaders" in adopting innovation. Later on, he introduced the concept of diffusion in 1903 (Kinnunen, 1996). The study of diffusion of innovations started in the subfield of rural sociology in the United States in the 1920s and 1930s, especially in the field of agriculture technology.

Diffusion of innovations has later been applied to many areas, such as medical sociology, communications, marketing, development studies, etc. When incorporating the concept within communication research, Everett Rogers, a professional rural sociologist, linked these findings back to the concept of two-step flow (Lazarsfeld et al., 1944). After synthesizing more than 500 diffusion studies across fields, Rogers (1962) published *Diffusion of Innovations* in 1962, in which he created the adoption of innovations theory among individuals and organizations.

Diffusion of innovations has raised the importance for understanding public responses to complex innovations. In Rogers' four-step process of diffusion, individuals might reject an innovation at any time during or even after the adoption process. Therefore, it is critical for any innovation to understand how the four key elements or variables might influence the diffusion of innovations.

Two segments are critical in the process of diffusion: innovators and early adopters. Innovators are mostly cosmopolitan, they have necessary skills to overcome the problems accompanying the introduction of innovations, and they can financially afford the risk of betting on an innovation. On the other hand, early adopters are often well-respected persons within local networks and open to new ideas. Early adopters, rather than innovators, are considered the gatekeepers of innovation. If they adopt, their environment will follow. It is fair to say that early adopters (opinion leaders) play an important role in determining the likelihood that the innovation will be adopted or not in a society.

Summary

Since social media are an unfolding terrain, more effort is needed to study how social media may shape social movements. It is naïve to think that the use of social media will automatically bring about the social changes we expect, but it is also problematic to overlook the power of social media in social movements. This chapter analyzes how social media speed up social movements around the world, like the Arab Spring and Black Lives Matter movements. It also examines how social media use helps mobilization and coalition building in those social movements. Three perspectives concerning the relations between social media and democracy are presented, which are the optimistic, pessimistic, and neutral perspectives. We should never forget that terrorists, racists, and those defending dictatorships are also on social media. They will have no hesitation in employing social media as weapons to suppress and disrupt democratic demonstrations and protests that lead to social change.

Looking Ahead

The next chapter will address the future development of social media. Several trends of social media use in business settings will be identified and highlighted, which should be insightful for readers who hope to make good use of social media as business and marketing tools.

Discussion

1. Give an example of how citizens make use of social media for social change either in your workplace or neighborhood. The example can be what you or your friends have experienced or what you read in the news or on social media.
2. Discuss the role of social media in the above activities and the lessons you have learned.
3. Why can social media be effective in motivating peripheral groups to join a social movement? Do you think their participation can become a game changer for a social movement?
4. Among the three scholarly perceptions – optimistic, pessimistic, and ambivalent – about the relations between social media and social movements, which one do you think makes more sense than others?

References

Alba, M., & Kamisar, B. (2021). New campaign filings show Trump's fundraising haul off claims of voter fraud. *NBC News*. https://www.nbcnews.com/politics/meet-the-press/blog/meet-press-blog-latest-news-analysis-data-driving-political-discussion-n988541/ncrd1250011#blogHeader.

Barberá, P., Wang, N., Bonneau, R., Jost, J. T., Nagler, J., Tucker, J., & González-Bailón, S. (2015). The critical periphery in the growth of social protests. *PloS One*, 10 (11), Article e0143611. https://doi.org/10.1371/journal.pone.0143611.

boyd, d. (2010). Social networke sites as networked publics: Affordances, dynamics, and implications. In Z. Papacharissi (Ed.), *A networked self: Identity, community and culture on social network sites* (pp. 39–58). Routledge.

Castells, M. (1996). *The rise of the network society*. Blackwell Publishers.

Castells, M. (1997). *The power of identity*. Blackwell Publishers.

Castells, M. (1998). *End of millennium*. Blackwell Publishers.

Castells, M. (2009). *Communication power*. Oxford University Press.

Castells, M. (2012). *Networks of outrage and hope: Social movements in the Internet age* (2nd ed.). Polity.

Christensen, C. (2011). Twitter revolutions? Addressing social media and dissent. *The Communication Review*, *14*(3), 155–157. https://doi.org/10.1080/10714421.2011.597235.

Gladwell, M. (2010). Small change: Why the revolutuion will not be tweeted. *The New Yorker*. Retrieved September 22, 2019, from https://www.newyorker.com/ magazine/2010/10/04/small-change-malcolm-gladwell.

Granillo, G. (2020). The role of social media in social movements. *Portland Monthly*. https://www.pdxmonthly.com/news-and-city-life/2020/06/the-role-of-social-media-in-social-movements.

Griffiths, J. (2019). Blocking social media would be "the end of the open internet of Hong Kong." It also wouldn't work. *CNN*. https://www.cnn.com/2019/08/29/tech/hong-kong-internet-block-emergency-powers-intl-hnk/index.html.

Hassanpour, N. (2013). Media disruption and revolutionary unrest: Evidence from Mubarak's quasi-experiment. *Political Communication*, *31* (1), 1–24. https://doi.org/10. 1080/10584609.2012.737439.

Howard, P. N. (2010). *The digital origins of dictatorship and democracy: Information technology and political Islam*. Oxford University Press.

Khamis, S., & Vaughn, K. (2012). "We are all Khaled said": The potentials and limitations of cyberactivism in triggering public mobilization and promoting political change. *Journal of Arab & Muslim Media Research*, 4 (2–3), 145–163. https://doi.org/10.1386/ jammr.4.2–3.145_1.

Kidd, D., & McIntosh, K. (2016). Social media and social movements. *Sociology Compass*, 10 (9), 785–794. https://doi.org/10.1111/soc4.12399.

Kinnunen, J. (1996). Gabriel Tarde as a founding father of innovation diffusion research. *Acta Sociologica*, *39*(4), 431–442. https://doi.org/10.1177/000169939603900404.

Lazarsfeld, P. F., Berelson, B., & Gaudet, H. (1944). *The people's choice: How the voter makes up his mind in a presidential campaign*. Duell Sloan and Pearce.

Lotan, G., Graeff, E., Ananny, M., Gaffney, D., Pearce, I., & boyd, d. (2011). The revolutions were tweeted: Information flows during the 2011 Tunisian and Egyptian revolutions. *International Journal of Communication*, 5, 1375–1405. https://hdl.handle. net/1721.1/123460

McLuhan, M. (1964). *Understanding media: The extensions of man* (1st ed.). McGraw-Hill.

Morozov, E. (2012). The net delusion: The dark side of internet freedom. *Public Affairs*. http://ezaccess.libraries.psu.edu/login?url=http://ebookcentral.proquest.com/lib/ pensu/detail.action?docID=625147.

Mundt, M., & Ross, K. (2018). Scaling social movements through social media: The case of Black Lives Matter. *Social Media + Society*, *4*(4), 1–14. https://doi. org/10.1177/2056305118807911.

Murthy, D. (2013). *Twitter: Social communication in the Twitter age* (2nd ed.). Polity.

Papacharissi, Z. (2013). On networked publics and private spheres in social media. In J. Hunsinger & T. M. Senft (Eds.), *The social media handbook* (pp. 144–158). Routledge.

Pinckney, J. (2019). Can Hong Kong's extradition protesters succeed without a leader? *South China Morning Post*. https://www.scmp.com/week-asia/politics/article/3014605/ can-hong-kongs-extradition-protesters-succeed-without-leader.

Rogers, E. M. (1962). *Diffusion of innovations* (1st ed.). Free Press.

Rogers, E. M. (1983). *Diffusion of innovations* (3rd ed.). Free Press.

Rogers, E. M. (1995). *Diffusion of innovations* (4th ed.). Free Press.

Sengupta, S. (2019). Protesting climate change, young people take to streets in a global strike. *New York Times*. https://www.nytimes.com/2019/09/20/climate/global-climate-strike.html.

14

The Future of Social Media

LEARNING GOALS

This chapter will help you understand:

- What is the future of social media?
- What is the two-stage model of social media development?
- How important will social media skill become as part of digital skills required at the workplace?
- What are the major implications of social media ethics?
- What is the most important prediction for the future of social media?

KEY CONCEPTS

Digital skill	Soft skill
Model of two-stage development	Social connectivity
Social media ethics	Future of social media

Overview

Young and Old Fish

David Foster Wallace told a fish story at the beginning of his commencement speech to the 2015 graduating class at Kenyon College (see Figure 14.1):

> "There are these two young fish swimming along, and they happen to meet an older fish swimming the other way, who nods at them and says, 'Morning, kids, how's the water?' And the two young fish swim on for a bit, and then eventually one of them looks over at the other and goes, 'What the hell is water?'"
>
> (Wallace, 2009)

Some graduates in the audience quickly got it, but others took a bit more time. Let's pause for a minute and think: What's your takeaway out of this fish story?

Social Media Communication: Trends and Theories, First Edition. Bu Zhong.
© 2022 John Wiley & Sons, Inc. Published 2022 by John Wiley & Sons, Inc.

Figure 14.1 This is water: A story about two young fish and one older fish (Illustration by Moxin Qian).

In his speech, Wallace explained, "The point of the fish story is merely that the most obvious, important realities are often the ones that are hardest to see and talk about." Nearing the end of his speech, Wallace elaborated more on the fish parable:

> The capital-T Truth is about life BEFORE death.
> It is about the real value of a real education, which has almost nothing to do with knowledge, and everything to do with simple awareness; awareness of what is so real and essential, so hidden in plain sight all around us, all the time, that we have to keep reminding ourselves over and over:
> This is water.
> This is water.

The fish parable from Wallace is particularly inspiring when we examine the future of social media use. As we are heading to a new stage of social media development, it is the moment to think why we spend so much time glued to a screen and a big chunk of that time is devoted to social media. Just like the young fish, the more we look, the less we see. The more you use technology, the less you notice it. Suddenly, we see more people are using social media anytime, anywhere. We hold a smartphone wherever we go, or we cannot go anywhere if we do not carry a phone. No, we do not use the phone to call anyone most of the time, we use it mainly for social media. Simply, we cannot put down the phone. If we do, we leave social media behind, which can be awfully nerve-racking.

Two Premises

In the future, more and more people will be on social media as we deeply care about what is happening on social media. What we are really doing on social media is seeking, filtering, and interpreting information – above all, searching for meaning. In this sense, social media help us to find and verify the meaning of our lives and our interactions with others and the world. At Kenyon College, Wallace pointed out, "This is water." In the social media era, his words should remind us that this is social media.

Social media will be everywhere and we may stop noticing how much they are influencing us. This should be our first prediction for the future of social media.

The two young fish may make us laugh, but we should not mock them. There is no old wise fish in the social media era. Each of us may be as susceptible to misleading information circulated on social media as anyone. After reading this book, we may still focus more on the information that reinforces our previously held beliefs and stereotypes. We could still passively ingest all kinds of social media content without any motivation to verify it. We waste so much time using social media for no clear purpose, but still get distracted by updates and notifications. We know it is not a productive social media habit, but our fingers cannot stop scrolling and swiping on the endless feeds. For these reasons, we should be cautious of anyone who self-claims to be the wise old fish with a special understanding of how social media should be used.

If someone has the fantasy of being immune to the pitfalls of social media, he is most likely to fall into a trap sooner or later. The best policy is being vigilant about social media effects, in particular, having a mind equipped to deal with the complexity of social media content. In the water of social media, much of what we are swimming in is still new and strange, requiring us to work hard to figure it out together. This can be our second prediction for the future of social media. In sum, social media will be everywhere and no one can ignore their existence and impacts. Though it is unrealistic to think we can avoid all the negative effects of social media use, we can be smart users who know how to cope with them if we keep learning. For those who are fully prepared, social media will bring them unique benefits that they could hardly get somewhere else. What is good or toxic about social media use will be the result of deliberate choices by all of us.

The Model of Two-Stage Development

The first social media site, SixDegrees.com, was born in 1997 (see Figure 14.2). For the first time in history, users could set up their own profile pages on SixDegrees, creating lists of connections and sending messages within networks. Its functions

Figure 14.2 The screenshot of SixDegrees website taken in January 27, 2021.

make it the first true social media site in the world. At its peak, it had around one million users, and its website is still viewable on the internet. In those early years, few predicted that social media would have developed into such a big industry. Almost no one imagined that social media use would be central to people's media routines in the 2020s. Since then, it is clear that social media are here to stay. Some have become tech giants like Facebook or Twitter, some are growing like Slack and Discord, and the rest are either defunct like Yik Yak or suspended like Parler and Gab. As a whole, the social media industry is booming. In 2020, for example, Facebook and Instagram had 2.6 billion users and the social media giants pocketed $86 billion in revenue (Ovide, 2021).

The power of social media has been widely recognized in the twenty-first century as their influence has penetrated every corner of human society. No one can afford to underestimate the influence. Rather, the use of social media has been a part of internet users' media routines. In the coming years, social media will become an inseparable part of political, social, and business strategies. The future of social media development is predicted to follow the model of two-stage development.

The first 25 years of social media development, or Phase 1, has proven that social media can function as productive information tools for individual users, marketing tools for businesses, and weapons of mass destruction for governments and other malicious actors. As a result, social media can provide benefits to social lives and business growth as well as deliver devastating damage to opponents in substantial ways. Done well, social media will be important platforms for not only social networking – generating engagement and meaningful interactions, but also knowledge collaboration – producing significant collective intelligence in the age of internet civilization.

Specifically, Phase 1 covers social media development from 1997, when the first social media site was developed, to 2022 when the COVID-19 pandemic will perhaps be put under control. In general, the first phase was full of uncertainties marked by an unstable initial growth of social media and there will be more stable growth in the second phase. In the economic world, the two-stage model has been used to examine the development of various modern industries. In most cases, the first stage may have a positive, negative, or volatile growth rate and will last for a finite period, whereas the second stage is assumed to have a more stable growth rate for industries.

As Phase 2 – the next 25 years of social media development – is unfolding, social media will play a bigger role in human societies as internet connection becomes automatic and permanent. In Phase 1 (1997–2022), social media played a central role in connecting us to each other and the world. In Phase 2 (2023–2047), the impact, scope, and complexity of social media use will be unprecedented, though the general growth trend will be stable and positive. This phase will be saturated with more pervasive use of social media, leading to everlasting changes to people's media routines and communication patterns that have never been seen before. As social media bring people more benefits, their negative outcomes will become a growing social concern, such as invasion of privacy, fake news, hate speech, data leaks, tech addiction, FOMO, and phubbing.

Overall, social media are no longer perceived as just platforms for socialization and congregation, but are being acknowledged for their ability to encourage aggregation for shared goals (Kapoor et al., 2018). Social media will provide more venues to inspire social learning – learning that can easily occur in various social contexts – in which new learning behaviors and patterns emerge based on observing other people's social media activities. Thus, social media will further promote knowledge sharing and collaboration (e.g., creating Wikipedia). All of these will make the future of social media more exciting for positive individual and social outcomes. These positive outcomes, of course, may not completely change the digital media landscape, but they can help make the world a better place in which to live.

Digital Skills at the Workplace

Can you major in social media at a US university? A few years ago, it became big news when a Pennsylvania college offered a Bachelor's degree in social media. In 2017, Kutztown University started to offer a new Bachelor's degree called "Social Media Theory and Strategy." In fact, numerous US universities had started to educate students about getting the most from online platforms before that. The University of Florida's College of Journalism and Communications, for example, has had a 38-credit online Master's program in social media (Somers, 2016). Other schools with social media offerings focus on providing Master's degrees. The University of Southern California (USC) offers a similar Master's program – "MS Digital Social Media" – at its journalism school. The MS degree, according to USC program's website, "Teaches you leadership and management of social media, digital media, and online communities," and allows students to "develop expertise in the practice, theory, and strategies that are essential for success in today's business and social landscape" (USC, 2017).

What the US universities are offering aligns with employers' needs in the job market, which emphasize digital competency consisting of a range of emerging digital skills like social media, data analytics, and communication techniques. These digital skills help college students to achieve job-market success for both STEM (science, technology, engineering, and mathematics) and liberal arts majors (e.g., journalism, communication). Acquiring the right mix of skills could help people to be more competitive in the job market and avoid or escape underemployment. Future technological progress will lead to a robust growth of high-skilled and high-paying jobs, but almost all of the new occupations require digital skills. One of these digital skills is making good use of social media for business purposes.

A Harvard study found that jobs requiring soft skills, such as social skills and digital skills, have seen the largest growth in employment and pay in the past decades (Deming, 2017). A study by Burning Glass Technologies, a Boston-based company that analyzes job-market trends, concluded that if liberal arts graduates gain proficiency in digital skills like social media or data analysis, their prospects of landing entry-level jobs increase substantially (Burning Glass Technology, 2018).

Another study finds that about eight in 10 middle-skill jobs require digital skills and digitally intensive middle-skill occupations are growing faster than other middle-skill jobs (Burning Glass Technology, 2015). Digitally intensive middle-skill jobs pay more than middle-skill jobs that do not require a digital component. Moreover, digital skills provide a career pathway into middle-skill and high-skill jobs. Digital skills are particularly helpful to workers who are motivated to grow from a middle-skill position to a high-skill one. As a digital skill, social media use at the workplace reduces the worker-specific cost of coordination with others. Workers with high social media skills can trade tasks at a lower cost, enabling them to work with others more efficiently.

Do college students and other workers realize the importance of using social media as a digital skill? Maybe. If not, they will get it or have to get it in the coming years. In the higher education system, it is increasingly clear that any colleges that leave students unaware of how to develop their digital skills, like using social media, could fumble the handoff from college to the job market, and even compromise their graduates' potential success in their future career paths. For workers without digital skills, they might lose plenty of growth and promotion opportunities. The trend will become more obvious in the coming decades.

Ethical Social Media Sites

There is no doubt that the future ecosystem of social media is different from what it is today. As we care more about privacy and fake news on social media, new social platforms will emerge that focus on protecting privacy and filtering out misinformation and disinformation on their platforms. This is not an easy job for tech companies, but as long as users strongly insist on them, some positive changes will inevitably happen. The new social media sites do not have to be subscriber-paid services because then only the wealthy will be able to afford them, limiting the ability of doing social good. We should be optimistic and hope that the advances of ICT and social innovation bring out such social media sites soon, though it is hard to predict how popular these new sites will be.

In the future, new social media sites will have two key features: (1) ethical and transparent and (2) better data security and privacy protection. In Phase 1, users suffered dearly in the unregulated digital world. Tech companies claimed they were not new media companies and so should not be held accountable like traditional news media organizations are. In the next decade, social media users and the tech industry should agree not to let a few companies wield too much power in people's digital lives. There has been a long and intense debate in civic, academic, and political spaces about how digital life is changing our society. As a result, the term "social media ethics" will be proposed and become a prominent topic when evaluating user activities and business strategies on social media. Tech companies are called to embrace the uptake of corporate social responsibilities. Some significant changes in the areas of guidelines and business practices will follow, such as privacy protection, data security, algorithm transparency, architecture design, and platform accountability.

The central challenge is that tech companies will not voluntarily engage corporate social responsibilities as long as they may affect their core business practices and bottom lines. They will respond when a large number of users insist that social media companies must face ethical quandaries and do the "right" thing. When users' criticism reaches critical mass, it will push companies to be more ethical and transparent, even if this many challenge business models and priorities. Embracing corporate social responsibilities also serves the bottom line in the long run. Without users, these companies are powerless. Any ethically questionable services or products could be a time bomb, threatening the survival of the company or even the whole industry.

Some initial efforts have been directed to hold tech companies accountable, for instance, changing algorithm designs to make social media use less addictive for children and adolescents or limiting users' screen time. They also invested more in fact-checking initiatives to fight fake news disseminated on social media. A few small victories have been achieved in Phase 1, but more are expected in the next phase. We believe more positive changes are coming because social media users, along with researchers, academics, and critics, have come to the consensus that social media companies must be more ethical and transparent in managing the consequences of digital technologies.

Fake News on Social Media

Another big concern about social media usage has been the pervasiveness of misinformation, disinformation, hate speech, and weaponized information on these digital media platforms. It is easy and low-cost for anyone to spread such information via social media. Platforms like Facebook and Twitter have noted that anonymity online has become a tool to spread misinformation and manipulate public thinking. It is predicted that social media companies will invest more in developing technologies to tracce social media misconduct anywhere on the internet.

When they take action, the results could be imminent. For instance, online misinformation about election fraud plunged 73% after several social media sites suspended former President Trump and key allies for one week in January 2021 (Dwoskin & Timberg, 2021). Zignal Labs, a research firm, reported that conversations about election fraud dropped from 2.5 million mentions to 688,000 mentions across several social media sites in the first week (January 8–15, 2021) after Trump was banned from Twitter. The suspension underscored the power of tech companies to limit the falsehoods poisoning public debate when they act aggressively.

In addition to the effort from tech companies, we predict that a new genre of "social media forensics" will come into sight, whose experts will trace users' privacy infringements through their data trails and even seek compensation on their behalf. When done ethically, this genre will create new job opportunities within the digital media industry. The experts in this new category will help the social media industry to grow and thrive in the future. More importantly, they help users to combat fake news and to build a heathier digital life. Quite likely, many of these experts will not belong to the existing social media giants. They may work independently as guards for user interests and put digital giants' power in check.

False and misleading information will not leave social media sites in the next decade. Unfortunately, social media will remain as hubs where a variety of fake news and conspiracy theories are incubated, reinforced, and disseminated. To address this issue, it is important to educate the public about social media literacy, especially the benefits and pitfalls associated with their usage. Educational systems and other social institutes will provide more training to the public and teach them how to recognize manipulations and manipulative techniques when they occur. Some changes have come from the initial efforts in Phase 1. In the next phase, social media companies need to realize that the dangers of data misuse and manipulation will not only hurt users but also themselves, including their bottom lines. Therefore, social media companies will increasingly realize that they can make more money by serving their users' needs properly and ethically.

In the coming years, social media users will be able to fact check, in real time, almost any information they encounter on various social media platforms. We are already seeing the advent of sophisticated fact-checking, image-validating, and information assurance initiatives. For example, Google image is not just an image search engine, but it can be used as a valuable tool to check against fake or forged photos. The fact-checking tools provided on social media will deliver a big blow to any deceivers, manipulators, and propagandists who, of course, will try to fool others. Efforts from users, educational institutes, and social media companies will help the public develop defense strategies against social media misuse. Will every social media company take action in fighting fake news? Probably not. Technology evolves quickly, and they need to be faster in how they adapt new business models because users will not wait long for them. As social media companies put truth and veracity as their core business values, they will win more trust from users, which, again, will help their bottom lines.

Social Connectivity

One of the main features of social media is social connectivity, enabling users to connect with others conveniently and regardless of geographic distance. No longer restricted by geographic location, people can provide emotional support, financial aid, and political advocacy for others around the world without leaving their own homes. In the next phase, social media will continue to bring people together so that they can share views and information with others around the corner or around the globe. After enjoying the initial benefits of social connectivity, people, naturally, expect that the power of this function will increase in the future. We predict that social connectivity will promote civic participation and social innovation in the coming decades. More importantly, social connectivity on social media will build up new user-managed communities among people with similar needs across local, state, and even national boundaries.

For decades, social media usage has been one of the most popular online activities. In 2020, over 3.6 billion people were using social media worldwide, and the number is projected to increase to 4.41 billion in 2025 (Tankovska, 2021). The trend will continue in Phase 2. After so many people are connected in countless virtual communities through social media for virtually every possible objective, a new trend will appear that online communities will further the civic participation and responsibility formed in the offline world, making them more effective and influential. Experts predict that new virtual communities will make the conditions ripe for an explosion of open creativity and innovation never seen before (Vogels et al., 2020).

In the next phase, the social media world is ready to welcome the next billion users who did not get in due to the digital divide. As a result, significant changes will happen in the technological, political, economic, and human-rights domains due to the deeper penetration of social media usage. The world may not know the exact futuristic impact of the creativity and innovation stimulated by social media use, but we predict the social media landscape will be totally different from what it is today due to new types of virtual collaboration.

Not all the changes brought about by extensive social connectivity are positive, even in the near future. Susan Etlinger insightfully points out that we must let go of techno-solutionism – the notion that the problems caused by technology can only be solved by more technology (Vogels et al., 2020). She calls for considering how social and civic innovation can inform our use of technology, including reducing data biases, improving algorithm interpretability, and promoting fairness and trustworthiness. Because so many algorithms are embedded in social media sites to collect user data, it is important to consider who decides what data gets mined and what criteria are used by such an algorithm.

As the world enters into a new economy that is growingly powered by digital technologies, it is crucial to consider the value of social connectivity powered by social media usage. It can be challenging to predict the future of social media as they will never stop evolving. When the consequences of social media development are collectively debated, people's perspectives will jointly generate creative and innovative solutions, which will help shape the future of social media. When billions of users join their hands together to search for a brighter future for social media, positive outcomes will happen and can overcome potential negative effects in the digital world.

If we narrow down to one prediction for the future of social media, it must be: human communication will progressively run on social media.

Summary

This final chapter tries to predict the future of social media. The first prediction is about the ubiquity of social media use – social media will be everywhere and users will stop noticing how much they are relying on them and how they are influencing us. The second prediction is that the digital life on social media is relatively new. People must keep learning about it to be smart social media users who may obtain unique benefits from social media use. It is also predicted that social media will follow a two-stage development mode in the future. The first 25 years of social media development from 1997 to 2021 has brought us both good and bad results in some substantial ways. In the next stage (2023–2047), more exciting and unprecedented changes will happen, though the general growth trend will be stable and positive. Meanwhile, more users will hold social media companies accountable for ensuring a healthier information environment on social media, setting a higher bar for social media ethics. The single most important takeaway from this book should be: the world is increasingly running on social media from now on.

Discussion

1. What are the two social media features mostly likely to happen in the near future?
2. Do you think the future of social media will follow the two-stage development model?
3. What is your prediction about social media as a digital skill required at the workplace?
4. How likely do you think ethical social media sites will emerge in the next decade?
5. What future changes do you expect regarding social connectivity on social media?

References

Burning Glass Technology. (2015). The digital skills gap in the workforce. *Burning Glass Technology*, 1–16. https://www.burning-glass.com/wp-content/uploads/2015/06/Digital_Skills_Gap.pdf.

Burning Glass Technology. (2018). Majors that matter: Ensuring college graduates avoid underemployment. *Burning Glass Technology*.

Deming, D. J. (2017). The growing importance of social skills in the labor market. *The Quarterly Journal of Economics*, 132 (4), 1593–1640. https://doi.org/10.1093/qje/qjx022.

Dwoskin, E., & Timberg, C. (2021, January 16). Misinformation dropped dramatically the week after Twitter banned Trump and some allies. *Washington Post*. https://www.washingtonpost.com/technology/2021/01/16/misinformation-trump-twitter.

Kapoor, K. K., Tamilmani, K., Rana, N. P., Patil, P., Dwivedi, Y. K., & Nerur, S. (2018). Advances in social media research: Past, present and future. *Information Systems Frontiers*, 20 (4), 531–558. https://doi.org/10.1007/s10796-017-9810-y.

Ovide, S. (2021, January 28). Facebook is hated – And rich. *New York Times*. https://www.nytimes.com/2021/01/28/technology/facebook-earnings-reputation.html.

Somers, D. (2016). You can major in social media? *U.S. News and World Report*. https://www.usnews.com/education/best-colleges/articles/2016-06-30/you-can-major-in-social-media.

Tankovska, H. (2021). Number of social network users worldwide from 2017 to 2025. *Statista*. https://www.statista.com/statistics/278414/number-of-worldwide-social-network-users.

USC. (2017). MS digital social media. https://annenberg.usc.edu/node?page=40.

Vogels, E. A., Rainie, L., & Anderson, J. (2020). Experts predict more digital innovation by 2030 aimed at enhancing democracy. *Pew Research Center*. https://www.pewresearch.org/internet/2020/06/30/innovations-these-experts-predict-by-2030.

Wallace, D. F. (2009). *This is water: Some thoughts, delivered on a significant occasion, about living a compassionate life* (1st ed.). Little, Brown and Company.

Index

A

addiction   66, 75, 88–91, 93, 94,
   101, 102, 180
adherence   142, 143, 145, 146
adolescents   65, 74, 75, 88–91, 94, 101–3, 138,
   146, 183
ads   109, 129, 151, 152, 155
adulthood   75, 89
adults   45, 57, 66, 68, 74, 88, 89, 91, 98, 102, 122,
   145, 147, 163
affordances   29, 169, 175
agenda-setting   123, 124, 127, 132, 134
algorithms   90, 96, 97, 101, 105, 120, 125–28, 133,
   134, 148, 149, 151, 156–60, 163, 182, 183,
   185
app economy   148–56, 158, 160–62
Arab spring   13, 33, 54, 60, 95, 162, 164, 165, 168,
   170, 174
artificial intelligence   25, 97, 144, 148, 150, 152,
   154, 156–63
Asia   130, 147
Asians   11, 47, 77, 80, 82
authoritarian   95, 96, 165, 171
automation   12, 17, 156–58, 163

B

Black Lives Matter movements   162, 168, 174
blog   59, 129, 145, 155, 163, 174
bloggers   170, 171
brains   41, 42, 51, 52, 89–91, 92, 93, 97, 100, 101,
   102
branding   110, 111, 117
brands   41, 107, 108, 109, 111, 118, 127, 160
Brexit   97, 102
broadband   18, 106, 119
BuzzFeed   128, 129

C

campaigning   54, 162
campaigns   1, 2, 96, 97, 101, 132, 138, 143, 152, 162,
   163, 167, 168

C (continued)

cancer   48, 136, 137, 139, 140, 146, 147
capitalism   16, 22, 61
China   6, 11, 82, 86, 139, 144, 145, 159, 176
Chinese   16, 80, 82, 85–87, 139
CNBC   56, 63
CNN   11, 12, 33, 45, 95, 175
cocaine   91
cognitive dissonance   40, 44, 49, 51
cognitive theory   53, 60, 62, 101
collaboration   61
collectivism   79, 81, 84
collectivist   77–79, 81, 82
communication technology   5, 6, 14, 18, 19, 26, 39,
   66, 69, 106, 132, 170
Computer-mediated communication (CMC)   21,
   24–32, 34–35, 36–39, 52, 58, 75, 85, 147
Confucianism   77
consumers   41, 46, 47, 57, 108–11, 121–24, 128,
   130, 138, 154, 157
Croatia   81
crohn's disease   139, 142, 147
crowdfunding   168
crowd-sourcing   106
cultivation theory   76, 83–85
cultural differences   73, 77–87
cyberbullying   3, 26, 98
cyber-troop   96

D

data analytics   96, 158, 181
data science   70–73
data scientists   70–72, 121, 126
data security   154, 182
decision-making   41, 42, 51, 52, 118, 125, 136, 137,
   141, 142, 145
democracy   3, 31, 95, 96, 131, 162, 164, 169–71,
   174, 175, 186
dictatorship   169, 172, 174, 175
diffusion   14, 26, 69, 76, 106, 137, 164, 172, 173,
   175, 176
diffusion of ICT   14, 26, 69

Social Media Communication: Trends and Theories, First Edition. Bu Zhong.
© 2022 John Wiley & Sons, Inc. Published 2022 by John Wiley & Sons, Inc.

diffusion of innovations 172, 173, 176
digitalization 1, 3–5, 8, 9, 12
digitization 1, 3–5, 8, 68
disinformation 2, 3, 96, 101, 130, 182, 183
dissonance theory 40, 49
diversity 3, 12, 76, 77, 84, 113, 119
doctor–patient relationship 142, 146

E

echo chambers 3, 166
e-commerce 26, 68
ecosystem 46, 56, 159, 182
efficiency 4, 126
e-government 114, 117
Egypt 33, 95, 96, 164, 167, 171
emails 10, 11, 22, 25, 26, 30, 32, 43, 68, 69, 106, 107, 109, 138, 139, 168
emotions 2, 42, 80, 90
empathy 48, 140, 141
Europe 16, 24, 95, 97, 102, 130
evolution theory 76
eye-tracking 160

F

Facebook algorithm 125, 127
Facekbook campaign 33
fact-checking 183, 184
FOMO 88, 93, 94, 97, 98, 100, 180

G

gambling addiction 88, 89
gaming addiction 91
gaming apps 150, 153
gaming disorder 88
gatekeepers 55, 121, 125, 173
generation gap 64, 68, 98
globalization 40, 51, 76, 81, 84
gun control 55

H

habits 50, 53, 55, 60, 70, 76, 81, 84, 91, 94, 98, 109, 117, 120, 121, 123, 126, 133, 154, 159, 160, 163
health behaviors 53, 56, 57, 60, 61, 63, 92, 135, 136, 137, 141, 143, 145
health belief 143, 145, 147
health communication 29, 133, 144–47
health literacy 135, 141
health misinformation 136, 143
hong kong's 24, 33, 164–66, 175, 176

I

individualism 18, 77–79, 81, 84
information age 9, 19, 22, 170
Information and communication technology (ICT) 5, 12–14, 18, 19, 21, 26, 30, 31, 36, 45, 46, 66–69, 76, 81, 100, 106, 117, 123, 170, 182

information cocoons 3
information overload 43, 46, 92
information processing 17, 21, 24, 29, 30, 35, 36, 39, 40, 43, 44, 50, 51, 113, 138, 145
information revolution 17
information society 16, 23, 74, 170
information sources 29, 33, 36, 57, 122, 170
information support 135, 140, 141
information systems 74, 118, 133, 186
information technology 4, 9, 17, 58, 86, 107, 120, 175
innovation theory 164, 172, 173
Internet privacy concern (IPC) 64–66, 68
iPad 18
Iran 171
Iraq 95
Irritable bowel syndrome (IBD) 139, 145
Israel 95

J

Japan 11, 78
job market 181, 182
job satisfaction 94, 102
job security 114, 119
journalists 14, 33, 54, 117, 120, 122–25, 127, 128, 130–34, 170–72
judgment and decision making (JDM) 36, 40–43, 45, 47, 50

K

knowledge civilization 23
knowledge collaboration 50, 53, 59, 61, 62, 180
knowledge economy 61
knowledge gap 148, 160, 161, 163
Korea 78, 159

L

Latinos 137
Lazarsfeld 161, 163, 173, 175
learning algorithms 160
Libya 164

M

machine learning 96, 148, 153, 156–60
manipulation, computational 101
mass communication 37, 38, 62, 87, 161, 163
mass communications 37, 99
mass media 16, 32, 58, 84, 109, 120, 122, 132, 134, 136, 148, 160, 163, 167
medical decision-making 137, 142, 145
medical intervention 133, 135, 137, 143, 144
mentality 1, 3, 8
misinformation 2, 3, 63, 95, 96, 120, 128–31, 136, 139, 143, 182, 183, 186
misinformation theory 120
mobile apps 144, 148–51, 152–55, 162
mobile commerce 68, 74, 153, 154

mobile technology   5, 14, 18, 21, 25, 69
mood modification   91, 98
mood regulation   51
motivation   16, 65, 78, 91–93, 102, 161, 179
multitasking   42

N
nationalism   67
Need for cognition (NFC)   71, 72
networked cultures   23, 38
networked publics   164, 169, 175, 176
news business   123, 131, 133
news consumption   46, 53–55, 60, 61, 117, 120–23,
            128, 133
news content   12, 41, 123, 130, 133
news decision-making   125, 127
news industry   54, 117, 120–22, 124, 126–28,
            130–34
news information   36, 45, 46, 50, 54, 55, 121, 124,
            125, 131, 132
news literacy   129, 134
news sources   129
nonverbal cues   27, 28, 30, 35
nonverbal information   27, 28, 30
NPR   45, 102

O
obesity   53
occupy central   33
Occupy Wall Street   164, 166–69
optimization   152, 156–58

P
pandemic   90, 115, 124, 131, 136, 149, 150, 180
patient–physician relationship   47, 143
patients' trust   141, 142, 145
pay-per-click   152
peripheral group theory   164
peripheral processing   72
phubbing   88, 93, 94, 97, 98, 100–102, 180
physician–patient communication   138, 139
physician-patient relationship   142
political advertising   99, 101
political campaigning   54
political campaigns   1, 2
pornography   53, 99, 102
privacy concerns   61, 64–66, 68–70, 71–75, 154
privacy protection   68, 75, 182
privacy risks   70
problematic behaviors   89, 98
problematic Instagram use   101
problematic internet use   89
problematic smartphone usage   102
problematic social media   90, 100–102
problematic use of   3, 54, 84, 88, 90–92, 94, 96–98,
            100, 102
proximity   94, 154

psychological distance   7, 9
publics   112, 164, 169, 175, 176

Q
quality communication   160, 162

R
racists   172, 174
radio   6, 10, 12, 22, 32, 35, 54, 67, 102, 125, 161,
            163, 173
reciprocity   113
recommendation systems   71, 158
Renaissance   16
robotics   25
robotization   17
robots   42, 157, 163
rumors   63, 111, 128
Russia   97

S
salience   19, 91, 132
selective exposure   3, 36, 40, 43–46, 50–52
self-assurance   97
self-awareness   81, 97, 98
self-control   88, 91–93, 97, 98, 100
self-efficacy   57, 92, 97, 101, 141, 143
self-esteem   44, 48, 52, 94, 97, 140, 141
self-responsibility   98, 100
sexting   88
smart devices   154
smart homes   5
smartphones   5, 18, 53, 66, 75, 89, 92–94, 101, 102,
            135, 144, 148, 149, 150, 151, 153, 154, 155,
            162, 178
smart wearable   153
social capital   100, 105, 112, 113, 117–19, 141
social changes   15, 24, 36, 107, 162, 164, 166–69,
            171, 172, 174
social endorsement   45, 46
social information   21, 24, 30, 33, 34, 36, 39
social media   1–6, 8–14, 17, 20–26, 28–38, 40–48,
            50–78, 80–86, 88–98, 100–103, 105–48, 150,
            151, 156, 158–62, 164–86
social movements   3, 13, 24, 32, 33, 162, 164–72,
            174–76
social network   12, 23, 29, 32, 36, 37, 39, 46, 48, 55,
            59, 81, 85–87, 105, 107, 108, 110–16, 118,
            119, 123, 127, 129, 140, 144, 175, 186
social networking   9, 31, 37, 39, 73, 74, 86, 94, 103,
            108, 111, 119, 171, 180
social norms   47, 65, 69
social psychology   36, 51, 52, 73, 74, 86, 146
social responsibilities   182
social support   48, 52, 57, 62, 78, 133, 135, 140, 141,
            144, 146, 147
social surveillance   68
stress   11, 44, 49, 77, 141, 146

students 10, 11, 20, 23, 27, 32, 54, 56, 58, 78, 80, 86, 87, 92, 94, 95, 169, 181, 182
support communities 48, 52, 140, 143, 147
support community 48, 59
support groups 48, 139, 140, 142, 145
surveillance 61, 64, 65, 67, 68, 72–75, 96, 169, 172
Syria 164

T
Taiwan 11, 78, 159
target audiences 77, 107, 133, 144
target customers 117, 144, 150–52, 156, 158–60, 162
target markets 150, 158, 159
tech companies 73, 92, 96, 97, 182, 183
technological determinism 8, 10, 19–21, 23, 66
technological innovations 14, 16
tech trend 153
teenagers 88, 91, 94, 138
telecommunications 20, 96
telephone 6, 106, 173
television 6, 12, 22, 32, 37, 45, 54, 58, 63, 83–85, 108, 109, 125, 173
tracking 55, 56, 68, 126, 154
Trump, Donald J. 9, 52, 97, 128, 168, 174, 183, 186
trust in doctors 142, 143, 145
trust in news media 129
Tumblr 11, 12
Tunisia 164, 170, 171
Turkey 33, 167
Twitter 10–12, 29, 31, 33, 54–56, 59, 62, 63, 69, 70, 94–96, 109, 114, 118, 126, 128, 129, 146, 156, 158–60, 165, 166, 170, 171, 175, 176, 180, 183, 186

U
Uber 154

Ukraine 33
Umbrella Movement 24, 165
Umbrella Revolution 164
uncertainty-accepting 79
uncertainty avoidance 77–79
uncertainty-avoiding 79
uncertainty-reducing 29
uncertainty reduction 21, 29, 30, 36, 38, 39
user-generated content 64, 70, 106

V
VCR 173
virtual collaboration 184
virtual community 13, 26, 68, 169, 184
virtual reality 13, 153

W
Watergate 128
weaponized information 97, 183
weaponized misinformation 2, 95
weaponized narratives 95, 96, 101
wearable devices 153
WeChat 11, 53, 55, 159
Weibo 11
well-being 59, 66, 75, 90, 92, 93, 98 102, 131, 140, 141

Y
Yik Yak 180
youth development 56, 62
YouTube 12, 43, 54, 59, 94, 110, 120

Z
Zappos 105, 106

Printed and bound by CPI Group (UK) Ltd, Croydon, CR0 4YY

16/04/2025

14658466-0003